D1418310

Guide to Internet Job Searching

Guide to
Internet Job
Searching

2008-2009 Edition

TWINSBURG LIBRARY
TWINSBURG OHIO 44087

Margaret Riley Dikel
Frances E. Roehm

0394 75162
Career
650.14
DIK
2008-09

McGraw
Hill

New York   Chicago   San Francisco   Lisbon   London   Madrid   Mexico City
Milan   New Delhi   San Juan   Seoul   Singapore   Sydney   Toronto

Copyright © 2008 by The McGraw-Hill Companies, Inc. All rights reserved. Printed in the United States of America. Except as permitted under the United States Copyright Act of 1976, no part of this publication may be reproduced or distributed in any form or by any means, or stored in a database or retrieval system, without the prior written permission of the publisher.

1 2 3 4 5 6 7 8 9 10 11 12 13 14 15 16 17 18 19   QPD/QPD   0 9 8

ISBN 978-0-07-149452-6
MHID   0-07-149452-9
ISSN 1527-7410

McGraw-Hill books are available at special quantity discounts to use as premiums and sales promotions or for use in corporate training programs. To contact a representative, please visit the Contact Us pages at www.mhprofessional.com.

This book is printed on acid-free paper.

Contents

Foreword

I read, the other day, that there are now an estimated 100 million websites out there. Apparently, no one knows for sure, because many sites have never been found by any search engine. It reminds me of the heavens above, and all the stars therein. We've hardly begun to catalog them, and no one is surprised when new ones are discovered.

With the heavens, we are dependent on astronomers. With the Internet, we are dependent on librarians. I have always found that they know more than anyone about information. Information of all kinds. And some of them came early to cataloging the Internet.

Among these are my own favorite librarians, Margaret Dikel (once Margaret Riley) and Frances Roehm. I know them both; in fact, I've known them for years. Margaret was writing The Riley Guide—rileyguide.com—when I first noticed the Internet (that was back in 1996). It was then and is now the most definitive Web guide to job-hunting sites that you can possibly find. I don't know how she does it. I picture her staying up long nights, burning the midnight oil, in order to keep up-to-date with what's going on out there on the Internet.

Later on, I met Frances Roehm and quickly became in awe of her skills, too. She put together ChicagoJobs.org on behalf of the Skokie (Illinois) Public Library.

I was one happy camper when I heard that both Margaret and Frances had joined with Steve Oserman on a book, eventually called *The Guide to Internet Job Searching*, copublished with the Public Library Association. I knew Steve, too, and was very sad when he unexpectedly died, very young.

Anyway, what have the three of them given us? This, which you hold in your hands: nothing less than a masterwork on job hunting and the Internet. Constantly updated, I might add. Are we ever blessed! This is as close to an encyclopedia of the Internet—for job hunters and career changers—as you will ever find, anywhere.

Note that, over the years, they have expanded their own community. They now draw on not only their own work but also that of two of my other favorite people—Susan Joyce and Susan Ireland.

What a wealth of expertise is in this latest edition of this book! Buy it! Read it! Use it! The job-hunting life you save will be your own.

Dick Bolles, author
What Color Is Your Parachute?

Preface

Would you believe that it was twelve years ago that the authors began working on a how-to guide for job searching on the Internet? Yes, the first edition of this book was published in 1996 at a time when we thought that "drinking from a fire hose" was a good analogy for the deluge of information available online. We listed telnet sites, Gopher servers, Usenet newsgroups, electronic journals, and some of the newfangled World Wide Web resources you might find. We were happy with monochrome monitors, 2,400-baud modems, 500-MB hard drives, and 8 MB of RAM.

We certainly aren't in Kansas anymore, but now we don't need to be. We can actually visit Kansas quickly and efficiently through the Web, perusing the many resources and services through online sites such as Kansas.gov and taking virtual tours of almost every part of the state with the click of a mouse. It is like that almost everywhere in the world. "Being there" is a state of mind now, since access is so, well, accessible.

This edition of the book was an interesting project. While we always anticipate a certain amount of change from the previous edition, this time it was different. As always, there is a reasonable degree of consolidation among job banks. Many have joined into networks, relying on one central database of jobs, while others merge to create an even larger entity with ever more market presence. Still others have shut down, having realized that after so many years of operation they cannot continue to compete in a market saturated with so many similar services. New niche sites proliferate as targeted services, associations, and organizations expand their online presence, offering good services and resources to the online public, while other small sites that were not so good from the start are dying off.

One major change we did not anticipate is the shutdown of America's Job Bank. When it went live in 1995, America's Job Bank was the first pillar in the suite of services that now make up CareerOneStop.org. It was also one of the first nationwide job banks. The launch of AJB signaled a new era in government employment services, not only bringing the strength of the U.S. Department of Labor's Employment and Training Administration into the world of online recruiting but also pulling the fifty states, the District of Columbia, and several territories and governances along with it.

Margaret was involved in AJB early on, creating the original Career Resource Library linking users to other resources and then assisting in the development of America's Career InfoNet and America's Talent Bank (the resume database). In 2007, the U.S. Department of Labor decided that cost and competition made the job listing service unwieldy and unnecessary, a decision that affected not only AJB's national market but also the states. Most states and governances relied on AJB's servers and service to support their own job banks. This move to terminate the site has forced many providers to reallocate personnel, funding, and technology to accommodate AJB's retreat. There are other services to take its place, of course, and you probably won't miss it, but AJB was one of the last of the "early runners" and the only one fully focused on you and your needs. It was truly your tax dollars hard at work serving you.

Nevertheless, the more things change, the more they stay the same. You still have access to millions of job listings, but now you must watch out for the ones that are scams designed to steal your money or your identity. You still need that great resume, but now you can consider the options of online portfolios and even "video" resumes. Your networking opportunities have expanded to include the many social and professional networking sites now available online that may help you reach others, but it's still the personal touch that will make that real connection. And while you are using the Internet to research employers, they are using it to research you. It is a strange and wonderful world, one that requires a little careful thought and preparation, but now that you are forewarned and forearmed, you can benefit from all it has to offer.

Acknowledgments

It's been twelve years since we teamed up with the late Steve Oserman to start this job-search journey together. Steve came up with the idea initially and early on provided much of the perspiration behind its success. His vitality and energetic personality were wonderfully inspiriting, and we continue to be inspired by his warmth and good works on behalf of job seekers and career changers. Since his passing, we have endeavored to uphold his vision for the book and to follow his example of service to the community.

We'd like to thank Richard Bolles, author of *What Color Is Your Parachute?*, renowned career expert, and good friend, for graciously agreeing to provide us with a Foreword. We are indebted to Susan Ireland, professional resume writer and author of *The Complete Idiot's Guide to the Perfect Resume*, fourth edition, for allowing us to use so much of her information on electronic resume formats in our book. And we owe a great deal to Susan Joyce, president of NETability and webmaster of Job-Hunt.org, who allowed us to quote information from her website and assisted with the editing of Chapter 2.

From Frances:

This guide would not be possible without the help and inspiration of many individuals. While it is not feasible to name them all, there are some who have provided so much in the way of encouragement, real-world experience, and technical support that I must extend a public thank-you.

Director Carolyn A. Anthony and the board of trustees of Skokie Public Library

The ChicagoJobs.org team: Mike Buhmann, business librarian and Web developer; Pat Gaines, reference librarian; Maxine Topper, supervisor, Career Development, Jewish Vocational Service; and Pam Neumann, resume specialist

Members of the SkokieNet group, especially "senior librarian" Jane Hagedorn

SkokieNet and SkokieTalk advisers, partners, friends, and volunteers

Sarah A. Long, Mary Witt, Alexis Sarkisian, and the Library Production Studio team

Colleagues and mentors such as Dick Bolles, Joan Durrance, Lola Lucas, Kathy Rolsing, the Illinois CLICKSters, and others who remind me that it's all about the people

And last, but certainly not least, Lenny, who keeps the home fires burning, and Christopher, Eva, family, and friends who make my world a better place

From Margaret:

Until you work on something like this, you never know how many people it takes to really create it.

Friends and colleagues such as Tony Lee, Dick Bolles, Joyce Lain Kennedy, Mary-Ellen Mort, Susan Joyce, and Susan Ireland are priceless. They not only keep an eye on what I'm doing but also introduce me to many more good people just like them.

I have had the good fortune of knowing the people at CareerJournal.com for many years, and I greatly appreciate their support.

Family is even more important, and my family is one of the true blessings I have. My parents have always been very supportive of me, as have my many brothers, sisters, aunts, uncles, and cousins.

Many thanks go to my husband, David Dikel, for his patience and love.

1

Pounding the
Virtual Pavement:
Using the Internet
in Your Job Search

Using the Internet in your job search is not necessarily easy. The online job search crosses a variety of services and information resources. No single website, online service, or electronic resource will contain everything you need for a fully effective online job search.

What Is a Complete Job Search?

Many people think they are working hard on their search for a new job when they religiously scan the Sunday classifieds each week. Unfortunately, what they are really doing is expending 100 percent of their effort on only 25 percent of the possibilities.

A complete job search involves four activities:

1. Networking

2. Researching and contacting employers about possible opportunities

3. Reviewing job leads

4. Preparing a resume or curriculum vitae (CV) and distributing it

Incorporating the Internet into your search means that each activity has two facets—off-line and online:

Job-Search Activity	Off-Line	Online
Network	Attend association meetings; have friends and colleagues introduce you to others	Participate in appropriate mailing lists and chat forums, and arrange to meet at local meetings or national conferences
Research and contact target employers	Use telephone books and business directories, and then make telephone calls or send letters	Use telephone books, business directories, association links, industry sites, employer websites, and search engines, and then initiate contact via e-mail or telephone
Review job leads	Use newspapers, recruiters, association journals, job postings on bulletin boards	Use online job banks, recruiter websites, newspapers, association journals, and employer websites
Distribute your resume	Mail copies to employers and networking contacts	E-mail copies to employers and networking contacts; post on online databases

Remember that as you search for opportunities, you must not put all your effort into just one activity or one facet. A success-oriented job search includes all of the activities and both facets in the appropriate measures, spending more time where you will get more value and focusing less on activities that produce poorer results. You are the only one who can measure your comfort level with any activity or environment, but avoiding some of the more difficult ones in favor of others that seem easier will only hurt you in the long run. Look at it this way:

- Networking off-line by attending local association meetings means meeting the people best positioned to help you with your search.

- Reviewing job listings online allows you to peruse lots of listings in a short time.

- Telephoning potential employers puts a person behind your name or electronic resume and lets you talk about possibilities and how you can help.

The Internet Advantage

Here are some ways the Internet enhances your job search:

- You can access current information when it's convenient for you, even if that means doing it at night after the kids go to bed.

- The Internet doesn't take holidays; the whole network doesn't go down all at once, so if one site is unavailable, there are always others you can use.

- There are no geographic limits online, so you can take your job search far beyond your regular boundaries. Many employers prefer to hire from the local area, but that doesn't mean you can't set up interviews before moving.

- You can dig deeper into your local area and perhaps find the smaller employer within walking distance from your house who needs someone just like you.

- Using the Internet in your search demonstrates computer skills to employers.

- No one can see you sweat. The Internet lets you meet new people and initiate new relationships with others in your profession or region without the usual "first date" stress.

- You can explore career alternatives and options that you might not have considered. Not quite happy with your current job? Explore! What sounds like fun? Are there any ways to apply your current skills in a new direction? You will find self-assessment tools, career guides, and even lists of local career counselors and career centers to help you if you feel you need it.

But Before You Go Online . . .

You need to know what keywords to use as you search, which means knowing what you want to find. Most of the online job banks and other directories allow you to search their listings using keywords, so to use them effectively, you have to know what you want to search for. To compile your list of keywords, ask yourself these three questions and jot down the answers:

1. What do you want to do? What can you do? (skills and occupations) For instance: *I can type seventy words per minute; I like working with my hands; I'm licensed to drive a forklift.* Along with your list of specific skills, put down general occupations that interest you. Don't focus on job titles, such as "chief medical officer" or "vice president of international sales"; think "doctor" or "sales" instead.

2. For whom do you want to work? What industries interest you, and what type of employer? (Industries and Employer Preferences) For instance: *I want to work for an Inc 500 company; I'd like to find a family-friendly employer.* Add any specific companies for which you've always wanted to work.

3. Where do you want to live and work? (location) Is there a particular city, state, region, or country you are targeting? For instance: *Southern California; Maryland; Someplace with good golf courses and very little snow.* If you are thinking about a particular city, find out what other cities and municipalities surround it, what county it's in, and if the region has a geographic nickname, like "Silicon Valley" or "Tristate Region," and add all this to your list. Local maps or an atlas can help you here, as can the online telephone books and map services. Your local librarians can point you toward even more useful materials.

JOB-SEARCH TIP: DERIVE KEYWORDS FROM YOUR RESUME

The best way to compile your list of keywords is to prepare your resume. This exercise forces you to define your skills and qualifications, outline your work experience, and determine how you want to market yourself, all of which will help to identify the keywords you will use in your search. You also need to have your resume ready once you begin your job search. Resources to help you write your resume are included in Chapter 2.

If you are having trouble coming up with answers to the previous questions, try the following approaches:

• **Scan some online job banks.** Search some of the job-lead banks listed in Chapter 3 for jobs that appeal to you. Read the job descriptions, note the skills and qualifications the employers are seeking, and then use these words in your search.

• **Ask a friend.** Friends can frequently see traits in you that you can't see yourself. They might also contribute some worthwhile ideas and overlooked options for you to consider.

• **Read some good books.** Check your local library for *What Color Is Your Parachute?*, by Richard Bolles (Ten Speed Press), or *Cool Careers for Dummies*, by Marty Nemko (For Dummies). These books contain information and exercises designed to help you identify your skills and interests, and they suggest some related occupations to consider. Your local career center, public library, or employment service center can recommend additional books and resources.

• **Ask a librarian.** Librarians are usually adept at this kind of exercise, plus they can steer you to other helpful books and resources.

• **Talk to a counselor.** If you are truly having trouble figuring out what you want to do, consulting a career counselor should be your next move. A counselor can help you learn more about yourself and your interests and guide you through the process of deciding where to go. We have resources to help you reach career counselors in Chapter 14.

The "Dirty Dozen" Online Job-Search Mistakes

Before we delve into where to go and what to look for, let's talk about common mistakes made by many people who use the Internet as a job-search tool. Susan Joyce, webmaster of Job-Hunt.org (job-hunt.org), put together the following list of common errors she encounters as she works with both job hunters and hiring managers. Review the entries so you can avoid making the same blunders.

1. **Posting your resume without worrying about privacy.** Protect your identity (and your existing job, if you are currently employed) by limiting access to your contact information.

2. **Using only the big-name Web job sites.** In tight budgetary times, employers save money by using their own websites along with less expensive "niche" sites that may have exactly the applicants they want, such as an association's site or an industry- or location-specific site.

3. **Using the "fire-ready-aim" method of distributing your resume.** Posting your resume at hundreds of job sites or "blasting" it to hundreds or thousands of recruiters and employers is a self-defeating strategy. Most recipients will probably consider it spam.

4. **Limiting your job-search efforts to the Internet.** People are hired by people, so the Internet is useful primarily as a way to reach the people with the job opportunities. Use the Internet as a *component* of your job-search tool kit.

5. **Applying for jobs without meeting the minimum qualifications.** Taking advantage of the simple application procedure to apply for every job that looks interesting, even if you don't satisfy the minimum qualifications, means you will be training recruiters and employers to ignore you.

6. **Depending on e-mail as your only method of contact.** The sad truth these days is that most employers have "spam filter" software that screens e-mail before it

reaches their eyes. Your messages may look like spam and get deleted, unread, without notice to you.

7. Assuming that you have privacy with e-mail and Internet use at work. Inappropriately using company assets, violating the company Internet "acceptable use" policy, and/or simply revealing to your employer that you are job hunting may cost you your job.

8. Not leveraging the Internet's extensive research resources to assist your job search. Use the Internet to identify potential employers, evaluate them, and contact them. Customize your resume and cover letter based on your research, and then dazzle company representatives in the interview with your insight into their products and services, market, competitors, and so forth.

9. Assuming that e-mail is an informal, *private*, temporary medium. Using a crazy, cute, or weird e-mail address (e.g., "WonderWoman@yahoo.com" or "BigStud@hotmail.com") undermines your credibility and almost guarantees that your message will be deleted or ignored. You also want to be careful of the content of your messages. Before you hit Send, think: would you be comfortable if a potential employer read this message on the front page of the *New York Times* or found it in Google tomorrow or two years from tomorrow?

10. Sending a virus-laden "surprise" with your e-mailed resume. An e-mail message containing a virus is usually quarantined and deleted. It's not viewed! And, it leaves a very bad impression. Buy and use anti-virus software, and keep it up to date!

11. Expecting someone else (the job sites, a recruiter, your outplacement counselor) to do the work. A job hunt is a do-it-yourself project! No one is as invested in your future as you are, and no one else knows what you want as well as you.

12. Forgetting that a personal resume Web page or portfolio is a business document. Stick to business-related information that will enhance, rather than hurt, your job search. Focus on the skills and accomplishments that are relevant to the job you want. Demonstrate your writing skills, but not in a political diatribe (unless you want a job as a political commentator).

Job-Hunt.org is filled with insightful and helpful articles designed to guide you to a better job search. We urge you to visit this site and take advantage of the free guidance provided, including several simple things you can do to stand out from the crowd in your search, as well as ways to protect your privacy and identity online.

Now that you know where you can go wrong, let's talk about where you can go right—into an employer's view and onto the payroll—starting with finding the information you need.

Make Your Search Less Work: Easy Ways to Find Anything Online

There are two simple ideas that will help you find anything on the Internet:

1. Move from general to specific. The more general sites such as Yahoo! will help you to find the more specific sites. When you are reviewing job listings, you want to check the big job sites such as Monster and the smaller, targeted sites such as ChicagoJobs.org.

2. Browse to learn, and search to find. Browsing allows you to look over a site at your own pace, learn the language it uses and what it includes, and get comfortable with it. Searching gets you to the heart of the matter quickly and efficiently, but to search, you must have something specific to find.

Time to Browse

If you are unsure of where to start or what to look for, browsing is the way to go. It's also helpful in cases in which you have already started looking online but aren't finding what you want. Browsing works well when you have a basic idea of what you want but could use some suggestions or adjustments to move you in the right direction.

Browsing is a general search-and-scan process. You use broad terms from your keyword list to search Internet libraries or directories for information and resources on your choice of occupations or industries, and then you scan the resulting list to see what came up. It's like searching the catalog in your local library: you find a book title that looks promising and go to the correct shelf to pull the copy, but while there, you look around to see what else might catch your eye. Similarly, you don't look just at the list of links to other sites and resources; you're also interested in the categories of information produced so you can scan the "shelves" and see what you might discover. In most cases, you should start gathering information and resources almost immediately, along with suggestions for more paths to explore. You can find job sites, potential employers, links to industry or occupational information, and pointers to resource guides.

Browsing also lets you test your keywords so you can see which terms from your list lead you in the right direction or even give you more keywords to use. You also learn which words don't work as well and which are taking you in the wrong direction and should be removed from your list. In any case, it is not a wasted activity.

Start the Search

Searching comes into play when you have your objectives identified, you've developed your keyword list and settled on the best terms defining your needs and objectives, and you have your resume prepared. You know you are ready to search when you have a list of specific terms defining your skills, the types of jobs you are seeking, and the companies or organizations for which you want to work—a list that was built while browsing. You are not looking for long lists of possibilities, but rather the most specific and best-matched ones.

Searching has the advantage of speed and accuracy. You cover more ground online because you move faster and with more determination. You get into and out of the major job-lead banks in ten minutes or less, you're able to review loads of information about an employer in preparation for an interview in twenty minutes or less, and you aren't wasting time scanning hundreds of job leads. Your searches produce a limited number of highly qualified leads and highly qualified employer lists with a minimum of mismatched job-lead spam.

Through browsing and searching, you have already begun to move from general data to specific information. The next task is to start expanding this approach to the online resources needed for your search.

Stepping Through the Internet Research Process

Now let's apply the ideas of moving from general to specific and browsing before searching to your search for information online.

Step One: Check Those Virtual Libraries and Internet Directories (very general)

Virtual libraries and Internet directories are large collections of information arranged in broad topics by human editors. Because they cover many subjects, they act as general guides to the Internet. They are useful for identifying the best search terms and for beginning to locate helpful resources. Start out by browsing their main categories, and then use their search features, scanning the resulting lists for ideas.

Try this: Browse *education* or *finance* in the following libraries and directories to glean information on these topics. Make a note of employers you find and topics you discover.

Librarian's Index to the Internet	lii.org
The Scout Report	scout.wisc.edu
University of Delaware Subject Guides	www2.lib.udel.edu/subj
Yahoo!	yahoo.com

Many of the search engines listed under Step Three also maintain directories of information you can browse.

Step Two: Review Online Resource Guides (becoming more specific)

Online resource guides are sites or documents dedicated to a specific topic or industry. As with print directories or encyclopedias that focus on only one topic, they are much more specific in identifying industry and employer information and are usually more inclusive of resources. The virtual libraries and Internet directories listed in Step One will point you toward online resource guides (look for the indexes or directories under any topic). The best resource guides are those created by organizations or people who are specialists in the particular subject.

To judge the value of a resource guide, look for information on who has compiled it, the creator's expertise in this area, and why the guide was created. Resource guides can take many forms, as you can infer from this short list:

Hoover's   hoovers.com (business information)

NewsLink   newslink.org (newspapers worldwide)

The Riley Guide   rileyguide.com (employment information)

Step Three: Search Those Search Engines (very specific)

While a Web directory usually directs you to a whole website, a search engine is a searchable database of keywords retrieved from individual Web pages, and these databases are huge. For this reason, it's best to not use the search engines until you are as specific as possible about what you want to find. Use them to locate hidden information on any topic (occupation or industry) or employer. Each search engine is different in how it works and what it indexes, and none of them, even the biggest, has indexed the whole Web. Use two or three in your search, and compare the results. Try them all, and then settle on the ones you like the best. Don't feel obliged to use the ones that your friends, the local librarians, or even this book might recommend. It's a personal choice. Once you've culled your favorites, become an expert searcher by learning all the advanced commands so you can really *search*!

Try this: Search the names of employers you found in Step One as well as specific topics or occupational fields, using the following tools:

AlltheWeb   alltheweb.com

Ask.com   ask.com

Google   google.com

Now that you know how and when to browse and search and where to look for what you want, you can start your online job search. We'll go through each job-search activity—networking, researching, reviewing job leads, and preparing a resume—and talk about how you can incorporate the online facet of each into your project. Just remember to also work on each activity off-line too for the best results.

INTERNET TIP: BROKEN URLS

If you have trouble connecting to a Web page, try cutting the address, or URL (uniform resource locator); go back one slash mark from the right end. The file or directory you are seeking may have moved, and by backing up one level at a time, you may be able to find the new location. For example, *rileyguide.com/careercenter/dob.html* becomes *rileyguide.com/careercenter* becomes *rileyguide.com*.

Step One for Your Search: Network

In their sixth annual "Source of Hire" white paper, Gerry Crispin and Mark Mehler of CareerXroads.com report that in 2006, 34 percent of all openings filled by hiring from outside an organization were filled by employee referrals. (The full report is available on their website at careerxroads.com.) Regular surveys of candidates in transition programs at various outplacement agencies confirm, from the job seeker's point of view, what experts repeat ad infinitum: *Networking is the best way to find a new job.* However, networking is also the most stressful of the four activities in the job-search process, which is probably why it is the least pursued. Fortunately, the Internet can make a difficult situation a bit easier by allowing you to network online.

Advantages of Online Networking . . .

• You can "break the ice" before meeting someone in person. No one can see you sweat.

• You can listen, engage, or be engaged as you wish. You won't feel like a wallflower, because no one can see you standing off by yourself.

• Many recruiters follow the discussions to help locate interesting and qualified candidates for positions they are trying to fill.

• Many employers and recruiters use subject-specific groups to post jobs targeting a defined set of potential applicants.

. . . and the Disadvantages

• Although making first contact is easier, establishing a true personal relationship online takes more time because you do not have the "personal touch" or a handshake.

• First impressions count more than ever, so be careful with your public postings, since any posting may be the first time someone learns about you. You must be even more professional and polite than you are in person, and conservative with your language.

- Strict etiquette and behavior rules apply, and they can differ widely from group to group. Any behavior that appears rude or obnoxious will get you blacklisted faster than you can imagine.

- The content of each group differs. Some allow job announcements; some don't. Some post only professional scholarly announcements. Know what is permitted before you post by reading any available FAQs (frequently asked questions) sections.

- The contents of public forums and lists are often indexed by the search engines and viewable by anyone who searches, at any time in the future. Don't reveal anything or write anything that you would be uncomfortable having a potential employer see.

JOB-SEARCH TIP: BE DISCREET ONLINE

In a survey by CareerBuilder.com, 26 percent of hiring managers said they have used Internet search engines to research potential employees. More than one in ten admitted to using social networking sites in their candidate-screening processes. Fully half of hiring managers who used search engines to research candidates rejected a person based on what they found, and 63 percent of managers who browsed social networking sites found something that caused them to dismiss a candidate. So, network online, but be cautious in your communications, and always maintain a professional presence. For a link to this report, as well as other material on this topic, see the resources lists at the end of the chapter.

The Fine Art of Netiquette

As we said earlier, the stress of making new connections is greatly alleviated through the Internet, but the Net isn't a fast track to the hidden job market. It is important that you begin these relationships in the right way and maintain them properly. Because you can't use your voice or body language to express yourself, you are limited to making sure that the words used, as well as how they are presented, properly represent your intentions. And this warning is not just for folks new to the Internet. Many Internet experts need a reminder that the real people behind the electrons make real decisions based on your electronic communication. To all of you, we humbly offer this bit of advice: *Do not go boldly where you have never gone before!*

Online networking gives you a unique opportunity to connect with people in hiring places. Take the time to learn some simple rules of netiquette, otherwise known as the fine art of correct behavior on the Internet. These precepts can mean the difference between stepping out in style and stumbling off the online block.

- **Stop** and learn the respective rules of conduct and desirable topics of discussion for any particular mailing list or community forum, and then follow them!

- **Look** for a list of FAQs so you don't pose the same questions that everyone else has and frustrate the other users.

- **Listen** patiently to the groups and forums you have joined, and learn the tone, language, and culture of the group before you start posting.

- **Never** post your resume or ask if anyone can help you land a job unless you are participating in a forum dedicated to this activity.

Think of each online discussion forum as an association meeting or an office party where you are the new person in the crowd. You must introduce yourself to everyone, and you want to make a good first impression. Step carefully, speak well, and learn as much as you can about this group of people before you make yourself known to them. Adhere to the three principles of good networking:

1. Public participation is necessary to get networking contacts. If you don't make yourself visible, no one will know you are there, including recruiters and potential employers.

2. Your participation must count. Enhance the discussions with your knowledge, but limit your responses to topics you know. Offer truly helpful advice or information when you can, but do not overwhelm the others by responding to each and every question asked. Earn your place and the respect of the others.

3. Networking is a two-way relationship that must be beneficial to both parties. You must give in order to receive. If you aren't helping others on the list, then it is unlikely they will be willing to help you.

We have books and resources on networking listed at the end of this chapter, but we offer the following articles as required reading before you start strutting your stuff online:

- Shea, Virginia. "The Core Rules of Netiquette" (albion.com/netiquette/corerules.html). Excerpted from her book *Netiquette*, this is a rundown of ten general guidelines to follow for communicating effectively online.

- The Writing Lab & OWL at Purdue University. "Email Etiquette" (owl.english. purdue.edu/handouts/pw/p_emailett.html). A nice guide to proper e-mail communication, particularly in a businesslike setting, this is one of the many good handouts on writing and communications from the Writing Lab at Purdue, which includes the Online Writing Lab (OWL).

Identifying the Good Contacts and Making That First Call

Once you are in an online discussion group, how can you identify the people who might be your best contacts? First, look for postings by participants who seem knowledgeable about the topic being discussed. This, of course, requires that you know the topic yourself, but beyond that, look for people who seem not only to be authoritative but also to have the respect of others. You want to pay attention to the contributor about whom others say, "Yes, listen to this person." Then check the person's organizational affiliation. You might be able to decipher this from his or her e-mail address, but it might also be in a signature at the end of the message. These signatures usually give a person's name, employer and job title, and more complete contact information. While such signature information is not a guarantee of merit, it's at least a statement that the writer is not afraid to identify him- or herself and the affiliate organization.

After you have selected some forum participants to contact, prepare your approach carefully. Because you know them from the Internet, your first contact should be through the Internet, specifically by e-mail. Be sure your message is professional and especially polite, and double-check for grammar and spelling errors before sending it. In addition:

• Contact each person directly, not through the list or open forum.

• Be concise, identify yourself, and state why you are initiating contact. Specify some of your interests and where you noticed some correlation with the person's postings. Never use this contact to ask for a job or for leads on employment opportunities.

• Request a follow-up to your message, via phone or e-mail, but give the recipient the choice of how to continue. Do not use the "Return Receipt" or confirmation-of-receipt feature in your e-mail software to verify that your message was read. Many people find these requests to be rude and may delete your e-mail in response.

• If you are contacting more than one person, do not copy the same message to each of them. Send each person a separate e-mail message. It not only looks better but also avoids the possibility of fueling any hidden rivalries that might work against you.

Where to Network Online

The numerous places to network online include mailing lists, chat rooms and Web forums, and social networking websites. The principles regarding netiquette and making contact with participants that we outlined earlier apply in all of these areas. All of these online forums offer a great way to begin those casual relationships that later turn into great opportunities. Various forums are used to announce meetings, projects, proposals, and products, and participants also discuss recent developments in their occupation or industry and ask questions of one another. Anyone involved in a job search or career exploration can benefit from following these online public discussions, learning about current trends and developments, and sharing the interests and concerns of those involved.

Among the thousands of discussion forums, the best ones for your job search will be those dedicated to professional topics germane to your particular employment field or the industry that interests you, or research topics in your field of study. For example, while the *ShowDogs-L* mailing list is a promising place to get to know other dog lovers, it will truly benefit only dog handlers, breeders, or sitters in terms of networking for employment. Once you identify the forums that carry discussions for your field or industry, it's also possible that you'll find job announcements crossing these forums, making these yet another targeted service for your job search.

Web Forums and Chat Rooms

Web forums and chat rooms, sometimes also called online communities or message boards, are discussion groups that operate through the Web. Many sites offer them, and the easy Web interface makes them popular with users. Many corporate, college and university, and military groups also operate Web forums to stay connected with their alumni; in these cases, membership is limited to true alumni, and your identity will be verified. To participate in these forums and chats, all you need is usually a valid e-mail address (for registration purposes) and a Web browser. Check out the Web forums and chat rooms at these sites to see what they offer:

Fast Company's Company of Friends	fastcompany.com/cof
Vault.com Message Boards	vault.com
AOL PeopleConnection	peopleconnection.aol.com
Company and Military Alumni Networks	job-hunt.org/employer_alumni_ networking.shtml

Social Networking Sites

Social networking sites work the "six degrees of separation" concept to the nth degree by using the Internet to turn who you are, whom you know, and what you know into a monster-size spider net of connectivity. They differ from chat rooms and mailing lists in that they are intended to be expanded contact lists, not solely discussion or support groups. Note that some networking sites are dedicated to business and professional connections, while others are intended for social contacts only. Obviously, your job search will benefit from the former much more than the latter.

Many job-search experts are not fully supportive of these sites, but you may find them to be useful. Be sure to read each site's privacy policy and user agreement carefully, and be honest about your reason for joining. To participate, you need a valid e-mail address (for registration purposes) and a Web browser. Here are examples of the service:

Friendster	friendster.com
LinkedIn	linkedin.com
Networking for Professionals	networkingforprofessionals.com

Mailing Lists

Mailing lists are discussion groups that operate through e-mail; anyone with an e-mail address can use them. A central computer (sometimes called the Listserv, listproc, or majordomo) runs the list. (The name varies according to the list-manager software being used.) To participate in a mailing list, you must first subscribe by sending a message to the list's host computer asking to be added to that particular list. The computer will then send you back a message to let you know your status. Once it says you are successfully added, you will automatically begin receiving the messages from that mailing list in your e-mail account. This ease of use and delivery fuels their popularity.

As with other online discussion forums, mailing lists cover a broad variety of topics and fields. They carry occasional job postings, usually in advance of print announcements, and they are a good resource for networking contacts, industry trends, and other developments. Mailing lists are particularly popular among the academic and research professions, making them especially useful for persons looking for work in colleges and universities.

INTERNET TIP: FREE E-MAIL

If you don't have an e-mail account available where you access the Internet, or if your account is through your employer, you can register with one of these free Web-accessible e-mail services:

| Google Gmail | gmail.google.com |
| Yahoo! Mail | mail.yahoo.com |

The following two directories will help you find relevant mailing lists for your networking. They can be searched using keywords that describe the subject or occupational area in which you are interested or can be browsed by major topic. They will also tell you if the list's postings are archived online and if you can view them before you join to get a better feel for the group.

| Catalist | www.lsoft.com/lists/listref.html |
| Yahoo! Groups | groups.yahoo.com |

There's one more thing you must remember about mailing lists, and that is how to control them. When you are first added to a list, you should receive a brief message with explanatory commands, including the ones you need in order to suspend mail while you are on vacation or to unsubscribe to the list should it not be right for you. Save this message somewhere, along with the e-mail address of the person who manages the list! Other members do not appreciate it when people have to write to the list to ask for this information.

To learn more about the basics of mailing lists, along with the rest of the Internet, we suggest you contact your local public library to sign up for an Internet Basics class, or read *The Internet for Dummies*, by John R. Levine et al. (For Dummies). It is updated frequently, so look for the most recent edition. If you cannot find it, ask the librarians what books they might recommend.

Step Two for Your Search: Research and Target Employers

The Internet is a huge collection of databases just waiting for you. Tap the resources provided by the thousands of companies, colleges and universities, governments, and news and information services to do extended research into your target occupations, industries, and employers.

Would it make sense to go into a hardware store and ask the manager if there are any job openings for day care providers? It wouldn't, because you know it is unlikely a hardware store would have any need for someone with those skills. This is why you research employers, to find those that have a need that you can fill. You want to know what they do, how they function, and how you might fit into the organization.

In the same vein, if you are invited for an interview, you cannot walk into an employer's office and say, "So, what is this job I am interviewing for, and how do I fit into your organization?" Employers today expect you to know who they are, what they do, what the job entails, and how you would fit into the company structure and culture, before you arrive. Researching the employer in advance will get you past the small talk and into the real purpose of your interview, convincing the employer that the company needs you and that you will be a valuable addition to the team who is worth more than the nominal salary.

Think of a job interview as a sales pitch: you have a product to sell (yourself). You need to know who is buying (the employer) and what the buyer needs (what skills are required in what jobs). Once you've determined the situation, you send in your marketing brochure (the resume and cover letter), noting the company's needs and specifying how your product fills those needs. If you've done it right, you'll be invited to make a live presentation (job interview), and possibly make the sale (be offered a position). All it takes is some advance research. You know the constant refrain by heart: 80 percent of all jobs are never advertised, not even on the Internet. Well, researching the employers and contacting them is one way to get connected to that "hidden market." (The other way is through networking.)

To start your search, you first need lists of companies to review, and then you must research the companies to weed out those that don't interest you, leaving only two or three. These few must be aggressively researched until you home in on the points that match your desires and, hopefully, the right people inside for you to contact.

Business directories and yellow pages directories, such as the following, are reliable sources for compiling lists of companies. Many of these online sources will include links to the company's website, if available. The business directories will also give you some information about the company so you can begin to cross off those that do not interest you and highlight those that do.

Business.com	business.com
Superpages	superpages.com
ThomasNet	thomasnet.com
Yellowpages.com	yellowpages.com

Armed with your list of possible employers, you can begin the three-part process of researching at the company level. It is through this process that you selectively pare your list to arrive at a small core of companies to target.

1. **Start your employer research at the employer's website.** The company website is a book about the employer by the employer. Read it "cover to cover," and print out the pages that interest you or have information you want to double-check.

   - Look at anything that says "News" or "What's New" for the latest information on what is happening and possible clues on new areas or projects where you might be able to help.

   - Read all mission statements or descriptions of services to learn how this organization describes itself. Use this knowledge to customize your cover letter to the company's interests.

   - Look for an annual report or strategic plan, and read it carefully. These documents will tell you where the company is going and how it plans to get there.

   - Check out the human resources area for more information on current or ongoing job openings and the benefits offered by this company.

   - Look over the whole site. What does the design of these pages say to you about this organization? Is the tone conservative or freewheeling? Are the pages well organized or difficult to follow? Companies want their websites to reflect the business's corporate image, so the site can say a lot about the institution with few words.

2. Check business directories and other employer information sources for outside profiles of the employers. This area, as exemplified in the following list, includes brief profiles with financial information such as those found in Hoover's, as well as insider profiles such as those from Vault.com and WetFeet .com. The reference librarians in your local library can suggest additional print and electronic resources to support your research.

Edgar (10K reports)	sec.gov/edgar.shtml
Hoover's	hoovers.com
Vault.com	vault.com
WetFeet.com	wetfeet.com

3. Fire up the search engines. Look for more information on an employer anywhere you can pursue it. Search the employer's name, the company's products, the names of any people in the organization, and so forth, in your favorite search engine. Why? As one job seeker put it, "The employer's website told me what they wanted me to know, but I found what I wanted to know by doing more searching online." Anything you spot can be useful in your initial search, your sales pitch, or even your decision on whether it's worth contacting this employer about opportunities.

Step Three for Your Search: Review Job Listings

While searching for employers and opportunities, look for job listings at several levels, again always thinking about moving from general to specific.

• Start with the large recruiting sites to get the broadest overviews and largest database searches you can.

• Review the online journals, newspapers, and job banks for your target location, industry, and occupation or discipline. Look for recruiters who specialize in a particular industry or occupational group, or who concentrate on one geographic area.

• Scan the various professional or trade association websites for job listings marketed to your particular job areas, occupational fields, industries, and geographic location. There are also websites for numerous diversity and affinity groups with which you might identify yourself, many of which carry job announcements.

• Visit employer websites, even if you have seen the companies' jobs listed in other locations. Many employers use the major job-lead banks to advertise generic jobs that they are always looking to fill but post the specific openings, along with even more job categories, on their own sites. You may also come upon a way to contact their human resources departments to learn about any opportunities they haven't posted.

Job Listings 101: Generally Start with the Internet Job Guides

Online resource guides for job and career information contain links to hundreds of Internet employment resources. Using these, you can quickly identify places to begin your job search. The Employment or Jobs/Careers sections of the virtual libraries might also be useful, but you'll likely find these targeted guides better organized and more in-depth. This short list will get you started, but a more complete list with descriptions is provided at the end of Chapter 3.

JobHunt	job-hunt.org
JobHuntersBible.com	jobhuntersbible.com
The Riley Guide	rileyguide.com

Job Listings 102: The Great Job-Lead Banks

Job-lead banks feature hundreds or even thousands of job announcements in numerous fields and occupations. The online classifieds of most major newspapers fall under this category (smaller regional and local papers are generally considered targeted sources, the next category). Almost all of these sites and sources have a keyword searching capability, allowing you to scan all the job listings in a few minutes instead of a few hours. A sample listing follows; a more complete list of the great job-lead banks along with descriptions is in Chapter 3.

Monster.com	monster.com
NationJob	nationjob.com
CareerBuilder.com	careerbuilder.com
JobCentral	jobcentral.com

Job Listings 103: Targeted Sources

Many sites are set up to serve a particular industry, occupation, geographic location, or group of people. Professional and trade associations, all trade and industry publications, and even the mailing lists and community forums discussed in the earlier section on networking fall into this category. This book contains hundreds of these sites, so select the chapters that address your needs, and scan the index for topics you hadn't thought of. This is just a small example of the variety of targeted resources available online:

American Academy of Forensic Sciences	aafs.org
ChicagoJobs	chicagojobs.org
JobAccess (jobs for people with disabilities)	jobaccess.org
Power Marketing Association	powermarketers.com

Job Listings 104: Employer Websites

As explained earlier, you need to create lists of employers for specific industries, filter the list to just those names that match your job criteria, and make contact. Business directories and telephone directories can be useful in this part of your job search, as can your local public library or job service office.

Step Four for Your Search: Post Your Resume Online

Yes, you can post your resume in hundreds of databases online with the hope that you will be "discovered" by a super employer and offered your dream job. The problem is that it is highly unlikely that this will ever happen to you, especially in the current job market. That's not to say that posting your resume is not worth your effort. Many people have posted their resumes online and got calls that turned into successful new jobs. Articles about such people have appeared in various national publications, and many successful posters have even sent us accounts of personal experiences or events they have witnessed, but these cases are an extremely small percentage of all those who are posting.

While we feel that posting your resume online is the least effective way for you to find a new opportunity, it is a way for you to become known to potential employers, so we want you to do it. We just don't want you to spend a lot of time on this activity when you could be doing better things, such as networking, researching employers, and even reviewing job-lead banks.

If you decide to post your resume online, you must do it correctly. Your resume must be in the right form and format. Also think about the ramifications of your decision to pursue this activity, and there are a lot of them. Because this discussion covers many topics and requires your full attention, we have devoted all of Chapter 2 to how, why, where, and what to do about posting your resume online.

How to Select the Good Stuff

Now that you've rounded them up, how do you decide which resources are the best and will fit your needs? You will have to make the final decision yourself based on your needs and preferences, but following are questions to ponder as you review everything you collected.

What Are You Finding There?

- Is it advertising, or is there information applicable to your search? A site that is merely advertising its services isn't giving you any help right now.

- Is it information from experts in this field, or comments submitted by others? While some lay users may contribute useful tips, articles from experts will have more authoritative and reliable information.

- Are there lists of employers, including businesses, colleges and schools, or nonprofit associations? These can be helpful for targeting key firms or linking you to organizations of which you were unaware.

- Are there job listings, job-search tips, and other helpful items? While job listings are always good to find, you may prefer a site with articles on writing cover letters and resumes at a time when you are struggling through this process.

Do You Know People Who Have Used This Service?

- For what purpose did others use the service (posted a resume, reviewed job leads, worked through the career exploration exam)? How well did it work for them (got calls from recruiters, found good job leads, gained some valuable insight from the exam)?

- Did they like what they found? Were the recruiters who called professional? Did they feel comfortable with this service?

- Do they feel it was helpful and worth the time spent here?

What About the Job Listings?

- Are there real jobs listed here, or just "sample lists of jobs we are currently trying to fill"? Samples are OK, but when you're ready to "buy," pay for only the real thing, even when it comes to free job listings.

- Do the job listings include the date they were added? It is frustrating to you and to the employer to waste time on a job that was filled six months ago.

- Can you look at the job listings without registering your personal information and/or resume? While it may be reasonable for the employer's contact information to be blocked, you should be able to review listings before you register, just to be sure that the jobs are current and relevant to you. We advise users to avoid sites that demand your personal information and/or resume before allowing you to see even a sample of the job database.

Who Operates This Service?

- Is there information about the people who run this site? A simple profile is not hard to provide, especially for a group with nothing to hide from visitors.

- What are the operators' backgrounds (recruiters, industry specialists, librarians, etc.)? Many online job-search services are now being run by people who have no background in what they are doing but hope to make money at it from you.

- Is there a name, address, or phone number for contacting them with questions? Legitimate services will provide this information, not just a form to fill out and submit. They want to hear from you, and they will also respond if you send an e-mail.

If There's a Fee for This Service, Is It Worth the Cost?

- Can you substitute other sites and providers that offer an equal service at no cost? Don't just pay for this service; be a careful shopper and compare it with others.

- What will your money get you? Access to job listings is one thing; access to exclusive listings and additional features such as help with resume creation and employer research is another.

- What is the refund policy if you're not satisfied? Again, look for who is running this site, where they are located, and how to contact them.

What Promises Are They Making, and Are These Promises Reasonable?

- Do they offer guarantees? If so, the Federal Trade Commission will want to speak with them. Nothing in a job-search process is guaranteed. There's no exclusive access to the "hidden job market," and there's no guarantee that shooting hundreds of copies of your resume to employers through e-mail will result in your getting an interview, let alone a job.

How Old Is the Other Information Posted There?

- Are articles and resource lists accompanied by dates so you know the last time the operator reviewed and revised them? These items can become "stale," just like job postings.

- Are the site's owners updating and adding new materials regularly (daily, weekly, monthly)? If they are not posting anything new, it's unlikely they are working on maintaining anything else on this site, such as the job listings.

- Are the articles retained for an extended period, or are they deleted when new material is added? While it's not necessarily a mark of higher quality, an archive of the older articles is a nice touch.

If You Send These People an E-Mail Message Asking for More Information, Do They Actually Respond?

- If they never contact you, consider this a warning that saved you some money.

- If they do contact you, then judge them using your own criteria based on the information they provide. Be sure to ask them all the questions that are important to you, and don't let anyone bully you into buying.

INTERNET TIP: ONLINE PAYMENTS

When paying for any service through the Web, always use a credit card. Never send a check or money order, and we don't recommend using a debit card either. Credit cards offer you more protections and recourse should you not receive the services or products advertised. When making a purchase online, look for a locked-padlock icon in the status bar at the bottom of the browser before you enter your credit card information into a Web page. If the padlock icon is open or unlocked, the data transmission is not secure, and you should not trust it with your credit card information. If you don't want to "transmit" your credit card information over the Internet, call the company from which you want to purchase and relay the information over the phone. If the company will not accept your payment information in this way, take your business elsewhere.

As we said at the beginning of this section, the final decision on whether to use any site or service online (or off-line) is yours alone. Be a careful consumer and buy wisely. If you get lousy service somewhere or pay for services that are not provided in the manner that was promised (or do not produce the promised results), don't take it lying down. Notify the Better Business Bureau (bbb.org), the Federal Trade Commission (ftc.gov), your state's attorney general, and, if it is an online service, the Internet Crime Complaint Center (ic3.gov). After you inform all of them, please send us an e-mail (rileyguide@yahoo.com), because we want to know about it too!

Managing Your Time Online

People frequently tell us that they always start searching online in the same place, and well, heck, they spend so much time with those pages that they never get anywhere else. So, we herewith offer some tips to prevent you from slipping into the same bad habit.

Every time you connect, start someplace new. Pick out a select list of general resources, use them to find more specific resources, and keep moving. Things change, but not so rapidly that you will miss something important if you check there only twice a week. Plan your online job-search strategy so you don't get stuck in one place and waste time and money.

Here's an outline of what we think is your best plan for spending your time online wisely. It's based on our simple idea of moving from general to specific, but it's up to you to remember to move!

1. Visit the large information databases first. These include virtual libraries and large recruiting sites such as CareerBuilder (careerbuilder.com) and all the other sites listed in Chapter 3. Look for links to information in your chosen field or industry. Repeat this search every few days—for example, Monday and Thursday.

2. Move on to the smaller, more exclusive resources and services, including online resource guides and sites dedicated to your field or industry. You want to find links to employers or collected information in your field that can give you leads or networking contacts. Repeat this search every few days—say, Tuesday and Friday.

3. Use the search engines to locate new and hidden resources specific to your occupation and field. If you are interested in a certain company, search on the company name, any variations or nicknames by which it is known, and names of its major products. Repeat this search every few days—maybe Wednesday and Saturday.

4. Finally, shut off the computer and spend some time with your family, your friends, and yourself. Take a day to relax, re-center, and remind yourself that there is a world out there and people to talk to. You can update your resume or prepare some cover letters, but don't go online. Take the kids to the park, play with your dog, scratch the cat, and sun the iguana, or substitute time with whatever pets you have. Searching for work is a stressful process, and you need to take time for yourself to maintain your health, both physically and emotionally. This positive action will reflect in your search and in interviews.

Probably the Most Important Statement in This Entire Book

The Internet should not be the only resource you use for your job search!

You must continue to utilize all contacts, information resources, and services available to you for the most effective and efficient search for employment. Attend local meetings, use the resources of your local library to help unearth employers you may have missed online, and pick up the telephone and call people. Despite all the potential of the Internet, it still doesn't connect everyone everywhere, nor does it contain all the knowledge of the universe.

Limit your time online to 25 percent of the total time you can dedicate to your job search. For information technology and networking professionals, this portion may increase to 50 percent of your time, but make sure your skills are current in order for you to be your most competitive.

Suggested Reading for Your (Internet) Job Search

Listed here are a few of the many books and online resources available to help you with your job search, both off-line and online. Your local public library or career service center may have many of the books in its collection, along with other titles. Ask librarians for their recommendations. If you'd like your own copy of a particular book to tear apart, mark up, or personalize in other ways, then check your local bookstore or any of the online bookstores. Many of these titles are updated every year or two, so always look for the most recent editions.

Job-Search Books

Bolles, Richard Nelson. *What Color Is Your Parachute?* Ten Speed Press (updated annually).

Pierson, Orville. *The Unwritten Rules of the Highly Effective Job Search.* McGraw-Hill, 2007.

Krannich, Ron, and Caryl Krannich. *The Blue Collar Resume and Job Hunting Guide*. Impact Publications, 2007.

————. *The Ex-Offender's Job Hunting Guide: 10 Steps to a New Life in the Work World*. Impact Publications, 2005.

Job-Search Guidance Online

JobHuntersBible.com

jobhuntersbible.com

This website incorporates Richard Bolles's megalist of job resources online with many of his self-assessment exercises and job-searching advice from *Parachute*, but he still refers to it as a companion to his book.

Joyce Lain Kennedy's Careers Now

featureserv.com

Joyce Lain Kennedy has been answering questions on career and employment issues for more than thirty years. She has written many books on careers and job search that have influenced the way thousands of us think of this process, and her syndicated column appears in more than one hundred newspapers. Tribune Media Services maintains a ninety-day archive of her columns, free to all viewers. Under "Business," look for "Workplace" and select "Joyce Lain Kennedy—Careers Now."

Ask the Headhunter

asktheheadhunter.com

"America's Employment System is broken. Everything you know about job hunting and hiring is wrong. Throw away your resume or job description and Ask the Headhunter." No, it is not your traditional job-search advice, but Nick Corcodilos, a former recruiter, does offer some interesting and thought-provoking commentary.

Knock 'em Dead Online

knockemdead.com

This companion to Martin Yate's *Knock 'em Dead* series of career books offers excellent articles and advice for your job search.

CareerJournal from the Wall Street Journal

careerjournal.com

CareerJournal offers hundreds of articles and information resources covering all aspects of your job search at this site, including all degrees of experience from entry level to chief executive. You'll see mentions to this site many times throughout the book as a top-rated source.

Strategies for Starting Your Online Job Search

job-hunt.org/starting.shtml

Susan Joyce, of Job-Hunt.org, walks you through your online job search step by step, pointing you to the relevant sections of her website along the way.

How to Job Search (The Riley Guide)

rileyguide.com/execute.html

This page acts as a gateway to all the job-search guidance in The Riley Guide, including topics such as protecting your identity and avoiding scams.

Networking Advice

Refer back to the discussion on networking earlier in this chapter for additional resources.

Darling, Diane. *Networking for Career Success*. McGraw-Hill, 2005.

Fisher, Donna, et al. *Power Networking: 59 Secrets for Personal and Professional Success*, 2nd ed. Bard Press, 2000.

Online Networking Advice

Knock 'em Dead Networking Advice

knockemdead.com/networking.php

Martin Yate, author of the *Knock 'em Dead* career books, has created one of the better collections of networking advice available on the Internet, including a discussion of online networking.

Networking Tips

rwn.org/misc.asp

Authored up by the Rochester (New York) Women's Network, this article is a nice guide to face-to-face networking and includes tips on working a room and even a table during a dinner event.

Haefner, Rosemary. "The Internet and Your Professional Image." (CareerBuilder.com)

careerbuilder.com/jobseeker/careerbytes/cbarticle.aspx?articleid=573

This article explores current trends in applicant background checks and how to protect your image online.

Maher, Kris. "Networking Web Sites: A New Job Search Arena." (CareerJournal.com)

careerjournal.com/jobhunting/usingnet/20040109-maher.html

This article discusses these services, showing both their positive and negative aspects and offering advice on the best way to utilize these new resources.

Lorenz, Kate. "Warning: Social Networking Can Be Hazardous to Your Job Search." (CareerBuilder.com)

careerbuilder.com/jobseeker/careerbytes/cbarticle.aspx?articleid=533

Not all employers search candidates and employees online, but the trend is growing. This article discusses one person's experience and offers tips for avoiding problems.

Needleman, Sarah E. "Tips for Safeguarding Your Online Reputation." (CareerJournal.com)

careerjournal.com/jobhunting/usingnet/20070131-needleman.html

This article is a gateway to several articles all relating to the topic of how employers are researching you online and how you can best protect yourself.

2

Your Resume on the Internet

When professionals evaluate the job-search process, distributing a resume or CV is rated as the least effective of the four primary activities that make up a complete search. Job seekers, however, rate it as the second most productive thing they believe they can do online (reviewing job listings is number one). We de-emphasize this element because, in terms of landing you a new job, it is not as effective as networking, researching and targeting employers, or even reviewing job leads. While we want you to create a top-notch resume for yourself and post it online, we don't want you to assume that doing so will bring you job-search happiness.

Writing your resume, actually creating the document that employers and others will review, is one of the most important tasks in a job search. Take the time to do it right, devoting mental effort to pinpoint what you want to attain before you start pounding the pavement. Notwithstanding how ineffective it is to post a resume in the many databases online, if you are going to post yours—and we think you should—you ought to do it right.

Your resume is your personal product brochure, the printed item that summarizes all the benefits of you and why the employer should "buy" you. An excellent resume can help you win the position you want. A bad one will likely knock you out of consideration, no matter how qualified you are. You must have a resume that serves you well, but we are not the ones to instruct you on accomplishing this mission. At the end of this chapter we list selected books and online workshops from experts in this field. They are the ones to help you compose a resume. Your local librarians, career counselors and coaches, and bookstore managers can recommend even more books and resources, so don't hesitate to ask around should nothing here suit you.

What we're good at is helping you take that resume and get it online, so that is what this chapter will cover. We'll address the problems associated with posting a resume, how to format it so posting it in websites and e-mailing it to employers is fast and easy, and how to select where to post it. We encourage you to read this chapter before you create your resume and then come back to these pages when you have it ready to go. Consider the issues and advice we present here, and apply what you've learned as you are working on your resume. And remember, you do not need to limit yourself to just one resume. You can have several that are presented in different ways. If you have access to a computer with word-processing software, you are limited only by the available space on your storage medium.

The Myth About the Internet Resume

Many people infer that the advancement of online resume databases, resume-management systems, and keyword searching requires you to produce one resume for paper but an entirely different resume for online. *This is not true!*

When done correctly, your well-written, well-prepared resume will contain all of the necessary keywords to attract attention whether it is being read by a hiring manager or scanned and searched in any database, online or off-line. You still need only one resume, but now you want to have it in several formats, ready to produce in the proper form as needed, including these:

1. **A designed hard-copy version:** a good-looking printed resume with bulleted lists, bold and italicized text, and other highlights, ready to send to contacts through the mail

2. **A scannable version:** a neat, word-processed and printed resume without bullets, boldface, italics, or other design highlights, written in a standard font and printed on white paper to send to employers who use scanning systems

3. **A plain-text version:** a no-frills, plain-text file that you keep to cut and paste into online forms and for posting in online databases

4. **An e-mail version:** another no-frills, plain-text file, but one formatted to meet the length-of-line restrictions of most e-mail systems, making it easy to copy and paste into an e-mail message and forward to an employer or recruiter in seconds

INTERNET TIP: HOW TO CUT AND PASTE

The cut-and-paste feature in all text-based programs (word processing, e-mail, online databases, etc.) allows you to quickly take text from one place and add it to another. The problem is compatible formatting, which is why we do not recommend you cut text from your Word resume to place in your e-mail message or the online forms found in most resume databases. The way the text appears is not the same. However, once you've created the plain-text and e-mail versions of your resume, you can easily and quickly use cut-and-paste to copy the text of your resume from Notepad to the online resume database or your e-mail message.

To cut-and-paste, using your mouse, place your cursor at the beginning of the text you want to copy. Click and hold the left button while pulling your mouse over the text to highlight it. Release the left button. Now place the cursor over the highlighted text. Click the right button for Options, and select Copy. Move your cursor to where you want to add the text you just copied, right-click your mouse again, and select Paste. You have copied and pasted the text.

You may also want to consider an HTML or web-page version of your resume. This version can be posted on a personal website or on any site offering this service. Many job seekers are creating HTML resumes in the hopes of being discovered. It can be an ideal reference for employers who want to see more than just that flat resume. This format works particularly well for people in a visual arts field, but if it is done correctly and for the right reasons, it could serve anyone who wants to present more than what is usually found on a standard resume.

Doing it "correctly" means creating a simple HTML version of your designed resume—not a hip-hop page of spinning-whirling gizmos, videos, and accompanying audio files better suited to impressing your friends. *Doing it "for the right reasons"* means turning your resume into an employment portfolio, complete with links to former employers, graphic samples, or projects that are already online. If you do this, be sure you are not violating any copyright or confidentiality clauses by putting project information online or linking to confidential resources.

The main drawback with HTML resumes is the too-much-information factor. Many job seekers make the resume a part of their personal website, where there is often a lot of information an employer does not need to know—for example, your marital status, ethnic background, or personal interests. Allowing an employer to learn so much about you can invite all kinds of problems, including discrimination against you for your physical appearance, political beliefs, religious practices, or even just the image you present. When you place your professional image online by posting your resume, it is essential to keep your presence entirely professional by never linking it to personal information of any kind. So, if you decide to add an HTML resume to your campaign, post it in a location separate from your personal website, and do not create a link between the two.

Rules for Responding Online

The fastest way to respond to Internet job listings is by e-mailing your cover letter and resume to the person or organization indicated. Your resume and cover letter are still your best means to winning an interview, but if you mess up the initial application process, those lovely documents won't get you where you want to be. The rules are short and simple, so take a couple of minutes to review them before you execute the Send command.

• **Format your resume correctly for e-mail.** If you try to copy and paste the text of your designed resume into the body of an e-mail message and then send it without preparation, by the time it reaches the intended recipient, the formatting will be such a mess that the text may be unreadable.

• **Always include a cover letter.** This rule applies whether or not you are responding to an advertised opening. Your cover letter should be the first few short paragraphs at the top of your message. Make that cover letter specific to the person or organization you are contacting, and make it interesting. If you are responding to an advertisement, note where the ad appeared and any relevant job codes. You can create and store a "standard" cover letter in plain text, but remember to customize it for each job for which you are applying, checking the format before you send it.

- **Send your resume in the body of the e-mail message.** Do not send it as an attachment unless you are specifically instructed to do so. You have only about twenty seconds to catch the eye of a recruiter or employer and to get him or her to read your resume. If you send your resume as an attachment, the recipient has to find it and open it before it can be read. Your twenty seconds are over before they begin. Put the resume right in the message so the reader will see it immediately upon opening the mail. This also helps you bypass e-mail systems that refuse attachments in this day of rampant computer viruses.

- **Use the advertised job title or code as the "Subject" of your message.** This makes it easier for the recipient to sort everything coming in and route your materials to the appropriate person. If you are "cold-calling"—trying to get your resume into someone's hands without responding to an advertised job posting— put a few words stating your objective in the subject line.

- **Read the application instructions in the job announcement and follow them exactly.** Some employers want applications sent to a specific e-mail address according to the job location. Others might require you to apply through the company website using a specific code. It's also possible they will request that you attach your resume in Word. Whatever they say, do it. You don't want your application to be delayed because you sent it to the wrong address or person, and you do not want to be perceived as someone who cannot follow directions.

Always remind yourself of this fact as you prepare to e-mail your resume to an employer: *it takes only a couple of seconds for someone to delete an e-mail message.* Don't let that happen to you. Read and think before you respond!

E-MAIL RESUME TIP: RENAME THAT FILE

If you have been instructed to submit your resume in MS Word as an attachment to an e-mail, the file name of your resume document should include your name! For example, rename *resume.doc* to read *MDikelResume.doc*. This will enable the recipient to readily identify your resume among the many others in his or her attachments folder.

E-Resumes Are Not Just for E-Mail

Besides the need to have a well-done plain-text resume for e-mailing, there are hundreds more reasons to take the time to create an e-resume—namely all those places online where you can post it. True, almost all sites have a copy-and-paste option for getting your resume online. Some even let you create your resume right on the site. However, resume expert Susan Ireland doesn't endorse using these forms. Here's why:

1. **Typos galore.** You're almost bound to introduce typos if you key directly into the site's form. Working first in your word-processing program (with its spell-check function) significantly improves your chances of having a perfect presentation.

2. **Format impositions.** The form may force you to use a resume format that you don't like. Most online resume builders insist on a chronological resume, a format that focuses on work history. This puts career changers at a disadvantage because the system doesn't allow you to build a functional resume, a format that focuses on skills.

3. **One-time use.** You cannot easily save your resume for other uses, because the resume bank is on a website. That means you must repeat your resume-building efforts on each site where you want to post.

The best way to post your resume online is to copy and paste it from a prepared version you have already formatted to look sharp online. For the most favorable results, that means transforming the hard-copy version before you copy and paste it into the website's resume form.

JOB-SEARCH TIP: PROTECT YOUR PRIVACY WHEN CUTTING AND PASTING

Susan Joyce, from Job-Hunt.org, notes that people frequently sabotage their own privacy by copying the top of the resume—with all of their contact information—into the body-of-the-resume blocks on Web forms. While the site may well prohibit access to the contact information that is input into specific labeled fields, careless job seekers inadvertently publish the information in the text block fields of the form. Be heads-up with the copy-and-paste process!

Preparing a Perfect Plain-Text Resume

Preparing a resume for e-mailing and posting is not difficult, and anyone creating a standard resume should invest the extra few minutes needed to generate a plain-text e-resume while still at the computer. Most word processors and resume-writing programs will let you save a file to plain text. The next step, altering the format, is simple. The instructions in this section, prepared by resume-writing expert Susan Ireland, explain how to turn that hard-copy resume into a perfect plain-text document for posting online.

Ireland even walks you through a handy way to format it for e-mailing. It is a slightly different process and means you will have two different plain-text copies of your resume, because e-mail has more formatting restrictions than most online resume databases. Fortunately, we know what those restrictions are. For more detailed instructions on creating resumes, cover letters, and even various formats for your e-resume, visit susanireland.com.

These instructions assume that your resume is in MS Word 2002 or 2003 for Windows. If your resume is in another word-processing application or another version of MS Word, you should consult your word-processing manual for specific instructions.

Step One: Check Keywords

Be sure your resume has all the keywords that define your job qualifications.

Step Two: Save as Plain Text

Plain-text documents work best for e-resumes because you can adjust the margins and formatting to suit the database or e-mail system in which you are working. To convert your MS Word resume to plain text:

1. Open the MS Word document that contains your resume.

2. Click File in your toolbar and select Save As.

3. Type in a new name for this document in File Name, such as "ResPlainText."

4. Under this is the Save As Type pull-down menu. From this list, select Plain Text (*txt). (You may need to scroll down the list to get to it.)

5. Click Save to perform the conversion.

6. Now close the document, but stay in MS Word.

7. Reopen the document you just closed by going to File in the toolbar: click Open, select the file named "ResPlainText.txt," and click Open. Do not exit MS Word and open the resume document by clicking on its icon in the directory; if you do, it will become a Notepad document, which is not what you want at this point.

After you've converted your resume to plain text, what appears in your document window is your resume stripped of any fancy formatting. You are now set to make a few final adjustments before posting it online.

Step Three: Delete Any References to "Page 2"

If your resume is more than one page, delete any indications of page breaks such as "Page 1 of 2," "Continued," or your name or header on page 2. You are making your resume appear as one continuous electronic document.

Step Four: Use All Caps for Words That Need Emphasis

Since the conversion to plain text stripped your resume of all boldface, underlines, and italics for highlighting words, use all uppercase letters to draw attention to important words, phrases, and headings. For the best overall effect, impose this treatment sparingly and judiciously.

Step Five: Replace Bullets with Standard Keyboard Symbols

Special symbols such as bullets, arrows, triangles, and check marks do not transfer well electronically. For example, bullets sometimes transfer as "&16707" or as ")" or as a little graphic of a thumbs-up. You avoid that fate by changing each one to a standard keyboard symbol. Here are three suggested replacements:

Hyphens (-)

Plus signs (+)

Single or double asterisks (*) (**)

Use the space bar to place a single space immediately after each symbol (and before the words). Do not use the tab key for spacing as you may have done in your original resume.

Also, allow the lines to wrap naturally from the right margin to the left margin below. Don't add a forced return (i.e., don't hit the enter key) if it's not the end of the entry, and don't indent the lines below with either the tab key or space bar.

Step Six: Use Straight Quotes in Place of Curly Quotes

As with other special symbols, curly—or "smart" quotes—do not transfer accurately and may appear as little rectangles on the recipient's screen. Replace curly quotes with straight quotes. To do this, select (highlight) the text that includes the quotes you want to change. Click Format in your toolbar, and select AutoFormat. Click Options, and make sure Replace Straight Quotes with Smart Quotes is *not* selected under both the AutoFormat and AutoFormat As You Type tabs. Click OK. Next, do a Find/Replace for a single quote and a double quote to change all the straight quotes to curly throughout the document.

Step Seven: Rearrange Text if Necessary

Do a line-by-line review of your document to catch any odd-looking line wraps, extra spaces, or words scrunched together in the body. Make adjustments accordingly. This cleanup may require inserting commas between items that were once in columns and are now in paragraph format because tabs and tables disappeared when the document was converted.

Step Eight: Copy and Paste Away

Now that you've prepared your resume, it's time to post it online. Just copy the text from your plain-text document and paste it into the appropriate field on the resume website, making sure to preview what you have done before you submit it. Almost all resume websites have a preview option, allowing you to eyeball your e-resume as it will appear on the recruiter's screen. Always choose this option so that you can proofread your writing and examine the formatting of the e-resume you pasted in. If you see anything you want to change, click the

Edit button and fix the error. Preview and edit as many times as necessary. When you're satisfied, click Submit or Send to dispatch your e-resume.

Making That Resume E-Mail Perfect

To be confident that your resume will be readable by almost any employer on the Internet, regardless of the Internet service provider, platform, or word processor, you will have to make a few final adjustments so your plain-text resume can be copied directly into your e-mail message for fast forwarding to an employer. It's a three-step procedure.

E-Mail Step One: Limit Line Lengths

Because each type of e-mail software has its own limit for the number of characters per line, your e-mail message may have longer line lengths than the receiver of your message allows. This can cause the employer to see line wraps in unusual places, making your document look odd and even illogical. To avoid this glitch, limit each line to no more than sixty-five characters (including spaces). Here's an easy way to make line-length changes in your document:

1. Open MS Word, click Open, select the file named "ResPlainText.txt," and click Open.

2. Select (highlight) the entire document, and change the font to Courier, 12 point.

3. Go to File in your toolbar, and select Page Setup. Set the left margin at 1 inch and the right margin at 1.75 inches. (Users of Yahoo! Mail should set the right margin at 2.5 inches.)

With the side margins set under these conditions, each line of your document will be no more than sixty-five characters and spaces.

E-Mail Step Two: Set Line Lengths

To save the line-length changes you made in the preceding step and make your resume e-mail ready, you need to convert your plain-text document to a Notepad document by doing the following:

1. With your plain-text resume open, click File on your toolbar, and select Save As.

2. Type in a new name for this document in File Name—such as "ResTextBreak"—and click OK.

3. When the File Conversion window appears on your screen, under Options click Insert Line Breaks; then click OK.

4. Click File on your toolbar, and select Save. Close the document, and exit MS Word.

5. Reopen the resume document ("ResTextBreak.txt") by clicking on its icon in the directory, allowing it to open as a Notepad document.

6. Select (highlight) the entire document, and change the font to Times, Arial, or another standard font you like. Don't worry that the margins automatically reset when you reopen your document. Your line lengths have been safely preserved by the paragraph returns inserted during the conversion.

E-Mail Step Three: Copy and Paste Your E-Mail Resume

Now that you've created your perfect e-mail resume, you're ready to insert it into a message and send it on its way.

1. Go online and open a new e-mail message.

2. Type the recipient's e-mail address into the "To" field, being mindful to spell out the address with 100 percent accuracy, including the use of upper- and lowercase letters. We recommend that you conduct a trial run by first sending the e-mail resume to yourself and a friend who uses a different e-mail program (e.g., your Yahoo! Mail to your friend's Outlook, or vice versa), to verify that all systems are go. If they aren't, open the resume document (ResTextBreak.txt) in Notepad by clicking on its icon in the directory and make any necessary changes to the document. Then try again.

3. In the subject line, type "Resume:" followed by the job title you're seeking (e.g., "Resume: Marketing Position").

4. Keeping the e-mail message screen up, open your ResTextBreak document in Notepad, and copy all the text in that document.

5. Go back to the e-mail message screen, and paste the document into the message window.

6. Now check the entire message to confirm that its appearance is exactly what you want the employer to see.

7. Click Send—and you're done!

RESUME TIP: THOU SHALT NOT STEAL

Never cite your current employer's street address, e-mail address, or phone number as your personal contact information on your resume. The personal use of company time and resources is widely considered to be stealing, and prospective employers may figure that if you'll do it to your current employer, you'll do it to the next one. Always provide personal contact points, such as a post office box, cell phone, and private e-mail account. Adopting this practice also counters your risk from possible monitoring by your current employer.

Where, Oh, Where Should That Resume Go?

With the thousands of possible posting sites now available online, you have ample opportunity to saturate the Internet with your resume. After all, don't you want to put it in front of every recruiter or employer you can, regardless of who they are? No, you don't.

Recruiters are tired of coming upon the same resumes for the same people in every database they search. They are even starting to ignore these resume spammers, refusing to give them any consideration for employment. There is also the danger that the further your resume spreads, the less control you can exert over it. So that you don't encounter these problems, limit your resume exposure by limiting your postings.

• Post it in only one or two of the large online databases, preferably ones attached to popular job sites. This will give you maximum exposure to many employers and recruiters.

• Post it in one or two targeted resume databases specific to your industry, occupational group, or geographic location. This will give you a targeted exposure to employers and recruiters looking for a smaller yet more highly qualified candidate pool.

If you don't get any responses to your resume within forty-five days, remove it from its current locations and place it elsewhere.

Resume Blasting: Should You "Scattershot" Your Resume?

Resume-distribution services, sometimes called resume broadcasters or blasters, are proliferating online. Some job databases even offer to "distribute" your resume for free or for a nominal fee after you have posted it in their database. While you may think this is a super way to get your resume seen, we disagree, for several reasons.

First, in reference to privacy, Susan Joyce, the editor of Job-Hunt.org, warns: "Such wide distribution may offer little, if any, control on where a copy of your resume could end up. Your name, address, and phone number, in addition to your education and work experience, could become completely public for a very long time."

Moreover, not all those who are on the lists of these services actually requested that they be placed on the list. Both of the authors of this book have received resumes broadcasted by these services, and neither of us has requested to be included. We have contacted some of the candidates whose resumes we received and learned that they were unaware of how their resumes were being distributed and who was receiving them. We have also heard from hiring managers who never signed on for these services but cannot get removed from their mailing lists (neither can we).

They may sound good, they may even make promises about how many responses you will get from your numerous contacts, but we urge you to avoid these scattershot techniques. Instead, focus your time, energy, and finances on a more targeted distribution method for getting your resume into the hands of persons you really want reviewing your qualifications.

Protect Yourself Online

Avoiding blasting services and restricting the number of posting locations is one way to protect your resume, but it is also important to select those few sites wisely. Susan Joyce encourages careful evaluation of the job sites you plan to use, because if you aren't careful, you risk a total loss of privacy. Not only could your resume become visible to anyone who comes across it, but also your personal information might be sold to people who have products and services to peddle. Joyce's article "Choosing a Job Site" (job-hunt.org/choosing.shtml) delineates fifteen critical questions to ponder in your evaluation of a site before you trust it with your resume, including the following:

1. **Have you heard of the site?** If a site is completely unknown to you, particularly if the operators send you an e-mail (spam) announcing their wonderfulness, be cautious. Do you know people who have used the site safely and successfully? Look for actual contact information on the site, meaning a name, address, and phone number, not just a form for visitors to complete to ask a question.

2. **Do you have to register a profile or resume before you can search through the jobs?** Be suspicious of a site that won't let you perform a job search before you register your profile or resume. You need to assess the site to determine if it has the jobs you want *before* you register.

3. **Does the site have a comprehensive privacy policy?** Look for a privacy policy, and *read it* before you register! The policy should disclose the information that the site collects and what the operators do with it (e.g., sell or rent your e-mail address). Pay particular attention to what happens to resumes.

4. **Who has access to the database of resumes?** The privacy policy should specify who has access to the resumes. In addition, check out the employer side of the site to see what controls are imposed on access. If resume access is free, or there is only a nominal fee (less than $50 per month or under $500 for a year), that's a sign that you should opt for a different job site.

5. **Can you limit access to your personal contact information?** The best sites provide you with options to protect your contact information (name, e-mail address, street address, phone numbers, etc.). Options range from blocking access only to the contact information to keeping your resume completely out of the resume database searched by employers. Choose the level that works best for you. If you are currently employed, limiting access can help you protect your existing job.

6. Are most of the jobs posted by employers or by agencies acting on behalf of employers? In general, jobs posted directly by an employer are preferable because you will be dealing directly with the people who can hire you.

7. Can you set up one or more "e-mail agents" that will send matching jobs to you when you are not at the site? E-mail agents typically compare your requirements with new employer job postings and send you the results via e-mail if they find a match. You don't need to revisit the site yourself and run your search; your agents will do the searching for you and send you the results.

8. Can you store more than one version of your resume so that you can customize it for different types of opportunities? Many sites offer you the ability to store several different resumes and apply for a job using the version that you have developed for that specific kind of opportunity.

9. Will you be able to edit your resume once you have posted it? Check to see if there is an "edit/update" option for you to access your resume. You can always seize on ways to improve your resume, and they should allow you to do it.

10. Will you be able to delete your resume after you have accepted a job? You don't want that old resume still available for view. If your new employer notices it, he or she may be concerned that you are getting ready to leave. The preferred job sites provide you with the capability to delete your resume and account or to put your resume in an "inactive" mode until you are ready for your next job search.

The bottom line when posting your resume is *you rule*. Many sites want your resume in their database. You can afford to be choosy about where you will place it and which sites you will use in your search.

Before You Post, a Few More Things to Think About

For some people, in some situations, posting a resume online is a great way to elicit new opportunities. In other cases, though, job seekers are burdened by the fear that their contact information will fall into the wrong hands, or that the wrong organizations—such as their current employer—will see their resume online and that problems will arise. We are also all familiar with news reports about stolen identities. You are the only one who can say how comfortable you are with this decision and how you want to approach the step of posting your resume. Before you begin, review "The 'Dirty Dozen' Online Job Search Mistakes" in Chapter 1, and then weigh the following questions carefully:

1. Are you ready to make your resume public? Once you have posted it, no matter where you place it, you should consider your resume to be public and, to some extent, out of your control. Anyone can look in the public databases and see what is there. Even the private resume databanks, as well as those offering confidential handling of your resume, may not let you dictate who can and cannot look at your resume.

2. Are you prepared for the consequences should an electronic resume come back to haunt you? Some job seekers fall victim to aggressive recruiters who grab their resumes from the Internet and unwittingly feed them back to the job seekers' current employers, with negative results for the employee. Others are finding their resumes posted in places they never put them, the victims of unprofessional resume services who copy the documents from other open venues. People have even been confronted by current employers brandishing copies of their online resumes, not realizing that the documents were more than a year old and part of the campaign to get the current job. You should always go back and delete any resumes posted during your search as soon as your search is over. However, you might not be able to remove every electronic copy in existence, so you may need some strategies to help alleviate this problem. You can include the date of posting at the very end of your resume as a record of when it was posted, or make slight changes to the wording of each copy you post, creating a code identifying where a copy originated. These small alterations will give you some ammunition should your resume float into the wrong hands at the wrong time.

We don't want to scare you away from posting your resume online, but you need to be aware of potential pitfalls. Susan Joyce has written two articles you should review before going forward with this task: "Your Cyber-Safe Resume," which offers tips on creating a confidential resume, and "Protecting Your Privacy," which is about ways to guard your identity when you're job searching online. Both articles and many more on this topic are available on her website, job-hunt.org. For more practical suggestions on keeping yourself and your identity safe during your job search we recommend "The Job Seekers' Guide to Resumes: Twelve Resume Posting Truths," by Pam Dixon (worldprivacyforum .org/resumedatabaseprivacytips.html), another of the respected Internet job-search pioneers. Many other articles and reports on the issues discussed here are available from the World Privacy Forum (worldprivacyforum.org).

Final Words of Wisdom: Scams and Schemes

It is unfortunate that you, the job seeker, have become one of the more attractive targets of scammers from all over the world. The Internet Crime Complaint Center (ic3.gov) lists among its "current and ongoing Internet trends and schemes" four well-known yet often repeated scams that are directed toward job seekers: reshipping, third-party receiver of funds, employment/business opportunities, and identity theft (more information on all of these is available at ic3.gov/crimeschemes.aspx). The World Privacy Forum has conducted several research projects on these problems, testing online job sites for their security procedures and tracking down fraudulent job announcements posted on many of the popular sites. Even the Better Business Bureau has articles on the many scams directed at people seeking employment and what to look for.

Along with the scams come the schemes, usually in the form of e-mail messages saying, "We saw your resume online, and we are contacting you because we can help," or "You should post your resume over here for the best results." Many of these are from so-called executive marketing or career management firms, but the truth is that a growing number of these organizations are in business not to help you, but just to make money. If you are contacted by a person or organization claiming to have seen your resume online and offering to assist you in your job search, likely for a fee, we urge you to merely delete the e-mail without responding. While you can try a background search on your own, just doing a search of the organization's name in Google may not give you a complete picture.

The Internet Crime Complaint Center, the Better Business Bureau, and the World Privacy Forum all issue free information on the many scams and schemes currently running, along with ways to spot potentially unethical services and where to turn if you become a victim.

World Privacy Forum	worldprivacyforum.org/workplace.html
Internet Crime Complaint Center	ic3.gov
Better Business Bureau	bbb.org/alerts/tips.asp (search using the word *employment*)

More information on this topic is obtainable from The Riley Guide at rileyguide.com/scams.html.

Help with Resumes and Cover Letters

Each of the following books and Internet services has valuable information and guidance for preparing your resume. Almost all will also walk you through the process of translating your designed resume into the necessary scannable and e-mail formats, and a couple will even take you into Web resumes. We've also included titles covering resumes for teenagers, international variations, and resumes for positions with the U.S. government. New editions of any of these may have been released between the time we created the list and when you are reading it, so check your local library or bookstore for the most recent edition.

Block, Jay A., and Michael Betrus. *101 Best Cover Letters*. McGraw-Hill, 1999.

Ireland, Susan. *The Complete Idiot's Guide to the Perfect Cover Letter*. alpha books, 1997.

————. *The Complete Idiot's Guide to the Perfect Resume*, 4th ed. alpha books, 2006.

Kennedy, Joyce Lain. *Cover Letters for Dummies*, 2nd ed. For Dummies, 2000.

————. *Resumes for Dummies*. 5th ed. For Dummies, 2007.

Thompson, Mary Anne. *The Global Resume and CV Guide*. John Wiley & Sons, 2001.

Troutman, Kathryn K. *Federal Resume Guidebook: Strategies for Writing a Winning Federal Electronic Resume, KSAs, and Essays*, 4th ed. Jist, 2007.

Troutman, Kathryn K., et al. *Taking the Next Step: Guide to Creating High School Resumes and Portfolios*. Delmar Thomson Learning, 2006.

Yate, Martin. *Resumes That Knock 'em Dead*. Adams Media, 2006.

Online Guides and Guidance

Online Writing Lab (OWL), Purdue University

owl.english.purdue.edu/owl

OWL was set up to help the students at Purdue with writing all types of documents. The Job Search Writing section includes help with resumes, cover letters, personal statements, and much more.

The Damn Good Resume

damngood.com

This is the online companion to the many resume books written by the late Yana Parker. It still offers her outstanding samples of good resume writing along with excellent advice on preparing your own resume or helping others with theirs.

The Resume Place

resume-place.com

The Resume Place is the resume-writing service operated by Kathryn Troutman, author of the *Federal Resume Guidebook* and other job-search guides. On her website you'll find free articles and advice on preparing what you'll need in order to create your resume. If you are considering applying for a job with the federal government, then you must review Troutman's information. She is an expert in the federal resume, which is very different from the resume you need for the private sector.

Susan Ireland

susanireland.com

Susan Ireland is an expert resume writer and job coach, and her website offers terrific job-search information and sample documents for you to review. You will enjoy her online guides for resume writing, e-resumes, and cover letters, along with the many samples. There is also a Spanish version, espanol.susanireland .com, specifically for Spanish speakers seeking jobs in the United States. Her blog, The Job Lounge (joblounge.blogspot.com), offers you an opportunity to review many job-search questions and answers drawn from her team of experts, or even ask your own question.

3

The Great
Job-Lead Banks

Job-lead banks are the sites and services on the Internet known for their collected job listings. They blanket multiple fields, industries, and occupations, providing leads for almost every line of work you can think of. While many are based in the United States, they do not necessarily confine themselves to listings for this country. This chapter is divided into three categories:

1. **Recruiting services:** recruiters and other organizations posting job announcements on the Internet

2. **Newspaper collections:** directories of links to newspapers from around the world

3. **Guides to the job hunt:** directories that refer you to complementary resources, including job-search and career advice

---

JOB-SEARCH TIP: MAXIMIZE TIME AND EFFORT IN ONLINE APPLICATIONS

If you visit one Internet job service frequently and have had luck plumbing for appropriate positions advertised there, consider registering your resume with that service. Some job databases automate the application drill, letting anyone with a registered resume at the site forward it in response to a job announcement with a single mouse click. It's also likely that the same recruiters and employers who post jobs here also search the resume database, increasing your percentages of being chosen.

Online Recruiting Services

Many of the sites described in this section include both U.S. and non-U.S. opportunities. Job banks that primarily serve non-U.S. audiences are contained in Chapter 12. Sites that are intended for minority or other diverse populations are in Chapter 13.

America's Job Exchange

americasjobexchange.com

America's Job Exchange (AJE) is the successor to America's Job Bank (AJB), which the U.S. Department of Labor (DOL) ceased funding on July 1, 2007. NaviSite, the vendor that operated America's Job Bank under contract to the DOL, is continuing to offer the same services enjoyed by users of AJB in the new AJE. Job seekers are encouraged to register for a free account, but registration is not a prerequisite to searching the job listings and applying for the positions. Also, as with the earlier AJB, AJE allows military personnel to search for civilian positions using their current Military Occupational Code. Links to additional career and job-search information from America's Career InfoNet are provided, keeping this site connected to the CareerOneStop suite. The site is also available in Spanish.

AfterCollege

aftercollege.com

AfterCollege is a service for college students and recent graduates who are looking for entry-level jobs, internships, or other opportunities in the United States and Canada, but at the time of review we also saw listings for people with more than five years of experience. You can elect to search just a subsection of the database, such as internships, government jobs, or jobs for Ph.D.s and postdoctorates, or search the full database by keyword, location, job type, or industry. You will need to register (free) to apply for the jobs, but we really liked what we saw and hope it will continue to grow.

CareerBuilder

careerbuilder.com

CareerBuilder has evolved into one of the larger and more dynamic sites for job and career information. Registering (free) with the site allows you to store your resume online without posting it in the database, and you can create up to five personal search profiles to track new jobs added to the database and have them e-mailed to you when a possible match appears.

CareerMatrix

careermatrix.com

This service, based in Michigan, rolls out jobs from all across the United States in numerous job fields. You can search for jobs by category, keyword, and location. While registration is not necessary to search and review job listings, you will need to register (free) and upload a resume in order to apply for some listings. Others might allow you to connect directly to the recruiter or employer. You can store more than one version of your resume here to pursue multiple avenues of employment.

CareerJournal.com from the Wall Street Journal

careerjournal.com

This free site brims with articles, information, and jobs. While some of the articles are from the *Wall Street Journal*, many are written specifically for CareerJournal.com. An impressive job bank is accompanied by terrific job and career content. This site has something for job seekers at all levels of experience.

SnagAJob.com

snagajob.com

SnagAJob.com calls itself "the number one source for hourly employment." You can search the large database of part-time and full-time hourly positions by simply entering your zip code, or scroll down the page to search by state or access the list of featured employers. The zip code search defaults to a twenty-mile radius, which is easily altered, and the results are sorted by distance, from nearest to farthest, a nice feature for folks looking to work close to home. You will need to register (free) in order to apply for positions here, but that will also allow you to store a profile for streamlining job applications.

College Grad Job Hunter

collegegrad.com

Don't let that the name fool you! This website, based on the book of the same title, is a cornucopia of resources and information to steer you through a complete job search. It has job databases for internships, as well as positions for both entry-level job seekers and experienced job seekers, along with a searchable database of more than eight thousand employers. To top it all off, it offers solid advice on careers, the job search, resume preparation, and more.

JobCentral National Labor Exchange

jobcentral.com

This website search engine enables you to search for jobs posted on many employer websites through this one source. You are then directed to the respective external sites to view jobs and apply directly to the employer. JobCentral offers a variety of channels—Diversity, Veterans, Executives, and Students—with a variety of partners, such as TheLadders.com and the National Association of Colleges & Employers, among others. JobCentral is also working hard to help replace the services of America's Job Bank, which ceased operations July 1, 2007. This site is operated by DirectEmployers Association.

EmploymentGuide.com

employmentguide.com

EmploymentGuide.com is the online companion to the free *Employment Guide* magazines published by Dominion Enterprises. The free website allows you to quickly search for part-time and full-time hourly positions, and you can easily target a specific city or region. One job from an employer will link to all others from the same employer, which is a handy feature. Some listings ask you to submit a resume via e-mail, while others merely run a phone number for you to call, so you will need to read the application instructions for each posting you want to pursue. Either way, we rate this as a top source for local hires.

Futurestep from Korn/Ferry

futurestep.com

Futurestep is a search service for midlevel management professionals brought to you by Korn/Ferry International. Registering with Futurestep is a free and confidential process and will cover more than just your standard resume. You will be considered for searches that the sponsors are conducting, but your information will never be given to hiring companies without your express approval. Interested persons can search the job database and even view full announcements before registering, but registration is required to apply for any position.

Yahoo! HotJobs

hotjobs.yahoo.com

Search for jobs by keyword, company, or location, or select a career channel and tailor your search to just the postings in this area. When presented with the results of your search, you can easily choose to view only jobs updated that day, in the past two days, or earlier. Further, since your results may cover multiple locations, you can easily select only jobs in your town, in the next town, or in another location close by.

Indeed

indeed.com

Indeed is a search engine that searches multiple sources with job listings, including newspapers, employers, and other job sites. The search results tell you where the job was found and how long ago that site was indexed. Developed by people who have created other job boards, it also allows you to constantly better define your search, including creating subcategories from your original broad search.

JobBankUSA.com

jobbankusa.com

A good site for many jobs in all kinds of fields, JobBankUSA.com offers information organized and accessible through a variety of means. You can search the job database by keyword, refining your search by location and position type (full-time, contract, etc.). You can also browse the jobs or scan the roll of featured employers and connect to their websites. Carefully review the privacy policy before posting your resume here. JobBankUSA.com is part of the Beyond .com family of job sites.

Manpower

www.manpower.com

Manpower is the largest employer in the United States today, and not just by virtue of placing secretaries and receptionists in offices. The world of the temp has opened up all the way to the chief executive's office. Assignments are searchable by location and include direct-hire listings from many employers. You will need to register (free) to apply for jobs listed here. Manpower has a presence around the world, so international candidates will want to look at what this company has to offer.

Monster.com

monster.com

Monster.com is probably the most recognized name in the online job-search industry. It hosts an enormous variety of job and career resources for everyone from college students to contractors to chief executives, and most are served with their own communities that include job listings and career advice. It has also instituted several industry/job-field communities, including health care, human resources, and finance.

MonsterTRAK

monstertrak.com

Formerly known as JobTrak, this Monster community is targeted to the college graduate. Your college or university must be a member of MonsterTRAK for you to gain access to the job postings on this site. Your career center can tell you if your alma mater is a member and, if it is, relay access information. MonsterTRAK has been noted as an excellent resource for executive as well as entry-level opportunities, so alumni can benefit at many stages from exploring this site.

NationJob

nationjob.com

This site is distinguished by an impressive collection of job openings, company information, and a variety of ways to find what you are looking for. Job seekers can search the entire database by keyword, category, and location, or opt to browse the listings collected in the many Specialty Sites (occupation-specific), Community Sites (local listings), or State Sites (local listings), as well as look at the many employers with Custom Sites here. NationJob has a long-standing tradition of excellence in online recruiting and job search.

Net-Temps

net-temps.com

Head over to Net-Temps for a searchable company database of temporary, temp-to-perm, and permanent full-time job listings derived from staffing companies across the United States and Canada. Search the full database by location and keyword, or select a smaller portion of the database that isolates your industry, state, or metropolitan area (if offered).

Recruiters Online Network

recruitersonline.com

This network is "an association of executive recruiters, search firms, and employment professionals around the world who have created a virtual organization on the Internet." Job seekers can search the database of openings contributed by the participating recruiters, post a resume for consideration by all members, and seek out recruiters working with a particular industry or occupational field for direct contact.

Top Echelon

topechelon.com

Top Echelon is a cooperative network of more than twenty-five hundred recruiters. It has good listings ranging from entry level to well into the six-figure range. You can also search the recruiter listings and contact some of the recruiters directly.

Online Newspaper Collections

Newspapers are an important component in your quest for employment. Reading local newspapers for your particular search location will help you learn about the community and its various employers, identify individual contacts within those organizations, and even connect with areawide job listings. Most newspapers in the United States and many around the world are now represented on the Web, making it easy for you to obtain and digest the news for your target location.

News and Newspapers Online

library.uncg.edu/news

This is an extensive directory of links to news and newspaper sources worldwide. You can browse the site by location or search by a variety of criteria. The directory is a free service of Walter Clinton Jackson Library at the University of North Carolina at Greensboro.

NewsDirectory.com

newsdirectory.com

This is a searchable directory of English-language media, including newspapers, magazines, television stations, colleges, visitor bureaus, governmental agencies, and more from around the world. You can also search the directory by publication title or search for U.S. regional news links by telephone area code.

NewsLink

newslink.org

NewsLink offers lists of and links to newspapers, magazines, and radio and television station websites throughout the world. This directory is operated by Congoo, a free real-time news, networking, and information portal.

NewsVoyager

newsvoyager.com

Operated by the Newspaper Association of America, this site calls itself "a gateway to your local newspaper." You can easily find the news you'd like by either browsing the contents or searching with keywords.

U.S. Newspapers

usnpl.com

U.S. Newspapers is a free directory of newspapers for each state plus the District of Columbia. The listings here include the local newspapers, college newspapers, radio and television stations, and magazines.

Online Guides to the Job Hunt

These Internet guides for the online job search, sometimes referred to as metaguides, gather information and resources to help you use the Internet to find employment. Some will give you notes about the resources, some will give you articles on the job search, but all will take you to more online information for your search.

Job-Hunt.org

job-hunt.org

One of the earliest guides to the Internet job search, Job-Hunt.org offers numerous well-selected links to job-search resources for the world. You can search for job sites by location, profession, industry, or job type. Susan Joyce, manager of this site, also provides users with excellent articles on job-search issues.

JobHuntersBible.com

jobhuntersbible.com

This online guide to the job search comes from the dean of career counseling himself, Richard Bolles! The site is a supplement to his bestseller *What Color Is Your Parachute?* and is spiced with his comments and observations on the job search and your decision-making process. His Net Guide, culling the best job-search and career-information sites online, makes this spot an excellent place for you to start your search.

JobStar

jobstar.org

JobStar began as a "California Job Search Guide," but it has always been a highly useful resource for everyone. This is one of the best places online to find out how and where to look for employment, both online and off-line. Among the wealth of information here are articles on the hidden job market, negotiating salaries, and numerous other topics that work to enhance the resources listed, selected because they are the best.

Quintessential Careers

quintcareers.com

This is a metaguide to everything you need for your job search created by the authors of *Dynamic Cover Letters*. From the initial "What do I want to do?" this site abounds with timely information and resources from both off-line and online publications. The job and career site lists are quite good, and there is also information for children looking for ideas.

The Riley Guide: Employment Opportunities and Job Resources on the Internet

rileyguide.com

One of the first guides to look at the Internet as a tool for finding new employment, The Riley Guide was established in January 1994 and has been going strong ever since. This site links you to hundreds of sources of information for job leads, career exploration, and potential employers. It even has information to help you explore new careers, new places to live, and new education and training options. In addition, you can check The Riley Guide for updates to listings in this book.

Yahoo! Employment and Work

dir.yahoo.com/business_and_economy/employment_and_work

Yahoo! links to more than fifteen hundred sites for job leads and other sources of employment information. Don't settle for just this list, though. Almost every category on Yahoo! has a separate employment category, so browse the shelves frequently.

Jobs in Business, Marketing, and Commercial Services

The resources in this chapter are geared to employment in business fields and commercial services, such as marketing, event management, and equipment leasing.

If you are pursuing a career in one of these professions, bear in mind that companies of all sizes and in all industries cannot do business without teams of accountants, sales representatives, and other support staff to keep them operating efficiently. Your opportunities can crop up everywhere, so your hunting grounds extend beyond what you see here.

Business Starting Point

MBA.com

mba.com

Created by the Graduate Management Admission Council, the people behind the Graduate Management Admission Test (GMAT), this site helps you to assess how earning an M.B.A. degree will impact your life. It also includes information on M.B.A. programs and the GMAT.

Accounting and Finance

AAFA: The American Association of Finance and Accounting

aafa.com

The AAFA is an alliance of executive search firms specializing in the recruiting and placement of finance and accounting professionals. Under the Offices header, you can choose a member firm close to you and then connect to that website to review current searches (if available) and obtain information on submitting your resume.

AICPA Online: American Institute for Certified Public Accountants

aicpa.org

AICPA is "the national, professional organization for all Certified Public Accountants." Go to Career Development and Workplace Issues for career guidance and insight on work/life balance, as well as the Job Search Tools section, with links to job announcements from various sources.

American Payroll Association

americanpayroll.org

This association website includes news and information for payroll, tax, and human resources professionals. The Career Center offers advice on finding work, but job announcements posted here are accessible only by members.

Association for Finance Professionals

afponline.org

The AFP's membership is made up of individuals representing a broad spectrum of financial disciplines. Under the Topics header, the Career Services area offers good information and resources to members and nonmembers alike. Registration (free) is encouraged but not required in order to search the jobs database, but you can opt to keep your posted resume private.

Bankjobs.com

bankjobs.com

Bankjobs.com is a trove of job and career information for qualified banking and financial services candidates in the United States. The database, which is open to all users, is easy to search and is filled with good-quality listings.

CFO.com

cfo.com

CFO Publishing's website features international news, articles, resources, and jobs for chief financial officers (CFOs), treasurers, and other senior financial executives in the United States and Canada.

Financial Job Network

fjn.com

This international site lists job opportunities for actuaries, controllers, auditors, chief financial officers, and many more finance professionals. Some jobs listed here require you to register (free) your resume in order to apply.

FinancialJobs.com

financialjobs.com

These are jobs for accounting and financial professionals throughout the United States. Select USA Jobs, California Jobs, CPA Jobs, or Featured Jobs on the Short List to view the respective listings. Some of the listings require you to register (free) in order to apply, but those on the Short List appear to be direct application.

JobsintheMoney.com

jobsinthemoney.com

This site offers pertinent job and career material for financial professionals covering an extensive international market. Browse or search the job listings to be sure there are ones that match your desires before registering your resume. Registration (free) is necessary to apply for some listings here.

National Banking and Financial Services Network

nbn-jobs.com

This is a large association of recruiting firms with job listings in the United States and Canada. The site includes jobs in finance, banking, and credit as well as many more opportunities within this industry. You must register your resume in order to search the listings, but you can do so anonymously, and it is free.

Robert Half International

rhi.com

Robert Half International is the parent company of Accountemps, Robert Half Finance and Accounting, Robert Half Management, and four other divisions offering staffing and consulting services in various business areas. Select the Specialized Services header to enter the various division websites, each with its own job listings, or select Careers to review jobs with this company.

TaxTalent.com

taxtalent.com

This site features job listings and career information for tax professionals.

Actuaries

Actuary.com

actuary.com

This is a directory of resources and services for experienced as well as prospective actuaries, including a free job database. All postings indicate the level of achievement desired, ranging from "entry level with no exams" to "fellow."

Northstar International Insurance Recruiters

northstarjobs.com

Northstar is an actuarial and underwriting recruiting service with listings from student positions (those still lacking certification) to executives.

Advertising, Communications, and Public Relations

Ad Age TalentWorks

adage.com/talentworks

AdAge.com, the website companion to *Advertising Age*, offers career advice and lists job openings for media and advertising professionals in its TalentWorks area.

The job database is open to all, but some positions require you to register (free) with TalentWorks in order to apply.

AdWeekJobs

adweekjobs.com

AdWeek, the magazine for ad agency executives, shares this career site with *BrandWeek, Billboard, MediaWeek, The Book Standard, Editor & Publisher,* and the *Hollywood Reporter*, to aggregate job announcements from all these publications into one central source. Users can easily browse the listings by category or search using keywords, and most announcements allow you to apply directly if you prefer not to post your resume here, which is free.

Commarts.com Network

commarts.com

This site is devoted to people engaged in the communication arts: graphics, marketing, artwork, and other visual methods for communicating with others. It hosts an impressive collection of resources for the industry and the individual, along with a job bank stocked with openings for graphic designers, Web project managers, and writers.

International Association of Business Communicators

www.iabc.com

The IABC represents writers, editors, public relations directors, and other advertising and communications specialists. The job bank is open for all to review and draws jobs for public relations specialists, technical writers, editorial staff, and directors of corporate communications. Many chapters also maintain individual job banks.

Public Relations Society of America

prsa.org

At the PRSA website's open job bank, even nonmembers may post a public resume for a fee; members post for free. A valuable list of links to industry resources also awaits visitors.

Appraisers

American Society of Appraisers

appraisers.org

The ASA is "committed to fostering professional excellence in its membership through education, accreditation, publication and other services." Persons interested in this field can learn more about training and certification opportunities, as well as the many appraisal disciplines and specialties available, and can review listings in the Job Bank.

Church Business Administration

National Association of Church Business Administration

nacba.net

This is "an interdenominational, professional, Christian organization which exists to train, certify, and provide resources for those serving in the field of church administration." The association sponsors training toward certification as a fellow in church business administration (F.C.B.A.) along with a number of workshops and conferences to assist others in this work. Among the website offerings are some terrific resources, including job listings and links to additional sources.

Customer Relations and Call Centers

CallCenterCareers.com

www.callcentercareers.com

CallCenterCareers.com is an online job site for the call center, telemarketing, and customer relationship management (CRM) industries. Visitors are greeted with job postings, a resume bank, industry news, and specialized career services. Registration is not required to search the database or apply for the jobs.

Equipment Leasing

Monitor Daily

monitordaily.com

Monitor Daily features news and information for the equipment leasing and finance industry. A service of Molloy Associates, recruiters for this business, the site also hosts two different listings of job opportunities: The Career Forum, with listings of current searches being handled by Molloy Associates; and The Classified Ads, with listings posted by various employers.

Human Resources

BenefitsLink

benefitslink.com

This site packs current information for anyone dealing with benefits, from the human resources manager to the actuary trying to figure it all out. You can read the latest news, check the industry links, and review the employment opportunities posted in the EmployeeBenefitJobs.com database.

International Foundation of Employee Benefit Plans

www.ifebp.org

The International Foundation of Employee Benefit Plans provides good resources for people in this field, including job postings. Jobs can be reviewed by posting date, location, or title, and nonmembers can post a resume here for a fee. Free to members.

Jobs4HR

jobs4hr.com

This site has jobs for HR professionals at all levels. Registration is not required to conduct a search, but the free registration allows you to customize certain features of the site. Some of the listings will require you to register in order to apply.

Society for Human Resource Management

shrm.org

The SHRM website is filled with information for human resource professionals. The HR Careers area is one of the largest databases of jobs for this field and is open to all users.

Insurance

Great Insurance Jobs.com

greatinsurancejobs.com

Head to this venue for lists of jobs in the insurance industry. Registration (free) is not required to search and view job listings, but some areas are open only to registered members. This site posts jobs from employers, while the companion site, GreatInsuranceRecruiters.com, permits you to search postings from recruiters for this industry.

InsuranceJobChannel

insurancejobchannel.com

This site is a portal to jobs in the insurance industry. You can choose Find a Job, with entries sorted by location and job function, or Find a Company, with entries sorted by name or industry segment and location. While it is not required, you can post your resume here at no cost.

National Insurance Recruiters Association

insurancerecruiters.com

This association of recruiting firms specializes in the insurance industry. The site includes searchable databases of job listings and recruiters. Interested candidates may also post a confidential resume for review by members of the association.

Also see the listings under "Actuaries" earlier in this chapter.

Meeting and Event Management

Professional Convention Management Association

pcma.org

This professional association website includes industry information, a job bank, continuing education opportunities, and much more.

Packaging

Institute of Packaging Professionals

iopp.org

The Institute of Packaging Professionals (IoPP) serves its members as an education and career-development resource. While the Career Center's job listings are accessible only by members, other visitors will appreciate the Industry Links (including recruiters) and the Chapter News and Info. Many of the individual chapters post job listings on their own sites.

Purchasing and Procurement

Institute for Supply Management

ism.ws

The ISM website displays the organization's publications, information on careers in purchasing management, and links to related resources. The job and resume databases are open exclusively to members, but the list of additional career resources is open to all. Many of the affiliate websites listed under About ISM have job banks.

SupplyChainRecruit.com

www.supplychainrecruit.com

SupplyChainRecruit.com is an international job board for purchasing, logistics, and supply chain management. At the time of review the vast majority of listings were in the United Kingdom, but other countries were also represented.

Quality Control

American Society for Quality

asq.org

ASQ is the leading quality-improvement organization in the United States, with more than 130,000 members worldwide. This website is a prime resource for people in this field. The ASQ Career Center is open for all to view the jobs, but resume posting is a membership perk.

Real Estate and Relocation

CoreNet Global

corenetglobal.org

CoreNet Global is an international association representing managers of corporate real estate. The Career Services section includes a job database that is open to all visitors as well as a list of executive recruiters in this industry.

Employee Relocation Council

erc.org

ERC is "a nonprofit professional membership organization committed to the effective relocation of employees worldwide." At this extensive website you can settle yourself in front of job listings in the relocation industry, a formidable online research library, and much more.

Sales and Marketing

Ludwig & Associates, Inc.

ludwig-recruit.com

This executive search firm specializes in the placement of sales and marketing professionals for consumer packaged-goods companies. Individuals in this industry are invited to review the list of current searches and contact the site at any time.

MarketingJobs.com

marketingjobs.com

To sample marketing, sales, and advertising employment opportunities in the United States, go to MarketingJobs.com. You will need to register your resume (free) to apply for most openings posted here.

MarketingPower, the American Marketing Association

marketingpower.com

The AMA's website, MarketingPower.com, supplies marketing professionals and AMA members with the information, products, and services required to succeed in their jobs and careers. The database of marketing jobs is open to all, and you can post a resume for free.

Training and Development

American Society for Training and Development

astd.org

ASTD is the premier professional association for the training and development community. Along with all the other excellent resources, a public job bank is available to all visitors. Non-ASTD members can forward their information to employers without adding a resume to the database.

Instructional System Technology Jobs

education.indiana.edu/ist/students/jobs/joblink.html

This site lists opportunities in all areas of training, including academic faculty, media developers, and corporate trainers. It is a service of the Department of Instructional Systems Technology in the School of Education at Indiana University, Bloomington.

Jobs in Law, the Social Sciences, and Nonprofit Organizations

The areas surveyed in this chapter have been grouped together for their interest in society and the public. The social sciences comprise many fields, including education, law, and economics, and many employers in these fields are nonprofit organizations.

Anthropology

American Anthropological Association

aaanet.org

Anthropology is "the study of humankind, from its beginnings millions of years ago to the present day. . . . Anthropologists may study ancient Mayan hieroglyphics, the music of African Pygmies, and the corporate culture of a U.S. car manufacturer." The website from this association includes information on meetings, publications, and careers, as well as job listings.

Archaeology

archaeologyfieldwork.com

archaeologyfieldwork.com

This site hosts several discussion boards having to do with various aspects of archaeology, including boards where people can post jobs and volunteer opportunities or ask questions about careers in this field. Links to additional sites with job listings for archaeologists are at the bottom of the front page.

Archaeological Institute of America

archaeological.org

The AIA is the oldest and largest archaeological organization in North America, with thousands of members around the world. The website includes information on jobs and fellowships, along with publications for all audiences from children to scholars.

Economics

Inomics Job Openings for Economists

inomics.com/cgi/job

This is a nice source for international jobs in this field as well as links to additional resources. Inomics, the host for this service, also maintains information on conferences, along with other good economics resources.

International Economic Development Council

iedconline.org

The IEDC serves economic and community-development professionals and people in allied fields. The website includes information on professional development, certification, and resources for funding and financial assistance. The Career Services area offers a job database for IEDC members, but nonmembers may sign up for a free newsletter that also lists jobs.

Job Opportunities for Economists

aeaweb.org/joe

Job Opportunities for Economists (JOE) from the American Economic Association is updated every month except January and July. The listings are grouped into U.S. academic, international, and nonacademic positions and subdivided into Full Time and Other listings. Each grouping is then arranged alphabetically by the name of the posting institution, eliminating the "University of" designation. Several months of listings are available at all times.

Education and Academe

This section is divided into categories based on the types of positions offered, but since many of the resources overlap categories, we suggest that you pore through the entire list.

College and University Level

Academic Keys

academickeys.com

Academic Keys lists faculty and administration positions in colleges and universities across the United States and internationally. Select your discipline to view jobs and other resources for that field. The database also lists graduate assistantships and fellowships.

Academic360.com

academic360.com

This site provides more than two thousand links to colleges and universities advertising their position announcements online in the United States and many other countries.

American College Personnel Association Career Connections

myacpa.org/car/car_index.cfm

These listings embrace jobs for resident advisers, directors of student programs, and others who support the students at colleges and universities.

Christian Higher Education Career Center

cccu.org/career/career.asp

This site posts faculty and administrative positions at the member and nonmember affiliate institutions of the Council for Christian Colleges and Universities. The most recent notices appear first. The full roster of member and nonmember affiliate colleges participating in this association is available.

Chronicle of Higher Education's Career Network

chronicle.com/jobs

This site includes career articles and job listings from the *Chronicle of Higher Education*, the weekly publication of higher education worldwide. Many international institutions as well as companies with research divisions advertise here. The job listings are updated daily and are free for all users. Anyone considering a teaching or administrative position with a college or university should look here.

Council for Advancement and Support of Education (CASE) Career Center

case.org/jobs

Specializing in administrative positions in academe and education, the CASE site lists positions in alumni relations, communications, development/fund-raising, public relations, major gifts, annual fund, government relations, information systems and advancement services, and advancement management.

HigherEd Jobs

higheredjobs.com

This website lists jobs in more than fifteen hundred member academic institutions for both faculty and staff. You can view the postings by category, location, or keyword.

Jobs.ac.uk

jobs.ac.uk

Jobs.ac.uk is the "specialist jobsite for careers in academic, research, science and related professions." All types of jobs in these institutions are listed here, including faculty, administration, and support services, and the listings are not limited to the United Kingdom. Users can smoothly target a search to particular subjects or job types or browse the list of posting institutions by name.

National Association of College and University Business Officers

www.nacubo.org

The National Association of College and University Business Officers represents chief administrative and financial officers at more than twenty-one hundred colleges and universities across the country. News, resources, and a link to its Career Headquarters are on the main page.

National Association of Student Personnel Administrators

naspa.org

NASPA is the leading national association for college and university student affairs administrators. NASPA's JobsLink includes openings for admissions, enrollment management, student affairs, housing, health, and much more.

THES Jobs: The Times Higher Education Supplement

thesjobs.co.uk

THES is a well-maintained pathway to jobs in higher education worldwide. It carries listings in all categories of higher-education job vacancies worldwide as advertised in the *Times* (London). New jobs are posted every Tuesday. Your free registration will allow you to save searches and sign up for alerts.

Women in Higher Education

wihe.com

The Women in Higher Education website offers news and information on issues affecting women on college campuses. Under the Position Openings header are several academic openings for faculty and chief administrators, and other areas of the site will connect you to many further sources of information for women.

Kindergarten Through Twelfth Grade

Academic Employment Network

academploy.com

The Academic Employment Network features job listings by state for kindergarten through college educators. Only the states with actual job openings are visible. You must register (free) in order to view the listings.

ISM: Independent School Management

isminc.com

This site hosts a Career Center with opportunities for administrators and teachers in private schools around the United States. There are no dates in the listings here, but information on the website states that "advertisements . . . remain online for a period of six weeks."

Jobs in Education/Emplois en Education

jobsineducation.com

This Canadian website offers job seekers and employers in the education sector an opportunity to meet. Users can easily review openings by subject, province, or international location and can also browse lists of Private/Independent Schools and First Nation Education Authorities that post here. As with all websites in Canada, this one is available in French.

Special Education

National Clearinghouse for Professions in Special Education

special-ed-careers.org

The NCPSE is "committed to enhancing the nation's capacity to recruit, prepare, and retain well-qualified diverse educators and related service personnel for children with disabilities." The website offers a number of resources for people involved in or considering a career in special education, including an overview of what special educators do, how to enter this field, links to employment resources, and information on financial aid.

Recruiting New Teachers

These services encourage people to consider teaching as a profession and to make the transition from other careers to this field.

Teach for America

teachforamerica.org

This nonprofit organization recruits college graduates of all academic majors to teach for two years in an underserved urban or rural public school. Applicants at all age and experience levels are welcome, and certification is not required, but your knowledge of a specific subject will be tested.

Troops to Teachers

jobs2teach.doded.mil

Troops to Teachers provides referral and placement assistance to military personnel interested in a second career as a teacher. This site includes employment resources and listings, information on how to obtain certification, and a list of mentors.

English as a Second Language/English as a Foreign Language (ESL/EFL)

ESLJobs.com

esljobs.com

This site presents jobs for teachers of English as a second or foreign language. You can select a world region to review or opt to look at all recent advertisements.

ESL Cafe's Job Center

eslcafe.com/jobs

This site, presented by Dave Sperling, provides a wonderful list of resources for ESL educators. The Job Center includes jobs wanted, jobs posted, discussion boards for ESL/EFL teachers, a journal of job experiences, a teacher-training forum, and links to even more resources.

Fund-Raising and Philanthropy

Chronicle of Philanthropy's PhilanthropyCareers

philanthropy.com/jobs

The *Chronicle of Philanthropy* is the leading news source for development professionals. Its online PhilanthropyCareers distributes employment opportunities, compensation news and trends, career information for people interested in fund-raising, and much more. Some areas of this site are limited to paying subscribers, but the job listings are open to the public.

Philanthropy News Digest from the Foundation Center

foundationcenter.org/pnd

Philanthropy News Digest's website includes articles and information from its print publication. The Job Corner provides listings of current full-time job openings at U.S.-based foundations and nonprofit organizations. Job seekers will also want to follow the links to information resources provided by the Foundation Center for more leads to potential employers.

PNN Online

pnnonline.org

Information on the nonprofit world is featured here, including a nice Career Center.

Law, Paralegal, and the U.S. Judiciary

FindLaw Career Center

careers.findlaw.com

FindLaw is a marvelous resource for legal information as well as for job and career information on all aspects of legal work. Positions listed here run the gamut from summer clerks, legal secretaries, law librarians, and attorneys in practice or academic positions to functions that support the operation of a legal practice.

HG.org Worldwide Legal Directories

hg.org

HG.org is a wonderful source of legal information. The Legal Employment Center includes jobs, a tremendous amount of information on job searching, notes on changing jobs, a list of recruiters, and more to boot.

National Federation of Paralegal Associations

paralegals.org

This website offers terrific information on work as a paralegal, including how to get started, where to study, legal resources, continuing education, and links to international associations and information. Under the CLE header, the Career Center offers a job database that is open to all visitors, but the "search" is not very friendly.

U.S. Courts: The Federal Judiciary

www.uscourts.gov

Consult this website for information on our federal courts, including employment opportunities in all areas supporting the U.S. courts, their services, and areas of responsibilities. You can review the listings by location, desired salary, or position title, or View All Jobs. Note that not all of the judiciary's employment opportunities are housed here; other announcements may exist on each court's website, in USAJobs, or in the Federal Law Clerk System. This site also links to the Federal Law Clerk Information System and the Supreme Court Judicial Fellows Program.

Resources for "Verbatim (Court) Reporters" are at the end of this chapter.

Library and Information Sciences

American Association of Law Libraries

www.aallnet.org

This website circulates information on law librarianship, professional development workshops offered by this and other organizations, jobs, and other good resources.

American Library Association

ala.org

The ALA is the oldest and largest library association in the world, and much of the website is open to nonmembers as well as members. Under Education and Careers are links to accredited programs, employment listings from various ALA publications, and much more. You can also look under Our Association for links to individual divisions, chapters, and roundtables, some of which operate their own career and employment sections.

ARLIS/NA JobNet

arlisna.org/jobnet.html

The Art Libraries Society of North America provides vacancy announcements for art librarians, visual resources professionals, and related positions.

Association of Research Libraries (ARL) Career Resources

www.arl.org/resources/careers

The ARL's Career Resources includes position announcements in ARL-member and nonmember libraries, and a database of research library residency and internship opportunities. Any visitor can review all listings currently posted, review only the entry-level positions, or search the listings by region, state/ province, or job category.

Jinfo: Jobs in Information

jinfo.com

Jinfo is an ideal place to prospect for information jobs. While most of the openings are in the United Kingdom, the site often hosts announcements from other countries. You can also sign up for the free monthly newsletter, filled with job-search and career tips and the CV makeover.

Library Job Postings on the Internet

libraryjobpostings.org

This guide, compiled by Sarah Nesbeitt, a librarian at Eastern Illinois University, attempts to link together all online sources for library employment listings. The site offers a Combined Jobs Database in cooperation with LISjobs.com, also described in this section.

Library Journal

libraryjournal.com

Library Journal is the trade journal of the library and information sciences profession. Persons interested in this field should visit the Careers area along with the Job Zone for job listings.

LISjobs.com

lisjobs.com

LISjobs.com is a guide to online career and job resources for librarians and information professionals that also hosts its own job and resume databases. The site is operated by Rachel Singer Gordon, a librarian and noted author on library careers.

Music Library Association

musiclibraryassoc.org

The MLA is the professional organization for music librarians in the United States. Among its many services is the Placement Service Job List, a monthly listing of open positions for music librarians across the United States.

Linguistics

Jobs in Linguistics from The Linguist List

linguistlist.org/jobs

This site is updated almost daily with job openings for linguists and features positions from all over the world. Because the site archives a huge number of listings, we suggest you select the Browse Active Listings and/or the Recent Listings area to limit your results to current announcements.

Ministry

ChurchStaffing.com

churchstaffing.com

ChurchStaffing.com advertises positions in Christian churches across the United States and Canada. You can search the listing by many criteria, including size of church and worship style. The most recent resumes are featured on the front page, so be prepared for a very public presence if you post your resume here.

MinistryEmployment

ministryemployment.com

This site lists jobs in Christian ministry primarily in the United States and Canada. The jobs cover the occupational spectrum from ministers to writers to business administrators, but all function in the ministry and are in organizations affiliated with various Christian faiths. It is operated by Providence College & Theological Seminary, Otterburne, Manitoba.

Resources for "Church Business Administration" are in Chapter 4.

Nonprofits, Associations, and Foundations

ASAE CareerHeadquarters

asi.careerhq.org

The American Society of Association Executives allows you to search its job database, post a resume, or learn about careers in associations. Your free registration will also allow you to save searches and apply online for positions advertised here. You are also welcome to review the many citations under Career-Related Articles and the Executive Recruiters roster.

CharityChannel

charitychannel.com

The CharityChannel includes information, resources, and much more for persons interested in working in nonprofits worldwide. The Career Search Online area lists current openings with various organizations, including postings from executive search firms.

Community Career Center

nonprofitjobs.org

This site lists nonprofit jobs all over the United States, from support staff to chief toxicologist to executive director.

execSearches.com

execsearches.com

This site helps nonprofit, education, health care, and public organizations recruit fund-raising, midlevel, and executive professionals.

Nonprofit Career Network

nonprofitcareer.com

The Nonprofit Career Network is dedicated to the nonprofit sector of today's business and economic world. The website features a nice database of jobs along with a Directory of Nonprofit Organizations.

The NonProfit Times

nptimes.com

The NonProfit Times is a business publication for nonprofit management. The website grants access to several special resources, including the NPT Power and Influence Top Fifty, the NPT Top 100, and a Salary Survey. Job seekers will want to review the NPT Jobs area with its numerous job announcements.

Opportunity Knocks.org

opportunityknocks.org

Opportunity NOCs (Nonprofit Organization Classifieds) was launched by the Management Center of San Francisco in 1986 as a print newsletter. Now a vibrant online resource, this site is a doorway to all levels of jobs in the nonprofit sector, accompanied by links to other nonprofit resources and services.

Psychology and Counseling

Mental Help Net

mentalhelp.net

Employers of all types can post their mental health positions free of charge at this site.

NACE JobWire

naceweb.org/jobwire

JobWire spotlights job announcements posted with the National Association of Colleges and Employers (NACE). Job listings for openings in human resources/staffing or career services are made available here for thirty days from the date of posting.

PsycCareers

psyccareers.apa.org

PsycCareers is a free service of the American Psychological Association and includes job and career information for all persons in this field. Anyone can register for free, but registration is not necessary to search the job listings.

Society for Industrial and Organizational Psychology

siop.org

The Society for Industrial and Organizational Psychology website includes information on this field of psychology, current and back issues of the quarterly newsletter (*TIP*), and the JobNet, with openings in academic, industry, or government settings, and internships.

Social Work and Social Services

National Association of Social Workers

www.socialworkers.org

The NASW maintains this website full of information for social workers, including careers in social work and jobs. You do not need to be a member to view the jobs, but members do have access to more features in this area of the site.

Social Work and Social Services Jobs Online

gwbweb.wustl.edu/careerdevelopment/jobsonline/pages/overview.aspx

This free website lists jobs in all facets of social work and links to additional resources for people in this field. It is supported by the Career Services Office at the George Warren Brown School of Social Work, Washington University.

Socialservice.com

socialservice.com

This is a fine place to look for a job in social services in the United States, Canada, and the United Kingdom. If you decide to register, you can customize job alerts and post your resume, all at no cost.

Verbatim (Court) Reporters

BestFuture.com

bestfuture.com

BestFuture is here to tell you everything you wanted to know about court reporting—how it is evolving and moving from the courtroom into new jobs in business and multimedia fields, and even how it is working to assist people who are hearing disabled through captioning technology. The Career Path section lays out the many career options such as scoping, medical and legal transcriptionists, and captioning as well as the more traditional courtroom services. This information is provided by the National Court Reporters Association.

NCRA Online, the National Court Reporters Association

ncraonline.org

The NCRA is working to advance the profession of "those who capture and integrate the spoken word to text." Its website is a reliable source for information on this profession, including education and certification resources. Members have access to The Job Bank.

Scopists.com

scopists.com

"This site is dedicated to the support of the professions of the scopist and court reporter by providing reference resources, word lists, employment opportunities, and just about anything of use to court reporters and scopists all over the world!" The site includes a directory of freelance scopists, a place to post job announcements, and links to useful reference sources for scopists.

Jobs in the Humanities, Recreation, Hospitality, and Personal Services

The purview of this chapter is occupations that provide a service to others, whether it's entertainment or assisting someone with a need. Persons searching for jobs in these areas will not usually see any that specify "English literature majors desired," so it's important for you to know how your skills can be parlayed before delving into job listings. The career-exploration resources in Chapter 14 will be of advantage here.

General Arts and Humanities Sources

H-Net Job Guide for the Humanities and Social Sciences

h-net.org/jobs

This guide takes you through positions in history and other fields in the humanities and social sciences, including rhetoric and communications. Most positions are in academic institutions.

"What Can I Do with a Major in . . . English?"

utexas.edu/student/cec/careers/english.pdf

This article spells out entry-level jobs for which graduates with a B.A. in English might be hired. It is divided into Direct Career Options (those closely matching the skills and qualifications of an English major), Less Direct Career Options (the fit is close, but some additional qualifications may be necessary), and Indirect Career Options (they may not appear to have a relationship with the study of English, but it is there). This article is a service of the Career Exploration Center, University of Texas at Austin, and is accompanied by many similar guides, including one for liberal arts majors (utexas.edu/student/cec/careers). This is a PDF (Portable Document Format) document and requires Adobe's free Acrobat Reader (adobe.com) for viewing and printing.

Acting and Entertainment

BackStage

backstage.com

The Internet presence for *BackStage*, the weekly newsmagazine of the theater community, includes reviews of various productions, a nice Career Advice section, various directories, and Casting Calls. The site is searchable by category and/or location (East Coast, West Coast, state, Canada, or another country). Some areas require a paid subscription, but most are open to all.

EntertainmentCareers.Net

entertainmentcareers.net

This site lists all kinds of jobs and internships within the entertainment industry, even news reporters and editors. Paying members have access to more listings.

Playbill

playbill.com

Playbill is a go-to source for listings of acting and theatrical support positions on and off Broadway, throughout the United States, in Canada, and around the world. Check the Casting and Jobs area for job opportunities.

ShowBizjobs.com

showbizjobs.com

This site raises the curtain on opportunities in all occupations in the film-, television-, recording-, and attractions-industry job markets. You can search the listings by region and job field or browse them by company or date of posting.

UK Theatre Web

uktw.co.uk

UK Theatre Web probably can tell you everything you could possibly want to know about the dramatic-arts scene in the United Kingdom, including what kind of employment opportunities exist.

Variety Careers

varietycareers.com

Variety is the trade publication of the media and entertainment industry, and its website is the source for "Media & Entertainment Industry Jobs Online." Anyone with a hankering to work in film, television, cable, publishing, home entertainment, or the like, can probably scout out something of promise here. This database spans the full range of jobs in this industry, from performers to producers to accountants and lawyers, and includes listings from not only *Variety* but also *Broadcasting & Cable*, *Multichannel News*, and *Video Business*.

Art and Artists

The Art Deadlines List

artdeadlineslist.com

This service lists "competitions, art contests, calls for entries/papers, grants, residencies, auditions, casting calls, funding opportunities, art scholarships, fellowships, jobs, internships, etc., in the arts or related areas (painting, drawing, photography, etc.)." There is a free list and a fee list, so if you find a lot here to interest you, a paid subscription may be to your benefit.

Greater Philadelphia Cultural Alliance

philaculture.org

Established in 1972 by nine Philadelphia cultural institutions, the Culture Alliance now boasts a membership of more than three hundred nonprofit arts and culture organizations from across the Greater Philadelphia area. Among the many services provided to members, the Culture Alliance operates a nifty job bank with numerous interesting opportunities for professionals and volunteers who want to work in the art and culture industry.

Cartooning

National Cartoonists Society

reuben.org

Are you the next Scott Adams? Well, the National Cartoonists Society wants you to know what it's really like to work as a cartoonist. Check out how to go from doodler to professional doodler from the folks who know the nitty-gritty, and learn how they got to where they are now. There are no job listings here, but there is information on how to advance in this field, rounded out with links to related associations.

Child and Elder Care

4aNannyJob

4anannyjob.com

4aNannyJob arms you with information on how to find work as a nanny or an au pair. In addition to a listing of training schools and professional associations, the site provides a set of questions that the nanny applicant should ask of any employer and a sample work contract that employers can copy and customize. This site links to NannyClassifieds.com for listings of open positions.

National Child Care Information Center

nccic.org

The National Child Care Information Center, a project of the Child Care Bureau, is a nationwide resource that links information and people to complement, enhance, and promote the child-care delivery system, working to ensure that all children and families have access to high-quality, comprehensive services. Among the many resources here is information on starting your own child-care business, complete with links to each state's agency for information on local regulations.

Culinary and Baking Arts

Bread Bakers Guild of America

bbga.org

This professional guild supports education in the field of artisan baking and the production of high-quality bread products. You can pull up recipes, tips, information on places to buy supplies and equipment, education links, and job listings at this site.

Escoffier On Line

escoffier.com

Escoffier On Line is for all food professionals, from bakers to chefs to food-service managers. This is a wonderful resource to tap if you are looking for a job, for education and training information in food-service hospitality or culinary work, as well as for other good industry links.

FoodIndustryJobs.com

foodindustryjobs.com

This site presents job listings and related information for the food, food-service, institutional hospitality, and related industries. You can search the job leads, review the employer or recruiter directories, or post your resume. Registration (free) is required if you want to post your resume and activate the Career Scout's automatic search-and-notification service.

PersonalChef.com

personalchef.com

A personal chef typically serves several clients and prepares multiple meals that are custom designed to meet the client's requests and requirements. These meals are packaged and stored so that diners may enjoy them whenever they choose. This site, a service of the American Personal & Private Chef Association, relays information on this growing field, including how you can turn your love of cooking into a profitable business.

Dance

CyberDance: Ballet on the Net

cyberdance.org

CyberDance is a resource guide with thirty-five hundred links to classical ballet and modern dance resources on the Internet. This compilation incorporates dance companies, news and information (featuring sources for events, auditions, and competitions), people, international information, and more.

Voice of Dance

voiceofdance.com

Voice of Dance is a directory of resources, news, and discussions on dance. Under the Community header are message boards listing auditions, jobs, and much more.

Fashion

The Apparel News

apparelnews.net

This site presents news for the industry along with loads of links to the players and buyers. The classified ads are accessible for a small weekly fee.

FashionCareerCenter.com

fashioncareercenter.com

FashionCareerCenter.com is a fit site for anyone in the fashion industry—models, sales representatives, pattern makers, and beyond. Look over the listings, or post your resume at no cost. You can also follow links to other fashion-industry career sites and industry news sources.

Women's Wear Daily

wwd.com

Women's Wear Daily (*WWD*) is "The Retailer's Daily Newspaper." Along with the articles and conference lists on the website, you have a link to FashionCareers.com, the online career center for *WWD*, *DNR* ("Defining Men's Fashion"), and *Footwear News*. You can search this combined source for job listings for free and then register your resume if you want to proceed with items that interest you.

Funeral Directors

FuneralNet

funeralnet.com

FuneralNet links to extensive information on funeral homes and funeral services nationwide. This site includes employment and internship opportunities.

National Funeral Directors Association

nfda.org

The NFDA has an excellent site with inside information on education and licensing requirements for this field. The site also features job announcements, facts on careers in funeral services, and details on scholarships.

Gaming

Casino Careers Online

casinocareers.com

Casino Careers Online offers a job bank and a resume database for people in the gaming industry. Only candidates matching the required qualifications will be added to the database, and only gaming companies that are registered users of this service can search the database. Qualified job seekers can post either an open or a confidential resume, which must be updated every six months to stay active.

National Indian Gaming Association

indiangaming.org

This association represents the tribes, businesses, and organizations engaged in tribal gaming enterprises across the United States. Persons interested in working in these casinos can review some listings posted under NIGA Information as well as use the list of member casinos to connect to available websites and review listings posted there.

Gender and Race Studies

National Women's Studies Association

nwsa.org

This organization is committed to the support and promotion of feminist teaching, research, and professional and community service. Among the many informative and helpful offerings through the website is a database of openings in women's studies and other academic appointments and fellowships. Scholarships and internships are listed under Student Resources.

Graphics, Multimedia, and Web Design

CreativeHeads.net

creativeheads.net

With the slogan "Jobs for the 'Right' Brain," CreativeHeads.net facilitates communications between employers and job seekers in the video game, animation, TV and film, and 3-D technology and software tools industries. (The "right" brain refers to the creative side of our minds.) This site hosts an amazing array of jobs posted by some of the most famous organizations. This is the official job board for ACM SIGGRAPH (Association for Computing Machinery's Special Interest Group on Graphics and Interactive Techniques), but you do not need to be a member to use this service.

RitaSue Siegel Resources

ritasue.com

RitaSue Siegel Resources is a search and consulting firm dedicated to recruiting and placing professionals in graphic design, industrial design, user interface/ Web design, interior design, architecture, fashion, textiles, and apparel at all employment levels from CEO to design staff. Its clients include consulting and design firms and leading academic institutions in the field of design. Interested job seekers can review job listings on the website.

Also see "Art and Artists" earlier in this chapter, as well as "Computing and Technology" in Chapter 8.

Hospitality

HCareers.com

hcareers.com

HCareers.com lists thousands of jobs in hotels, restaurants, casinos, resorts, cruise ships, and anything else in the hospitality industry. While this main site includes U.S. and international postings, you can opt to search the separate sites just for Canada and the United Kingdom and Ireland.

Hospitality Net

hospitalitynet.org

This site is a laudable source for news and information regarding jobs in hotels and restaurants as well as the food and beverage industry. The job listings are provided by WIWIH.com and require you to register for a free account to see the full announcement.

Museums and Archives

American Association of Museums

aam-us.org

AAM is the national service organization representing the American museum community. The website features information about the association, museums, and career and employment resources. While anyone can review the job listings, AAM members have access to additional career resources and services.

Museum Employment Resource Center

museum-employment.com

The Museum Employment Resource Center lists jobs for museums and other cultural resource institutions in the United States. You can also gather information on museum studies courses.

MuseumJobs.com

museumjobs.com

This site lists jobs in museums and galleries in the United Kingdom and the United States. You do not need to register (free) to view the listings, but registration will allow you to set up job alerts.

Music and Music Education

American Symphony Orchestra League

symphony.org

The ASOL provides leadership and service to American orchestras while communicating to the American public the value and importance of orchestras and the music they perform. The organization also matches qualified conductors and administrators with orchestras around the country. If you are interested in orchestra management, the Orchestra Management Fellowship Program is a must. Individual membership is encouraged for anyone planning to pursue music or arts management as a career, and it includes access to a special Careers area of the website with jobs.

MENC: The National Association for Music Education

menc.org

MENC (Music Educator's National Conference) provides music educators, students, and musicians with information on and links to education standards, career opportunities, financial aid, festivals, suppliers, teacher's guides, and more. Under the Jobs and Careers header, you will find information on careers in music and music education as well as the MENC Job Center. This lists current openings for teachers ranging from early childhood to college, and the listings are free for all to view.

Musical America

musicalamerica.com

Musical America covers the business of the performing arts industry and is probably best known for the annual *International Directory of the Performing Arts.* The website companion returns this venerable publication to its newspaper roots with current news, information, and resources on the performing arts. While many sections of the website are limited to paying subscribers, the Career Center with its numerous jobs and internships for managers and administrators (and an occasional musician) is open to the public.

Musicalchairs.info

musicalchairs.info

This website calls itself the "world's best site for classical music jobs." It lists audition announcements from organizations around the world and links to competitions, master classes, and much more. It also houses directories of organizations, conservatories, and musicians. This site is not just for instrumentalists, offering auditions and other resources for vocalists as well. It is very interesting and a nice way to review the international audition scene.

Philosophy

Canadian Philosophical Association

acpcpa.ca

The Canadian Philosophical Association, a learned society made up principally of teachers and students of philosophy, is devoted to professional philosophical activity in Canada. Among the many resources and services provided on this site are listings of jobs, along with announcements of fellowships and scholarships. Most of these opportunities are in Canadian universities, but not all are limited to Canada.

Jobs in Philosophy

www.sozialwiss.uni-hamburg.de/phil/ag/jobs

PhilNet, in Hamburg, Germany, is to be commended for this excellent worldwide list of jobs in philosophy in French, German, English, and Spanish.

Photography and Photojournalism

National Press Photographers Association

nppa.org

The National Press Photographers Association is dedicated to the advancement of photojournalism. The membership includes still and television photographers, editors, and representatives of the businesses that serve this industry. The public side of the website includes sections with information on careers, scholarships available from the organization, and schools and colleges offering courses in this field. The Job Info Bank is open to members only.

PPA's Photocentral

ppa.com

The Professional Photographers of America site offers certification courses for professional photographers, copyright protection assistance, and many other benefits. The website also includes good information for people looking to get into this business or expand their business presence, including free classified ads.

Publishing, Printing, and Bookbinding

Bookbuilders of Boston

bbboston.org

This is a "nonprofit organization dedicated to bringing together people involved in book publishing and manufacturing throughout New England." Its website is an excellent primer for interested job seekers, with information on education and training opportunities, resources for the industry, and a job bank.

Publishers Weekly

publishersweekly.com

Publishers Weekly is the "international news source of book publishing and bookselling." Visit this online companion to the print publication for weekly updates on news affecting the industry, in addition to other services and resources. Click on the Job Zone for slots covering the worldwide publishing industry.

Semper International

semperllc.com

This staffing agency specializes in the print, copy, and digital industries. To review job listings, select a regional office and then select a job area that interests you. At the time of review, it listed jobs in bindery, duplicating, large press, prepress digital, silk screen, and other areas.

Sports and Recreation

Cool Works

coolworks.com

Cool Works is the major source for jobs in our national parks, ski resorts nationwide, and other similar opportunities. Organized by state, the listings range from summer or seasonal to year-round permanent, and from parking attendant to manager of the resort.

FitnessManagement.com

fitnessmanagement.com

FitnessManagement.com is the online companion of *Fitness Management* magazine. Resources here include articles, news, product listings and reviews, and classified ads. Sell your equipment, buy new equipment, or track down a job here.

GolfingCareers.com

golfingcareers.com

This is a nice-looking site for the golfing industry. While the site is free for users, registration is required to gain access to many areas, including the specific details of the job listings. Once you have done this, you can set up a personal search agent, post your resume, and even search for employers. This site links to many of the golf associations around the United States.

Sporting Goods Manufacturers Association

sgma.com

The SGMA website includes all kinds of information on the sports equipment industry. There are job listings, links to member companies and their employment listings, and links to executive recruiters for this industry.

TazSport.com

tazsport.com

TazSport.com is your connection to high school and college coaching jobs. There is a fee for access to the job database, but you can review the list of jobs and employers before deciding to register. Your fee also includes listing your resume in the database. Along with the jobs, TazSport.com links to numerous resources for many sports.

Writing, Journalism, and Broadcast Media

Editor & Publisher Online

editorandpublisher.com

This site is the online companion to *Editor & Publisher*, the weekly print newsmagazine for the newspaper industry. The Jobs area is a shared service that combines listings from *Billboard*, *AdWeek*, *MediaWeek*, and other publications; it includes employment listings for academic, administrative, editorial, advertising, production/technology, and other facets of this industry. Your free registration is necessary to apply for listings shown here, but you can search and review the listings before registering.

J-Jobs Journalism Jobs and Internships

journalism.berkeley.edu/jobs

J-Jobs is a service to the journalism community provided by the University of California, Berkeley Graduate School of Journalism. Jobs are usually posted as they are received and are removed after about thirty days. Internships are generally considered permanent but are subject to verification each year. Follow J-Jobs links to additional job-search support and career resources for journalists.

National Diversity Newspaper Job Bank

newsjobs.com

Visit this site for jobs in all facets of the journalism industry. While the job bank is targeted to diversity populations, it is open to all users. However, you must submit your resume in order to get the free password needed to access the job database.

National Writers Union

nwu.org

The NWU is a labor union that represents "freelance writers in all genres, formats, and media." All working writers are eligible to join the union. Part of the service is the Job Hotline, a cache of writing, authoring, and multimedia jobs in the United States. While anyone can view the list of jobs, the identifying contact information for each employer is available only to members. Freelance writers will appreciate the many resources on the site, such as the Alerts from the Grievance and Contracts Division.

RadioandRecords.com

radioandrecords.com

Welcome to "the Radio and Record Industries Information Leader." This site turns you on to industry headlines, job announcements for production staff as well as radio personalities, and loads of directory-type listings within The R&R Directory.

Society for Technical Communications

stc.org

The Society for Technical Communications is an individual membership organization dedicated to advancing the arts and sciences of the field. Its twenty-three thousand members include technical writers, editors, graphic designers, multimedia artists, and others whose work involves making technical information understandable and available to those who need it. All visitors have access to the job database, but only members may view listings less than fourteen days old. Any visitor can download and view the free PDF guide "A Career in Technical Communication," found under Membership / Join STC / STC Brochures, or by going directly to stc.org/pdf_files/acareer.pdf. (This document rquires Adobe's free reader [adobe.com] for viewing and printing.)

SunOasis Jobs

sunoasis.com

SunOasis lists jobs and freelance opportunities for writers, editors, and copywriters. There are also links to additional sources and job sites. Be sure to check out the "CyberSearch Guide to Writing Jobs," a succinct tutorial on how to use the Internet to help you find work.

TVJobs.com

tvjobs.com

This is an impressive site with jobs and information for the entire broadcast industry. While you must pay to view the job listings and salary database, you can enter the call letters of target television and radio stations in the search box and find their websites (and locally posted job listings) for free. Other terrific resources here are free. TVJobs.com has a companion site for radio broadcasting, AMFMJobs.com.

7

Jobs in the Natural Sciences, Health, and Medicine

This chapter leads you through sources for the natural sciences, including agriculture and food sciences, physics, chemistry, and the earth sciences, as well as the many health and medical fields. Many of the natural science and health and medical fields overlap, so don't narrow your sights to just one particular heading. You should also page through Chapter 8 for related areas of interest.

General Resources

BioSpace.com

biospace.com

BioSpace.com is a "global hubsite for life sciences." Persons with an affinity for biotechnology and other life sciences are rewarded here with news, job openings, and career information. The job listings can be searched by location, keyword, and date of posting. The free registration is not required unless you want to store a resume, save your searches, or create a job agent.

Lifesciencejobs

www.lifesciencejobs.com

Put this site on your itinerary to scope out jobs in the worldwide life sciences industry. The News & Career area links to recruiting services, journals, and other online job sites.

MedZilla

medzilla.com

MedZilla is an established recruiting site for the biological and health care industries run by a recruiting firm with several years' experience. This site includes jobs and a resume database and does not charge job seekers for using it. Users will also want to size up the many discussion boards in the Community area, some of which deal with job search and career development and advancement.

Nature

nature.com

Nature, the weekly international journal of science, is the brains behind this site. Check out the latest enhancements, sign up for the daily update, and go to NatureJobs for news on career and employment issues, upcoming meetings and courses, announcements, employer listings, and jobs.

New Scientist Jobs

newscientistjobs.com

This site delivers the international employment listings from *New Scientist*, a major newspaper for the scientific community. Start your job search by selecting a world region, and then refine your search by field of interest. This is an excellent source for jobs in academic, industrial, and government settings. Registration for this service, which is free and optional, empowers you to create search agents and store listings, CVs, and cover letters.

Postdoc Jobs

postdocjobs.com

As you can infer from its name, Postdoc Jobs posts positions for holders of a Ph.D. The listings are open for all to view, but registering (free) grants you subscription to an e-mail notification list and other services and does not require you to post your CV. There are other good resources to probe, including information for non-U.S. citizens seeking positions in this country. Users can multiply their gains by visiting the partner sites, UniversityJobs.com (universityjobs.com) and ScienceJobs.org (sciencejobs.org).

ScienceCareers.org

sciencecareers.org

ScienceCareers.org is operated jointly by the American Association for the Advancement of Science and *Science* magazine. This site includes job and career information for persons pursuing a career in any scientific field, along with the precious GrantsNet database of research funding opportunities. The jobs can be browsed by company, position title, or date posted, or they can be searched by keyword. Users can also sign on for the free Job Alerts e-mail service.

Agriculture, Forestry, and Landscaping

AgCareers.com

agcareers.com

Here you have an outlet for jobs in all areas of agriculture, including working with animal health, teaching, natural resources management, and administration/sales. The listings take you to Canada, the United States, Australia, and other international locations. The site also links to additional resources.

American Agricultural Economic Association

aaea.org

Agricultural economics is the study of the economic forces that affect the food and fiber industry. Select the Careers & Education header for entreé to the AAEA Career Center, replete with job and internship listings, a resume database, the skinny on careers in this field, and then some. Most areas of the site are open to all users.

American Society of Agricultural and Biological Engineers

asabe.org

ASABE is an educational and scientific organization whose mission is the advancement of engineering applicable to agricultural, food, and biological systems. The Career Resources area unfolds to a public job database, profiles of career possibilities, and other germane career-development material.

ASA/CSSA/SSSA Job Listings

asa-cssa-sssa.org/jobs.html

This is a joint project of the American Society of Agronomy (ASA), the Crop Science Society of America (CSSA), and the Soil Science Society of America (SSSA). Users can browse the position announcements from *Crop Science, Soil Science, and Agronomy News* (*CSA News*) and from submissions received throughout the month. The listings encompass government, private, supervisory, international, and assistantship/fellowship opportunities.

Cyber-Sierra's Natural Resources Job Search

cyber-sierra.com/nrjobs

This wonderful source for jobs does double duty as a collection of links to resources for employment in forestry, earth sciences, and other natural resource fields. The maintainer goes the extra mile to add an excellent Read Me First file with tips on attaining work in these fields.

Tree Care Industry Association

tcia.org

Established in 1938 as the National Arborist Association, the TCIA "develops safety and education programs, standards of tree care practice, and management information for arboriculture firms around the world." Under the Publications header, the Classifieds carry help-wanted announcements, while other areas of the site feed you essential information on careers in this field as well as potential employers.

Weed Science Society of America (WSSA) Job Positions

wssa.net/WSSA/Jobs

The Weed Science Society of America is a nonprofit professional organization promoting research, education, and extension-outreach activities related to weeds and fostering awareness of weeds and their impacts on managed and natural ecosystems. This database lists permanent, term, postdoctoral, graduate student, internship, and summer positions in weed science.

Related information appears under "Farmworkers" later in this chapter. Also see the resources under "Architecture and Urban Planning" in Chapter 8.

Animal Sciences, Fisheries, and Marine Sciences

American Fisheries Society

fisheries.org

This society works "to improve the conservation and sustainability of fishery resources and aquatic ecosystems by advancing fisheries and aquatic science and promoting the development of fisheries professionals." The website includes a Job Board with employment and internship opportunities.

American Society of Limnology and Oceanography

aslo.org

ASLO is dedicated to "promoting the interests of limnology, oceanography, and related sciences." The website includes job listings with openings for biologists, aquatic scientists, postdoctorates, trainers, and administrators in academic and other settings. A second board lists student opportunities. This site also features guides to aquatic careers and interrelated fields.

AnimalJobs.com

animaljobs.com

AnimalJobs.com offers jobs for professionals who work with animals as well as animal lovers. While many of the jobs are management or retail positions in animal supply shops, there are numerous listings here for veterinarians, veterinary technicians, animal shelter management and staff, and groomers, not to mention several listings for individuals looking for that special someone to help care for their pets. The site is free and includes additional helpful resources for your search.

Aquatic Network

aquanet.com

Aquatic Network is a fountain of information on aquaculture, conservation, fisheries, limnology, marine science and oceanography, maritime heritage, ocean engineering, and seafood. Under Opportunities, users can cast their eyes on not only Jobs Offered, Jobs Wanted, and Grants/Funding Announcements, but also some businesses for sale and consulting opportunities.

Association of Zoos and Aquariums

aza.org

The AZA is a nonprofit organization "dedicated to the advancement of zoos and aquariums in the areas of conservation, education, science, and recreation." Persons interested in working in zoos and aquariums in the United States will find internships and employment opportunities in the Job Listings, including opportunities with non-AZA-accredited organizations. You can also learn about careers in zoos and aquariums under Kids and Families.

Equimax—Where Jobs and Horse People Find Each Other

equimax.com

Equimax provides job listings and resume services, both for a fee, to people whose employment interests lie among horses. Be sure to avail yourself of the free hiring and career advice, including the article "What It's Like to Work in the Horse Industry." Also, through the list of links you can rein in many more resources for your appraisal.

Also see the citations under "Veterinary Medicine" at the end of this chapter.

Astronomy

American Astronomical Society

www.aas.org

The AAS, the largest organization of professional astronomers in North America, promotes the advancement of astronomy and related sciences. The association's website offers public access to several good career resources, including the AAS Job Register and a guide to careers in astronomy.

For more resources see "Physics" later in this chapter.

Biology

Bio.com

bio.com

Bio.com is a resource hub for the life sciences community. The Career Center includes employment listings, career forums, and insightful articles on bettering your career and improving your job search.

Listings for "Biotechnology and Biomedical Engineering" are in Chapter 8.

Chemistry

AACC International

aaccnet.org

Formerly known as the American Association of Cereal Chemists, AACC International is a nonprofit organization of members who are specialists in the use of cereal grains in foods. Under the Membership header, check out the Career Placement Service's link to Useful Sites for your job search, the AACC International Members Offering Recruiting Services, and the job announcements. You also get the brochure "Careers in Cereal Chemistry."

Chemjobs.org

chemjobs.org

Operated by the American Chemical Society (ACS), this is a job and career information service for the chemical community worldwide. It is not the exclusive domain of ACS members, but some resources as well as some job announcements that derive from the most recent print issue of *Chemical & Engineering News* can be viewed only by ACS members. You do not need to be registered to use the Apply Now feature.

Chiropractics

Chirocareers.com

chirocareers.com

Chirocareers.com was started by a doctor of chiropractics who had a difficult time finding information on potential practice opportunities when he was first licensed. Today, chiropractic career seekers can post resumes, search jobs, and find practices for sale, all at no cost. At the time of review, the site was still small but it did contain very good job listings.

PlanetChiropractic

planetc1.com

PlanetChiropractic is a community where chiropractors can share information with one another, but it also serves students of this profession and potential patients. Among the many resources here are articles on a variety of topics authored by doctors and other professionals, resources for finding practitioners and equipment, and the Classifieds, with employment listings.

Dentistry

American Dental Association

ada.org

The ADA site is a good source of information on all careers in dentistry, including dental hygiene, dental assisting, and dental laboratory technology. Select the Dental Professional area from the front page to access the Resources and Publications section, where the Dental Careers and Job Listings await.

Entomology

Entomological Society of America

entsoc.org

The society hosts listings for jobs and internships in entomology. If you are drawn to studying bugs, or just want to figure out what entomologists do all day, you can sample guides to entomology, a FAQs section, and more under Resources.

Jobs in Entomology

insects.tamu.edu/jobs

The Department of Entomology at Texas A&M University posts listings for openings in this field, including assistantships. They also link to other websites that list job openings in this and related fields.

Environmental and Earth Sciences

Earthworks

earthworks-jobs.com

Work your way to Earthworks for lists of jobs in oil, energy, geoscience, environmental science, ecology, conservation, and other related positions. It is operated by a small advertising agency based in Cambridge, England, so the majority of postings are from the United Kingdom and Europe. The Links section gives way to hundreds of related resources to survey.

Ecological Society of America Careers & Certification

esa.org/careers_certification

The Ecological Society of America posts job announcements, internships, and funding opportunities that are submitted to the site. Visitors who are curious about a career in ecology will want to troll the many resources set forth under Teaching & Learning.

EnvironmentalCareer.com

environmentalcareer.com

This site from the Environmental Career Center in Virginia lists environmental and natural resources jobs from entry-level to senior management. To apply for jobs that are not direct applications on the employer's website, you will need to register (free) and post your resume, but it is not mandatory in order to view the listings and the employer's contact information.

Farmworkers

National Farmworkers Job Program

www.doleta.gov/msfw

This site from the Employment and Training Administration, U.S. Department of Labor, contains information on several programs that assist migrant and seasonal farmworkers with housing, job training, and much more.

Forensics

This field covers many disciplines and is adding new areas of study all the time.

American Academy of Forensic Sciences

aafs.org

This professional society is dedicated to the application of science to the law. Its membership includes physicians, criminalists, toxicologists, attorneys, dentists, physical anthropologists, document examiners, engineers, and others who practice and perform research in the many diverse fields relating to forensic science. You can review information on a career in forensic sciences, investigate employment opportunities, and look for educational institutions offering programs leading to this field, among other activities.

American Society of Crime Laboratory Directors

ascld.org

This nonprofit professional society advocates the improvement of crime laboratory operations through sound management practices. The website includes information on meetings and accreditation of labs, an overview of how these facilities are staffed and operated, links to additional forensic societies, and jobs.

Geography and Geographic Information Systems

GIS Jobs Clearinghouse

www.gjc.org

This site is a clear choice for seekers of jobs in geographic information systems (GIS) as well as remote sensing, image processing, and global positioning systems. It also links to additional information and resources. You can post a resume here gratis.

Internet Resources for Geographers

colorado.edu/geography/virtdept/resources/contents.htm

This collection of links to geography information is maintained by Kristina Klos Wynne and Kenneth Foote, of the Department of Geography at the University of Colorado at Boulder. Channels of information include journals, professional and research organizations, map collections, job and education resources, and much more for the practicing or budding geographer.

Health Care and Medicine

The following resources pertain to numerous job areas within the health care and medical fields, including medical school faculty, physicians, nurses, clinical researchers, therapists, and lab technicians. You should also direct your attention to the many specific career areas highlighted in this chapter, including Chiropractics; Dentistry; Hospice Care; Midwifery; Nursing; Pharmacology and Pharmaceutics; Physical, Occupational, and Massage Therapy; and Public Health.

Academic Physician and Scientist

acphysci.com

Academic Physician and Scientist, or *APS*, is a newsmagazine published ten times a year by Lippincott Williams & Wilkins, a publisher of professional medical information, and is endorsed by the Association of American Medical Colleges. This companion website lists open academic medical positions for U.S. medical schools and affiliated institutions in Administration, Basic Science, and Clinical Science areas. You can also read career articles from the print *APS* newsmagazine on this site.

Experimental Medicine Job Listings

www.medicine.mcgill.ca/expmed/emjl

Operated by the McGill University Department of Medicine, Division of Experimental Medicine, in Montreal, Quebec, this international job board hosts announcements for research scientists, medical professionals, postdocs, and even grad assistants in academic, government, and industrial settings. The list is divided into Montreal, the rest of Canada, and outside Canada. Be sure to note the dates on the announcements; at the time of review we saw some very old listings.

HealthCareSource.com

healthcaresource.com

This site brings you jobs in the health care industry, coupled with information on continuing education units and professional seminars.

JAMA CareerNet

jamacareernet.com

This searchable database is where to go for current employment listings from many of the publications of the American Medical Association along with employer-listed openings. You can select a specialty and browse all listings in that area, search the employers that post here, or use the Advanced Search to combine specialty, keywords, and locations.

MedHunters

medhunters.com

MedHunters lists jobs for health care professionals in a variety of settings all around the world. Select from Nursing, MD, Allied Health, or Other positions to browse the list of job fields, or scroll down each page to browse the same list of positions by location or "Lifestyle" (Sun, Snow, Mountains, Rural, etc.). You can also browse jobs by employer. You do not need to register unless you want to apply for one of the jobs.

Physicians Employment

physemp.com

Job listings for physicians make up the Physicians Employment site. The listings can be searched by specialty alone, so you do not need to complete the entire form to access the postings, nor do you have to register your CV. However, allowing the site to retain basic information about you will put you on the list for new and unadvertised positions.

Hospice Care

National Hospice and Palliative Care Organization

nhpco.org

The information here on hospice care will prove helpful to persons interested in this line of work as well as to those interested in utilizing these services. The NHPCO maintains an excellent searchable directory of hospices and links you to HospiceChoices, a career center for the hospice community (hospicechoices.com).

Meteorology

American Meteorological Society

ametsoc.org

The American Meteorological Society promotes the development and dissemination of information and education on the atmospheric and related oceanic and hydrologic sciences. Founded in 1919, it now has a membership of more than eleven thousand professionals, professors, students, and weather enthusiasts. The site includes publications from the association, a career guide for the atmospheric sciences, certification information, a directory of local chapters, and employment opportunities in a variety of organizations. All visitors are welcome to use the job board, but only AMS members can see listings that are less than fourteen days old.

Midwifery

MidwifeJobs.com from the American College of Nurse-Midwives

midwifejobs.com

This site holds employment opportunities as well as authoritative information on a career as a certified nurse-midwife. Users can register to store a resume here at no cost, activating the Reply Online feature that accompanies each job announcement. Registration is not required to search the database, and contact information for each employer is cited.

Nursing

Nurse.com

nurse.com

Nurse.com is operated by Gannett Healthcare Group (publisher of *Nurse.com*, *Nursing Spectrum*, *NurseWeek*, and *Today in PT*). This website offers visitors current news and information about the nursing field, details on continuing education courses, a Career area with employer profiles, a free Resume Builder, a Travel Nurses section, and a searchable job database.

Pharmacology and Pharmaceutics

InPharm.com

inpharm.com

Operated by John Wiley & Sons, InPharm.com is a specialist online recruiting service for the worldwide pharmaceutical industry. Job seekers can search this international database by location, type of business, or specific recruiting firm. You can also add to your knowledge base from the storehouse of industry news and information here.

Pharmacy Week

pharmacyweek.com

Pharmacy Week's website dispenses job postings, articles, and links to more information from the weekly print magazine. Browse the job listings by category, search for those in a particular location, or view all listings at one session.

Physical, Occupational, Speech, and Massage Therapy

American Massage Therapy Association

amtamassage.org

This site from the professional association for massage therapists presents a wealth of information on what massage therapy is and how you can become a practitioner, along with other news and information, including select articles from the association journal. It's a great resource for people considering this career option. The job bank is open to all users without registering (free).

RehabTime.com

rehabtime.com

This resources site is focused primarily on the "rehab team," including physical therapy, occupational therapy, and speech therapy. Users will appreciate the free job listings and information on continuing education, along with resources for those in this field.

Physics

Physics Today Career Network

physicstoday.org/jobs

Physics Today, published by the American Institute of Physics, reports on noteworthy events and news in the field of physics. The online companion includes a marvelous career center with job listings from academe, industry, government, and nonprofit organizations. This site also offers job-hunting advice and excellent career information for younger persons interested in this field. The site is open for all visitors to use.

PhysicsWorld

physicsworld.org

PhysicsWorld, sponsored by the Institute of Physics, is a bountiful resource for persons in this field. It contains news, product reviews, Web links, articles from *Physics World* magazine, and announcements of physics jobs. All the jobs advertised through *Physics World*, CERNCourier.com, and Nanotechweb.org are represented here. You can quickly and easily search through the listings to view quality positions in academia, industry, and government.

Public Health

Career Action Center

www.sph.emory.edu/studentservice/Career.html

The Career Action Center from the Rollins School of Public Health at Emory University is a free, public resource for relevant job and career information. The main feature of this site is the Public Health Employment Connection, a database loaded with jobs in the public health field. Interested persons can also register to post a resume here for free. The Career Action Center also offers information on continuing education opportunities, job-search tips, and insight into careers in public health.

Public Health Resources on the Internet

www.lib.berkeley.edu/PUBL/internet.html

This guide to information on public health is maintained by the Public Health Library at the University of California, Berkeley. It is a first-rate fund of material on the field and includes links to associations and other resources for professionals.

Veterinary Medicine

Association of American Veterinary Medical Colleges

aavmc.org

The Association of American Veterinary Medical Colleges represents faculty, staff, veterinary students, and graduate students studying and working in veterinary colleges, departments of veterinary science, and noted animal medical centers in the United States and Canada. Visitors will find information on preparing for a career in veterinary medicine, guidance on applying for admission to a veterinary college, and the AAVMC Career Center, a public job service operated by the Veterinary Career Network and routing jobs from all over the world.

American Veterinary Medical Assocation

avma.org

The not-for-profit AVMA represents more than seventy-five thousand veterinarians in private and corporate practice, government, industry, academia, and uniformed services. Visitors to the association's site can learn about this practice, review recent scientific and industry news that affects animal scientists, and familiarize themselves with careers in veterinary medicine. The free and public Veterinary Career Center is operated by the Veterinary Career Network, which offers the same service through the AAVMC, preceding. AVMA members can also access the classified listings from the *Journal of the AVMA* from this site.

VeterinaryLife.com

veterinarylife.com

This is a source of classified ads for veterinarians and vet techs from all over the world. These include veterinarian jobs offered or wanted, clinic jobs offered or wanted, and equipment and practices for sale.

VetQuest Classifieds

vetquest.com/classifieds

These classified ads are directed to persons in veterinary medicine. You can review all Positions Offered listings posted in the last twenty-four hours, forty-eight hours, week, or month, or select a category from the menu. These categories include Internships/Residencies and New Graduates, a nice option for users at these levels. Anyone wanting to take over an existing practice can search through the Hospital Sale Lease Buy listings.

Jobs in Engineering, Mathematics, Technology, and Transportation

Presented here are specs on sites for fields and occupations related to engineering, technology, and transportation. Under this canopy are all of the engineering specialties, as well as mathematics, construction, mining, public utilities, unions, and manufacturing. You may want to flip back to Chapter 7 for allied areas.

Multiple Fields

AEJob.com

aejob.com

Hall & Company operates this site, which lists jobs nationwide for architects, engineers, and environmental consultants.

American Society for Engineering Education

asee.org

The American Society for Engineering Education is a nonprofit member association committed to promoting and improving engineering and engineering technology education. Students are served with links to engineering societies, news of interest to engineers, and information on continuing education. Undergrads and grads alike will want to look under Publications for the link to Tech-interns.com, the ASEE source for internships and research opportunities. Other users will want to reflect on the *Prism* Classifieds, the position announcements published in *Prism*, the monthly magazine of the ASEE. Members can preview the listings thirty days before publication.

ContractJobHunter

cjhunter.com

This website from *Contract Employment Weekly* specializes in job openings for contractors and consultants in engineering, IT/IS, and technical disciplines. All the jobs from the print publication as well as those posted electronically are stacked here. Guests can register to search the job database for free, which allows you to view contact information for each listing, but paying members have access to many more services and features for a modest fee.

Engineer.net

engineer.net

This site integrates jobs for engineers in many fields, including aerospace, chemical, civil, electrical, industrial, manufacturing, mechanical, and software engineering. Entry-level job seekers will also draw a bead on some listings here.

Engineering Job Source

engineerjobs.com

This free site lists jobs for engineers and technical professionals. Browse the listings by state, or search by keyword. The site also hosts a resume database. We could not discern who operates this site, but it does sport attractive jobs.

National Society of Professional Engineers

nspe.org

The NSPE website provides a slew of career information for anyone with designs on an engineering specialty. Choose the Employment header for NSPE's Career Central, home of the NSPE Job Board, with listings targeting this professional group. All users are welcome to post a resume for free. Other regions of the site include more information on this career field, networking opportunities, and the P.E. (professional engineer) licensure. Membership is required to participate in some services here, but it is a thrifty investment.

SWE: The Society of Women Engineers

swe.org

The SWE's mission is to "stimulate women to achieve full potential in careers as engineers and leaders, expand the image of the engineering profession as a positive force in improving the quality of life, and demonstrate the value of diversity." The website bestows grand information and career/employment resources for women mulling or currently pursuing engineering careers. The job board is accessible only by members, but women in this field will realize a handsome return on the investment.

Aeronautics and Aerospace

American Institute of Aeronautics and Astronautics

aiaa.org

At this site, the association rolls out loads of nuts-and-bolts information for you to apply in your career or job search. The Industry News & Resources area pulls together much of what you'll need to circle prospective employers, plan a career path, and arrive at job opportunities, but take the time to tour the entire site.

Astronaut Selection from NASA

nasajobs.nasa.gov/astronauts

It's the chance of a lifetime. The National Aeronautics and Space Administration needs pilot astronaut and mission specialist astronaut candidates to support the space shuttle and space station programs. NASA is accepting applications on a continuous basis and plans to select astronaut candidates every two years, if needed. Men and women from both the civilian sector and the military services will be considered. This site supplies all the information you need on qualifications, applications, positions, pay, and much more.

Space Careers

space-careers.com

Space Careers loads its site with job listings and links to hundreds of sources for employers, industry news, and collateral information spanning the entire world. It is well organized and easy to review in short time.

Space Jobs

spacejobs.com

Space Jobs connects you with employment opportunities in the aerospace industry worldwide while keeping you up-to-date with happenings in the industry. Review the list of jobs currently posted, and refer to the write-up on each employer so you know who's who before you apply. Job seekers can also make use of the schedule of events to plan networking activities.

Architecture and Urban Planning

American Institute of Architects

aia.org

This site includes excellent career and job information along with many resources for professional development and networking. Anyone leaning toward a career in architecture will learn much from what is here.

American Planning Association

planning.org

Right this way for ready information on careers in planning and affiliated fields, in addition to jobs posted with this professional organization. APA's Jobs Online listings are open to the public and may run for as short a time as one week, so you should drop by this site weekly if it is a part of your search plan.

American Society of Landscape Architects

asla.org

The ASLA website includes information on careers in landscape architecture, a list of landscaping firms, notices of scholarships and internships, and job openings. In other words, it's possible to learn about this career field, find an accredited program, study the industry, and get a job right here. A resume database is available for members and nonmembers, but nonmembers pay much more for posting.

Architecture.com

architecture.com

This is the official home page of the Royal Institute of British Architects. The heart of the site is an indexed collection of hundreds of annotated links to architecture resources from around the world, though it focuses mainly on Britain (search the links by keyword or browse them by category/subject). The Careers section is a wonderful exploration of the field, from how it affects society to the training necessary and where to get the training. While this is all wonderful for any reader, much of the really good stuff (like where to study and how to pay for it) is dedicated to the United Kingdom. Other features here include a registry of architects in the United Kingdom, information on events and competitions, and a job board (ribaappointments.com).

Cyburbia, the Planning and Architecture Internet Resource Center

cyburbia.org

Established in 1994, Cyburbia is the oldest portal and networking site for urban planners and others interested in cities and the built environment. It has earned our respect for its longevity, expansive coverage of the resources in this field, and continued efforts to provide the best for this profession. The Cyburbia Forums are discussion boards in which anyone can participate (after registering for free), and the Resource Directory includes an area devoted to Career Development and Employment.

Job Hunting in Planning, Architecture, and Landscape Architecture

www.lib.berkeley.edu/ENVI/jobs.html

Created by the Environmental Design Library at the University of California, Berkeley, this is a selectively annotated guide to help job seekers in the professions of architecture, landscape architecture, and city/regional planning. Not a resource for job listings, this guide is an outline of the complete job-search process targeted to these career fields, with resources and links to job-lead sources. While many annotations and references are specific to the University of California, almost all can be retrieved through an outside public or university library. All comers to the site can gain from the introduction to the many resources available to assist in a job search.

Automation

ISA, the Instrumentation, Systems, and Automation Society

isa.org

Founded in 1945, ISA is a global nonprofit organization for automation and control professionals. Under the Careers header, visitors can learn about various pursuits in this field, read up on certification and other training and education programs, and look at ISA Jobs. The job listings are open for all to review, and ISA members may post a resume in the database at no charge.

Automotive

SAE International, the Society of Automotive Engineers

sae.org

Forming the ranks of SAE International are more than ninety thousand members in almost a hundred countries who share an interest in advancing the engineering of mobility technology. They include engineers, business executives, educators, and students. The website distributes information on the association, its conferences and training opportunities, and job leads. You must register to access the job leads, but this free service is open to all users.

Aviation

Aviation Employee Placement Service

aeps.com

The AEPS site is a source of jobs for all occupations and fields in the aviation industry, from executives to mechanics, with both general and corporate opportunities. Access to listings of current jobs requires a paid subscription, but a free trial subscription enables you to test out the database.

AVJobs.com

avjobs.com

In AVJobs.com you have an online resource that brings together employers and employees in the aviation industry. Offerings for paying members include a job database, a resume service, and other career-guidance resources. Free goods here include excellent career information on many specific fields within this industry. There are various fees for the different levels of membership, but they start at a reasonable rate.

Biotechnology and Biomedical Engineering

Medical Device Link

devicelink.com

This online information resource aims to serve the people who design, manufacture, and market medical devices. The Career Center includes a salary survey, a salary estimator work sheet, and job listings, while the rest of the site delivers news, events, extensive links to suppliers and consultants, and links to even more information. Registration is required to use the Apply Now feature of the job database as well as some other special features, but it is free.

There are more resources for this field in Chapter 7.

Chemical Engineering

AIChE, the American Institute of Chemical Engineers

aiche.org

The AIChE website is designed to help people considering a career in this field, students, and seasoned professionals. The CareerEngineer section includes job listings, information on managing your career, top employers of AIChE members, and much more. Some services and resources are available only to members, but many are open to the public, including the free registration needed to apply for jobs listed here.

Chimney Sweeps

Chimney Safety Institute of America

csia.org

The CSIA is "a nonprofit educational foundation that has established the only nationally recognized certification program for chimney sweeps in the United States." Persons interested in working in this field will find training opportunities here. Visitors can also check the site for consumer information on safe chimneys and how to find a certified professional.

National Chimney Sweep Guild

ncsg.org

This guild is an organization owned and managed by chimney service professionals dedicated to making life and business better for every sweep.

Civil Engineering

American Society of Civil Engineers

www.asce.org

The American Society of Civil Engineers represents more than 133,000 members of the civil engineering profession worldwide and is America's oldest national engineering society. Look under Kids and Careers for a description of civil engineering, how to get started in this field, and lists of colleges and universities conferring degrees in the many disciplines that make up this field. The Professional Issues area includes career-development information and job leads.

Also see "Construction and Public Works" and "Mining, Drilling, and Offshore" in this chapter, as well as "Environmental and Earth Sciences" in Chapter 7.

Computing and Technology

Association for Computing Machinery

acm.org

Most of the ACM online resources are a membership perk, but nonmembers will encounter several open areas on the site. The chapter directory will connect you to local professionals who share your interests, and many chapters maintain their own websites. The Career Resource Center and the job board are open to the public, but the application feature and employer contact information is reserved for members. ACM members also have access to a large array of career services, so you may want to give thought to joining.

ComputerJobs.com

computerjobs.com

This Internet-based advertising service posts technical job and career information for computer professionals. The site is divided into geographic and skill areas, making it easier for you to target the opportunities that appeal to you, but keyword searching is also possible. A nice feature here for non-U.S. citizens is the "Visa Sponsor" flag identifying opportunities posted by an employer willing to sponsor a work visa for the candidate; these listings can also be called up by selecting Visa Sponsor from the Select a Specialty menu on the front page.

ComputerWorld

computerworld.com

This website accompanies and expands on the eponymous weekly print IS/IT trade publication. If you are inclined toward a career in computing, or are an experienced professional who wants to keep up with the latest developments, this is the place to learn what to expect, where to go, and what to do once you get there. While you may want to home in on the Careers area, with its job listings, surveys, and career-related articles, the entire site has much to recommend it.

Computing Research Association

cra.org

The CRA is an association of more than two hundred North American academic departments of computer science and computer engineering, industrial and government laboratories engaging in basic computing research, and affiliated professional societies. The site includes public job listings for computer science, computer engineering, and computing research professionals.

DevBistro

devbistro.com

DevBistro features jobs for programmers and other technical types. Registration for this site is not required unless you want to post your resume here, and even then it is free. Check out the Tech Interviews, which spreads the word on questions asked during real job interviews.

Developers.Net

developers.net

Developers.Net is "a social marketspace and library promoting the exchange of ideas and connections among technology professionals and companies." The Careers area's free tech-jobs board has thousands of full-time technology career opportunities, each linked directly to the employer's website.

Dice.com

dice.com

If you search only one IT site, it should be Dice.com. This is probably the best single site for IT professionals and is consistently highly rated by recruiters looking for IT talent, which means they are using this site and liking it a lot. As a job seeker, you will appreciate the job listings, online resume database, and other good career tools. Some services will require you to fill out the free registration form.

ERP Jobs

erp-jobs.com

This is a place for enterprise resource planning (ERP), as well as supply chain management (SCM), execution management (EM), and many other software specialties and firms to advertise their career and contract opportunities and their availability. Jobs are categorized by enterprise area (SAP R/3, JD Edwards, Enterprise Asset Management, etc.).

Webgrrls International

webgrrls.com

"Webgrrls International provides a forum for women in or interested in new media and technology to network, exchange job and business leads, form strategic alliances, mentor and teach, intern and learn the skills to help women succeed in an increasingly technical workplace and world." Members of this organization can attend local networking events and meetings, access an online job bank, and participate in online forums regarding issues in their lives and work. All visitors can read the great articles in the Career section and consult the map for local chapters.

WITI4Hire from Women in Technology International

Witi4hire.com

WITI's purpose is to support women in reaching the upper administrative levels in all industries and encourage more women to pursue technical careers. The job board is open to the public and features an international database of listings.

Construction and Public Works

American Public Works Association

apwa.net

It's hard to beat the APWA site as a resource for information on the many fields straddling public works. It features a stellar list of links to related professional and trade associations. The association also hosts a nice job board, the APWA WorkZone, which can be searched by location and/or job category.

Builder Online

builderonline.com

This extensive website for construction professionals includes features such as the searchable Builder 100, a ranking of companies in the industry, with profiles and contact information for each. Users will also like the product database and industry news from the print magazine of the same title, among other sources. There is also a career center, BuilderJobs, which all users can search for free. Registered users (also free) can store a resume here, customize their search agents, and use the Apply Now feature. This site is highly recommended as a resource for project managers, purchasing agents, and similar fields in this industry.

Construction Executive

constructionexecutive.com

This is "a career advancement and leadership development center for CEOs and executives in the architecture, engineering and construction industry." There are job leads, a resume board, and other resources useful to your search.

Helmets to Hardhats

helmetstohardhats.org

The mission of this site is to inform armed forces veterans about the many trades that make up the growing building and construction industry. Use the Career Browser to learn about the various trades and locate apprenticeship and training programs operated by the trade unions. You can look around the site and search the careers database without registering, but free registration permits you to apply to opportunities quickly and directly and puts your resume where employers can see it. The program is administered by the Center for Military Recruitment, Assessment, and Veterans Employment and is headquartered in Washington, D.C.

MEPJobs

mepjobs.com

This site serves the broad construction industry with listings for jobs in engineering, electrical, plumbing, sales, office personnel, construction, estimating, and heating/ventilating/air-conditioning. You do not need to register to review and apply for jobs, but the free registration allows you to store a resume here and set up certain customized services.

Electrical Engineering

IEEE (Institute of Electrical and Electronics Engineers) Job Site

careers.ieee.org

IEEE members and others in electrical engineering can plug into jobs, job resources, and career advice at this outlet. While some services and resources are for members only, the job listings are open for the public to review. Just enter a keyword in the Search box at the top of the page. There is additional Career and Employment information available from the main IEEE page (ieee.org), along with resources from individual IEEE societies and councils.

Environmental Engineering

See "Environmental and Earth Sciences" in Chapter 7.

Explosives Engineering

International Society of Explosives Engineers

isee.org

The ISEE is a professional society that promotes the safe and controlled use of explosives in mining, quarrying, construction, manufacturing, forestry, and other commercial pursuits. Its website includes major legislative and society announcements, a calendar of events, information on training and certification, the chapter contact list, career information, and a small but nice job board that is open to the public.

Facilities Engineering and Maintenance

APPA, Serving Educational Facilities Officers

appa.org

Formerly known as the Association of Physical Plant Administrators, APPA is an international association dedicated to maintaining, protecting, and promoting the quality of educational facilities and other nonprofit organizations, such as public and private schools, military installations, and city/county governments. The Job Express's job listings are updated weekly (several weeks are available at any time), and the resume database allows nonmembers to post their information for a nominal fee.

Association for Facilities Engineering

afe.org

AFE is a professional organization of nine thousand members who ensure the optimal operation of plants, grounds, and offices at Fortune 500 manufacturers, universities, medical centers, government agencies, and innovative small firms around the world. The website's CareerNet offers free job listings for all users, and AFE members may post a resume here.

Finishing

Finishing.com

finishing.com

This website is dedicated to professionals of the metal finishing industry, those who coat, anodize, plate, and otherwise cover everything. There are chat rooms and links to technical resources, events, professional societies and related organizations, job shops, consultants, and suppliers, all of which are sources of potential opportunities. The site also hosts Help Wanted listings.

Fluid Dynamics

CFD (Computational Fluid Dynamics) Jobs Database

cfd-online.com/Jobs

The CFD Jobs Database is filled with employment opportunities in this field. The listings are sorted into industry, academe, postgraduate, Ph.D., full time, contract, and country/continent. This is a service of CFD Online, and you should examine the entire site for even more links to potential job sources and employers.

Food and Beverage Processing

FishJobs

fishjobs.com

This site lists employment opportunities in seafood, fisheries, or aquaculture companies seeking to fill sales, marketing, management, operations, or quality control positions. Entries are categorized by geographic region, and postings are retained for as long as six months. Many listings include direct contact information for the employer, while others require you to submit your resume to H. M. Johnson & Associates, the recruiters who operate this site.

Probrewer.com

probrewer.com

People drawn to the brewing industry can fill up on information at this cool site. The Classifieds will carry you to employment listings, but also check in with the Resources area for lists of suppliers, events, and profiles of registered users. Registration for the classifieds and discussion areas is free and is obligatory only to participate in the discussions. This is a handy industry resource with an international reach.

Winejobs from WineBusiness.com

winejobs.com

This site lists wine industry jobs from big-name wineries, distributors, universities, and more. You can browse the listings or search the jobs by keyword, category, location, and company. For even more industry goings-on, you will enjoy sampling the WineBusiness.com Directory.

Footwear and Apparel

American Apparel & Footwear Association

apparelandfootwear.org

The national trade association representing apparel, footwear, and other sewn products companies in the United States has assembled this site. Job seekers are fitted out with free access to the AAFA membership listings (under Membership), the Supplier Resource Directory (under Resources), and the industry Links. The AAFA Classifieds, with Positions Available and Positions Wanted, can be reached by scrolling down the front page or by looking under Resources.

Also see "Fashion" in Chapter 6.

Industrial Design

Core77 Design Magazine and Resource

core77.com

Industrial designers are the people who create toys, develop new TV sets, and even redo the entire Tupperware line! This site fills you in on the field and the benefits, offers advice for freelancers, and connects you with the education and training opportunities—and the jobs. The job board, Coroflot (coroflot.com), lets you post a portfolio as well as search for employment. Core77 also gives you a frequently updated list of design firms to contact for internships, co-ops, and employment.

Logistics

JobsInLogistics.com

jobsinlogistics.com

JobsInLogistics.com lists jobs and hosts a resume database for people in logistics-related fields (customer service, distribution, inventory management, supply chain, transportation, warehousing, etc.).

Maritime and Cruise Ships

Cruise International

cruiseshipjob.net

Cruise International is an employment agency for the cruise line industry, acting as a central source for you to reach several of the top cruise lines. As is the case with all of the employment agencies we've encountered that serve this industry, you must pay a fee to have your resume submitted for consideration. The site has good information on working in this industry, including a breakdown of the many jobs on a cruise ship, responsibilities for each, salary ranges, and general working conditions.

Seafarers International Union

seafarers.org

The Seafarers International Union, Atlantic, Gulf, Lakes, and Inland Waters District, AFL-CIO, represents unlicensed U.S. merchant mariners sailing aboard U.S.-flag vessels in the deep sea, Great Lakes, and inland trades, as well as licensed U.S. mariners in the Great Lakes and inland sectors. The SIU also sponsors the Paul Hall Center for Maritime Training and Education, a vocational training facility located in Piney Point, Maryland.

Mass Spectroscopy

spectroscopyNOW.com

spectroscopynow.com

A portal from Wiley Publishing, spectroscopyNOW.com includes news, features, conferences, book releases, jobs, and directories in various subdisciplines of this field. Registration is not required to view or apply for jobs here.

Materials and Metallurgy

ASM International, the Materials Information Society

asminternational.org

ASM International is a professional society for materials engineers and scientists. Guests can review much of the organization's online information, including journals, newsletters, directories of suppliers, and the Career Center. You do not need to register to view or apply for jobs, but registering gives you access to other services and is free.

Mathematics

American Mathematical Society

ams.org

This association website has many pluses for all mathematicians. The Careers and Employment area offers employment services for Ph.D. mathematicians, insight on careers in this field for newcomers, early preparation information for future mathematicians, and other guidance for visitors. The featured job database, MathJobs, is open for all to view without registering, but only registered MathJobs users can apply for positions shown here. Other job listings as well as links to additional sources appear throughout this site.

Listings for "Actuaries" are in Chapter 4.

Mechanical Engineering

ASME, the American Society of Mechanical Engineers

asme.org

This website for mechanical engineers includes information on professional development, industry news, and jobs and careers. A nice feature of the job bank is the ability to search jobs by career stage—internships, entry-level, and experienced. ASME also publishes several journals and newsletters that are well worth your review. Some may be accessed online for free; others will require a paid subscription.

Mining, Drilling, and Offshore

Drillers.com

drillers.com

At this site, a joint venture between the Drilling Research Institute and NRG Constancy Limited, you can stake out job listings as well as links to associations, recruiters, industry suppliers, and more.

InfoMine

infomine.com

What you have here is probably the most informative mining site on the Internet. You'll discover information on equipment, companies, education and training, events, countries, and a lot more. InfoMine's CareerMine includes many job listings from around the world, a recruiter roster, and a resume database. Many areas of this website (including most of the job listings) are limited to subscribers, but if this is your field, then the subscription is a wise investment. You can elect to subscribe to smaller sections of the site, a less expensive option.

Mining USA

miningusa.com

Here you can prospect for mining industry jobs in the United States and internationally. All of the ads carry the date of posting. Other practical information on the industry is also lodged at this site.

Thomas Mining Associates

thomasmining.com

Thomas Mining is a U.K.-based recruiter specializing in the worldwide mining and quarrying industry.

Musical Instrument Repair

National Association of Professional Band Instrument Repair Technicians

napbirt.org

NAPBIRT is "a nonprofit organization that supports the activities of quality professional band instrument repair technicians." Association membership is open only to school-trained technicians (in a NAPBIRT-approved learning situation) or technicians who have been on the job or have apprenticed for a minimum of five years. In addition, members must be working in a legal, licensed operating business. Beat a path to this website for information on approved training programs, a career in instrument repair, and more. NAPBIRT members have access to the Classified Ads area.

Occupational Safety and Industrial Hygiene

American Industrial Hygiene Association

aiha.org

This association represents the people who are concerned with occupational and environmental health and safety issues. All visitors can go to Career & Employment Services to search AIHA's CareerAdvantage for free. Students will want to look at the many career articles under Get Student Information. Some local sections of the association maintain their own job lists on their websites.

Optics and Photonics

Optics.org

optics.org

Optics.org is sponsored by the Institute of Physics. Within this rich resource is a great employment area with international job listings. Visitors willing to fill out the free registration form can also receive the Optics.org Jobswire, a free electronic newsletter sent out every two weeks on Wednesday nights.

SPIEWorks

spieworks.com

Operated by SPIE, the International Society for Optical Engineering, this public website offers professionals in optics, photonics, and imaging the opportunity to review job listings, check out employers, look for career fairs, and even get career tips, all without paying for membership or even registering a resume with the site. However, you can register for a free account, which allows you to post your resume and use other advanced features of the site.

Public Utilities

American Gas Association

aga.org

This trade association represents two hundred local energy utility companies that deliver natural gas across the United States. The AGA website gives you industry news, a list of member websites, a searchable handbook covering the publicly traded member companies, and more. In the Quick Tasks menu is a link titled Find an Industry Job; it will connect you to the AGA Jobline, a public database of opportunities posted by industry-affiliated companies.

American Water Works Association

awwa.org

An international nonprofit scientific and educational society, the American Water Works Association is dedicated to the improvement of drinking water quality and supply. Its more than fifty thousand members comprise treatment plant operators, managers, scientists, environmentalists, and others who hold a genuine interest in the water supply and public health. Membership includes more than four thousand utilities that supply water to roughly 180 million people in North America. This site is awash in job listings, links to water utility sites and to local AWWA sections, information on industry and government regulations, and much more.

Energyjobsearch.com

energyjobsearch.com

Energyjobsearch.com is an enormous worldwide site for jobs in the energy/power industry at all levels. You must register to view job details, but you can search for possibilities before doing so, and the registration is free. Your resume is not required during the initial registration.

NukeWorker.com

nukeworker.com

NukeWorker.com covers exactly what its name implies—jobs for professionals in the nuclear industry. As you might expect, most positions are in power plants, but there are some exceptions. Users must register to view the contact and application information for jobs listed here, but it is a free service. You will be required to upload your resume at this time, but you can elect to keep it hidden from employers who are searching the database. This site also offers other news of interest to persons in this field.

PowerMarketers.com

powermarketers.com

Here you have news, information, and employment opportunities for people experienced in managing and marketing power, courtesy of the Power Marketing Association. This organization represents the entire spectrum of the U.S. electric power industry, including independent power marketers and brokers, regulated utilities, unregulated utility affiliates, and providers of products and services to the industry.

Telecommunications

RCR Wireless News

rcrnews.com

Published by Crain Communications, RCR Wireless News is updated daily with a mix of breaking stories and in-depth analysis into the issues that mold today's wireless telecommunications environment. There are also select resources for the industry, including links to various associations and organizations. The Classifieds section has employment listings, but they do not carry posting dates.

Telecomcareers.net

telecomcareers.net

This site lists jobs in the telecommunications industry. Visitors can search and view the results list, but you must register and upload your resume to see the details of each job announcement. A neat resource section has helpful links to many telecom publications that may interest you.

Wireless Week

www.wirelessweek.com

This site is a companion to the weekly newspaper relaying all the business, technology, and regulatory news in the cellular, personal communications services, paging, specialized mobile radio, private mobile radio, wireless data, satellite, wireless local loop, and microwave fields. Click on Advertising to get to the Classifieds job listings. The many industry research resources available here will also spark visitors' interest.

Trucking

1800Drivers.com

1800drivers.com

Park yourself at this site—or call 2-800-DRIVERS by phone—if you're on the lookout for a good source of job leads and job information for the trucking industry. Visitors can start at ground level: there are many postings for companies willing to train people who are new to the trucking world. You get brief information on the jobs, but registration is required to view the full listings. No mention of fees is made on the site. Related information here includes lots of useful links for truck drivers as well as for others who might want to take a run at this business.

Union Hiring Halls

IBEW Construction Jobs Board

ibew.org/members/jobs

This is the official job network for the construction branch of the International Brotherhood of Electrical Workers. Select the location, scale, and/or date of posting of the job, and go. Job calls are posted directly by the local unions. All listings contain information on whom to contact for more information or to apply.

Union Jobs Clearinghouse

unionjobs.com

Union Jobs Clearinghouse lists union staffing and trade/apprenticeship positions across the United States. This site was set up to centralize these announcements. You can review the staffing listings geographically or alphabetically by posting organization.

Opportunities in Government, Public Policy, and Public Service

Help yourself to this bounty of domestic opportunities for employment in public service and in government agencies and the departments and institutions that work closely with them. For a world of employment opportunities with international governments through the Internet, turn to the appropriate headings in Chapter 12.

Defense Industry

ClearanceJobs.com

clearancejobs.com

At ClearanceJobs.com, job seekers holding active or current Department of Defense, Department of State, and Department of Energy security clearances are matched to hiring employers and recruiters looking for skilled cleared candidates. The jobs range through numerous fields, levels, and locations. You can search by keyword, minimum clearance required, and location, or just select All, which at the time of review brought up a dossier of more than three thousand listings.

The Defense Industry

marylandcareers.org/intel.html

This guide to employment information and opportunities in the defense industry is sponsored by Maryland Careers and Tom Coates, a local career consultant. The links here include industry information, recruiters, associations, and other job sources for the defense industry, connecting to national as well as local resources and associations for the District of Columbia area.

Jane's Information Group

janes.com

Jane's Information Group is a leading provider of intelligence and analysis pertaining to national and international defense, security, and risk developments. The website enspheres worldwide news and information on defense, transportation, aerospace, and security, rounded out by business and regional news affecting these industries. If you have a mind to serve in this industry, you must know Jane's.

Federal Government

The federal government is one of the largest employers in the United States and probably the most diversified. Opportunities can be sought in several free locations online, so it is unnecessary to pay to look at listings for government duty. The federal government requires that resumes fit a specific format and will also ask for personal and other information not usually disclosed on one's resume. Read the rules under Information on Applying at the sites and follow the instructions noted.

Federal Job Source

dcjobsource.com/fed.html

The Federal Job Source is a collection of links to the many sources of listings for federal jobs. This is a free service from The Internet Job Source.

Government Computer News

www.gcn.com

This companion to the weekly print magazine expands on the news and information provided there with additional reports, blogs, and updated headlines for any person whose primary professional interest is in govern-ment IT. Information technology and computing professionals interested in jobs with the companies that provide services to government agencies will want to search the jobs area, operated in conjunction with Washington Post.com.

The Resume Place

resume-place.com

Kathryn Kraemer Troutman, author of *The Federal Resume Guidebook* (Jist) and *Ten Steps to a Federal Job* (Resume Place), gives you great information on creating your private-sector resume as well as preparing your federal resume. She is considered to be the expert on the government's resume format and its new electronic resume system. If you are considering the federal government as a potential employer, then you must review Troutman's information. You will also appreciate her extensive list of links to federal job and career resources.

Studentjobs.gov

www.studentjobs.gov

Studentjobs.gov is designed to be a one-stop source for information on flagging down a job with the federal government. Special opportunities exist for high school, college, or graduate students—co-ops, internships, summer employment, the Outstanding Scholars Program, volunteer opportunities, and much more. This site's job-search and resume database services are similar to those of USAJobs, described in the following entry.

USAJobs

www.usajobs.gov

USAJobs is the official site for federal employment information and jobs listed with the U.S. Office of Personnel Management. Here you can learn about current openings in the government and related pay and benefits, download forms required for some applications, and review instructions for submitting an application. USAJobs also features a resume builder you can use to create and store your resume in the system. While most government agencies post their jobs here, not all are required to do so; USAJobs will link you to those agencies for information on their openings.

In addition to the foregoing sources, individual departments and agencies may post jobs on their own pages. There are also a few departments, as well as agencies, that are not required to post their openings with USAJobs. While USAJobs will point you to many of these sites, the following resources will also help you in locating the many departments, agencies, and services that make up the U.S. government:

USA.gov   usa.gov

Library of Congress   loc.gov/rr/news/fedgov.html

Also see the entry for U.S. Courts: The Federal Judiciary under "Law, Paralegal, and the Federal Judiciary" in Chapter 5.

Fire and Protective Services

National Directory of Emergency Services

firejobs.com

This site dispatches reliable information on jobs and training for people grooming themselves for careers in firefighting or police work. Access to the job leads is by paid subscription, but you can preview the database before buying. Other areas of the site are open to all visitors, including the list of training academies and the many articles under Job Strategies.

National Fire Protection Association

nfpa.org

Among the NFPA's membership are fire departments, building code regulators, emergency services, fire and safety associations, and anyone else you can think of who would have a part in fire protection and safety regulation in the United States and abroad. Operated by Monster.com, NFPA's Career Center lists jobs for fire protection engineers, inspectors, technicians with monitoring firms, and other professionals in this field.

Law Enforcement and Security Services

ASIS International

www.asisonline.org

Founded in 1955 as the American Society for Industrial Security, ASIS International is the world's largest organization for security professionals, boasting more than thirty-five thousand members worldwide. Visitors can look at the Career Center's main page and even review the job titles and numbers of positions listed in the job board, but access to the job postings is reserved for paid members of the association.

The Blue Line: Police Opportunity Monitor

theblueline.com

The Blue Line is a resource for persons of interest in jobs with law enforcement as well as fire and public safety. This enormous site has areas that are open to the public, including back issues of the monthly job newsletter, but the two most recent months of listings are accessible only by paying members (nominal fee). This is a good source for career and job information in this field.

Also see "Forensics" in Chapter 7.

Public Administration

PublicServiceCareers.org

publicservicecareers.org

The American Society for Public Administration, in partnership with the National Association of Schools of Public Affairs and Administration (NASPAA) and the Association for Public Policy Analysis and Management (APPAM), created this free website as a central source for job listings in public service and public administration. Eventually this site will also offer career and job information for anyone with proclivities in these areas.

Public Affairs and Capitol Hill

These resources include opportunities to work for members of the U.S. Congress or the political action groups, lobbyists, and various nonprofit or educational institutions whose dealings closely involve the government.

Congressional Quarterly

cq.com

One feature of the *Congressional Quarterly*'s website is the Hill Jobs, a list of openings in congressional offices or organizations that work alongside the government.

Opportunities in Public Affairs

opajobs.com

This site lists public affairs positions available in the District of Columbia metropolitan area spanning entry through senior levels. There are some free listings, but a paid subscription will get the full list sent to you each week. The Job Resource section includes well-written guides to job searching on Capitol Hill, preparing cover letters, and public affairs careers.

RCJobs

rcjobs.com

RCJobs is the free employment service from *Roll Call*, the newspaper of Capitol Hill known for dishing the dope on what's happening "inside the Beltway." Users can search for jobs or post a resume. Registration of your resume is not required, but it is free and facilitates forwarding of your information to employers.

Public Policy and Think Tanks

NIRA's World Directory of Think Tanks

nira.go.jp/ice

The National Institute for Research Advancement was established to conduct research from an independent standpoint and contribute to the resolution of complex issues facing contemporary society. The NIRA directory is a compendium of think tanks and other resources for policy research worldwide, annotated with descriptive information about each.

State and Local Governments

Careers in Government

careersingovernment.com

Careers in Government is a clearinghouse of information, resources, and jobs available in public-sector organizations in the United States and abroad. Search by job category, location, keyword, or other criteria.

Local Government Job Net

govtjob.net

Sponsored by the Local Government Institute, Local Government Job Net is a centralized online source of jobs available in local governments across the country. It also cites related executive search firms that recruit public servants.

Govtjobs.com

govtjobs.com

Govtjobs.com pledges to help individuals obtain the jobs they are seeking in the public sector. In addition to job listings, you get links to agencies, executive search firms, and resources for locating more opportunities.

Job Listings from the State Governments

The following columns set forth all the state government job pages. Unlike the state job banks in Chapter 11, these cites in this section strictly pertain to jobs working for the state government. Chapter 11 also contains other career resources for states, counties, and municipalities.

Alabama	personnel.state.al.us
Alaska	jobs.state.ak.us/statejobs.html
Arizona	azstatejobs.gov
Arkansas	www.ark.org/arstatejobs
California	spb.ca.gov
Colorado	www.gssa.state.co.us
Connecticut	www.das.state.ct.us/exam
Delaware	delawarepersonnel.com
District of Columbia	dc.gov
Florida	peoplefirst.myflorida.com
Georgia	thejobsite.org
Hawaii	hawaii.gov/hrd/main/esd
Idaho	dhr.idaho.gov
Illinois	www.cmcf.state.il.us/jobpost
	illinois.gov/gov/internships.cfm
Indiana	in.gov/jobs
Iowa	www.iowajobs.org

Kansas	jobs.ks.gov
Kentucky	personnel.ky.gov
Louisiana	www.dscs.state.la.us
Maine	maine.gov/bhr/state_jobs
Maryland	dbm.maryland.gov
Massachusetts	ceo.hrd.state.ma.us
Michigan	michigan.gov/mdcs
Minnesota	www.doer.state.mn.us
Mississippi	www.spb.state.ms.us
Missouri	missouri.gov/mo/stjobs.htm
Montana	mt.gov/statejobs/statejobs.asp
Nebraska	wrk4neb.org
Nevada	dop.nv.gov
New Hampshire	nh.gov/hr
New Jersey	www.state.nj.us/personnel
New Mexico	www.spo.state.nm.us
New York	www.cs.state.ny.us
North Carolina	www.osp.state.nc.us
North Dakota	nd.gov/hrms
Ohio	statejobs.ohio.gov
Oklahoma	ok.gov/opm
Oregon	www.oregonjobs.org
Pennsylvania	www.scsc.state.pa.us
Rhode Island	www.dlt.state.ri.us/webdev/jobsri/statejobs.htm
South Carolina	ohrweb.ohr.state.sc.us/ohr/
South Dakota	www.state.sd.us/jobs
Tennessee	tn.gov/dohr
Texas	workintexas.com
Utah	statejobs.utah.gov

Vermont	vermontpersonnel.org
Virginia	jobs.virginia.gov
Washington	www.dop.wa.gov
Washington, D.C.	*See "District of Columbia."*
West Virginia	www.state.wv.us/admin/personnel
Wisconsin	wiscjobs.state.wi.us
Wyoming	personnel.state.wy.us

The following resources can lead you to even more information on state, local, tribal, and territorial governments.

| Library of Congress: State and Local Governments | loc.gov/rr/news/stategov/stategov.html |
| State and Local Government on the Net | statelocalgov.net |

U.S. Military and the Department of Defense

Go Defense: Civilians Working for National Defense

godefense.com

Operated by the Defense Applicant Assistance Office, this site is designed to assist persons pursuing civilian positions with the U.S. Department of Defense (DoD). The site includes information on the many civilian occupations available and outlines opportunities for experienced professionals, new college graduates, veterans, and disabled veterans. You can search the full database of nonmilitary jobs in the DoD and its many agencies, link to the individual hiring pages for the agencies, or connect to the job sources for DoD Nonappropriated Fund (NAF) Morale, Welfare and Recreation (MWR) Programs and Military Exchanges.

Today's Military

todaysmilitary.com

Planning on serving some time in the military before pursuing a career in the private sector? If so, take the liberty of tapping this site for details on all enlisted and officer occupations, paired with the civilian counterpart for every applicable military occupation. It also describes training, advancement, and educational opportunities within each of the major services.

U.S. Armed Services

Connect to each service's website for more information on military service opportunities, benefits of a military career, and recruiter locations.

U.S. Air Force	airforce.com
U.S. Army	goarmy.com
U.S. Coast Guard	gocoastguard.com
U.S. Marines	marines.com
U.S. Navy	navy.com

10

Entry-Level
and Summer
Employment,
Internships,
and Co-ops

This chapter is targeted to college students and new graduates. If you're seeking information about cooperative or intern positions, your best course is to consult your department head and college career center before scouring these pages. Afterward, turn back to the major job-listing sites in Chapter 3 for leads, paying special attention to any areas set aside for college students or entry-level personnel. Then use the procedures suggested in Chapter 1 to identify other organizations in your major field, and solicit them about possible assignments. To further extend your horizons, go to the search engines and key in *intern, internship, co-op, cooperative education, summer employment*, and *temporary employment*. While you're at it, check Web servers of colleges and universities in the region where you would like to work for possible leads from local organizations, as well as the resources for your region in Chapter 11. There are a lot of ways to nail down these opportunities, but it will take some ingenuity on your part.

Internships, Co-Ops, and Student Exchange Opportunities

CollegeGrad.com

collegegrad.com

From the site's left menu, select Search Internships to refine your yield to just intern listings in the College Grad database. You can perform a quick keyword search or use the Advanced feature to delineate a specific location, industry focus, or other criteron.

Council on International Education Exchange

ciee.org

If you want the goods on international studies or internships, look up the programs and services offered by the CIEE. This organization's site offers information on summer employment and internship opportunities throughout the world, including listings of opportunities you can search, and will help you complete the legal paperwork necessary to get the proper work documents. There is a fee for participating in CIEE programs, but it's a bargain rate for the support you get.

Find a Job or Internship: The Russian and East European Institute

iub.edu/~reeiweb/placement/findajob.shtml

These are links to lists of websites of companies and organizations that frequently hire in the Russian and East European fields, divided by sector to help you better focus your search. Job sites in Hungarian, Polish, Czech, Russian, and Bulgarian are also included, and don't overlook the Career Night handout with its suggested resources. This service comes to you from the Russian and East European Institute at Indiana University, Bloomington.

Finding Science Internships from Sistahs in Science

mtholyoke.edu/courses/sbrowne/sistahs

Sistahs in Science, a Mount Holyoke student organization for minority women in the sciences, was founded in 2003 by a professor of chemistry, Sheila Browne, and her student LeAnn Williams. This site is designed to help science students find and obtain research internships in science. It offers information on resume preparation and career development and links to resources for internship opportunities.

GoAbroad.com

goabroad.com

GoAbroad.com is filled with information geared to college students, but it's also your ticket to learning anything you might want to know about going overseas. Search for internships, volunteer opportunities, teaching opportunities, study opportunities, travel information, and you name it. The site highlights featured programs under each area but also offers a full directory search starting with a target country. There are fees for many of the programs, but given the value of the assistance you receive, you're getting away cheap.

Idealist.org from Action Without Borders

idealist.org

This site matches idealistic job seekers with nonprofit and public-service organizations. You can search for your ideal job, internship, or volunteer opportunity by country or specialty.

International Opportunities Program—Non-Study Opportunities

www.cie.uci.edu/prospective/iopother/index.shtml

Put together by the Center for International Education at the University of California, Irvine, this page links to situations providing nonstudy international experience abroad. The specific situations are divided into five categories— work, volunteer, internship, research, and teaching—and each category lists websites you can visit as well as some of the better-known programs offering opportunities.

Internship Links, California Polytechnic State University

www.careerservices.calpoly.edu/students/coop/internshiplinks.htm

The Career Services Center at CalPoly developed this series of links to internship opportunities categorized under Agriculture & Environment, Arts, Business & Economics, Communication & Media, Experiential Education, Government & Washington DC, History & Museum, International, Nonprofit, Recreation & Sports & Fitness, Science & Math & Engineering, and General Internships. It also has some links to sources for summer jobs and an article on how to land your dream internship.

InternshipPrograms.com

internshipprograms.com

This site, sponsored by WetFeet, greets you with thousands of internship opportunities from near and far. You can search the database by location and/or job category, or you can browse the lists according to U.S city/state, international opportunities, company name, or "most popular" designation. Registration is not required to review the listings, but registering and submitting your resume will make your application process easier and will let employers find you.

JobWeb.com Information on Intern and Co-Op Programs

www.jobweb.com/resources/library/interncoop_programs

JobWeb.com, operated by the National Association of Colleges and Employers, offers career-development and job-search advice to college students and new graduates. Make this section of JobWeb your destination for articles on how intern and co-op programs can benefit you, how to get the internship you want, and interview and resume preparation.

MonsterTRAK

monstertrak.com

Formerly known as JobTrak, this Monster zone is dedicated to college students and new graduates. All users can review the career advice, but your college must be a registered participant in order for you to search out jobs and internships. Ask your college career center for the login and password. If the school isn't registered, you can request that it join.

Studyabroad.com

studyabroad.com

Studyabroad provides links and contact information for thousands of opportunities in dozens of countries. Search by country, or use the menu for language programs, internships, or summer jobs. Consult the StudyAbroad.com Handbook for tips on living abroad, including the section "Before You Leave Home." Contact the specific sites for more facts about their programs.

Washington Internship Institute

ielnet.org

The Washington Internship Institute, a project of the Institute for Experiential Learning, offers numerous internship programs, all of which are based in Washington, D.C.

Youth.gc.ca/Jeunesse.gc.ca

youth.gc.ca

Created to help prepare young people for the workplace and the job hunt, Canada's Youth.gc.ca is a partnership among several agencies of the Canadian government and the private sector. Visit this website for self-assessment tools and career resources, along with job opportunities and resources for starting your own business. This site is available in both English and French.

Government-Sponsored Student Work Opportunities and Internships

Corporation for National & Community Service

nationalservice.org

Established in 1993, the Corporation for National & Community Service engages more than a million Americans each year in service to their communities—helping to alleviate community problems. The corporation's three major service initiatives are AmeriCorps, Learn and Serve America, and the Senior Corps. The corporation offers its own opportunities for fellowships and internships in its offices across the United States, and you can learn about these programs and apply for any through that section of the website.

Peace Corps

peacecorps.gov

You'll find background information on the organization and access to a transition service for RPCVs (returned Peace Corps volunteers) at this site provided by the Peace Corps. Check the database for current positions, and then send in your application using the guidelines stipulated on the Web page. Graduate students may be interested in the Master's International program, which incorporates Peace Corps service into a master's degree program at more than forty colleges and universities, or the Fellows/USA program, which offers returned volunteers scholarships or reduced tuition at more than thirty participating schools.

Studentjobs.gov

www.studentjobs.gov

Studentjobs.gov is a site from the U.S. Office of Personnel Management and the U.S. Department of Education's Student Financial Assistance Office. As they say, "This website is designed to be your one stop for information you need to find the job you want in the federal government. Whether you're in high school, college, or graduate school, you could be eligible for a variety of special opportunities for students in the federal government." Most federal agencies are required to post vacancies in this database, but Studentjobs.gov has gathered information on the agencies that don't appear under Other Job Opportunities, "giving you the most comprehensive access to federal job opportunities available." The site adds: "Learn about co-ops, internships, summer employment, the Outstanding Scholars Program, volunteer opportunities, and plenty of temporary and permanent part-time and full-time jobs." You can search for jobs, post a profile to allow auto-matching with posted jobs, store your resume here, and learn about the many government agencies and departments.

The White House Fellowships

whitehouse.gov/fellows

The White House Fellows program spans multiple fields and provides gifted young Americans firsthand experience in the process of government, either in the Office of the President or in one of the cabinet-level agencies. Information about applying is housed right here.

Seasonal and Other Work Opportunities

Back Door Jobs—Exciting Career Adventures

backdoorjobs.com

This is a companion to *The Back Door Guide to Short-Term Job Adventures*, by Michael Landes (Ten Speed Press), where you can sift through some of the short-term exciting or adventurous job experiences depicted in the book. Even better, Landes uses this site to keep his material current. For a younger person, this could open some interesting doors. For an older person, it could be a welcome break from desk-jockey duty and give you that chance to follow your childhood dream of riding the range.

CollegePro Painters

collegepro.com

You've seen the signs—these people are painting houses all over the U.S. and Canada! Brush up on the availability of jobs and internships, as well as local franchises, here.

Cool Works

coolworks.com

Catch the wave of seasonal jobs at this website. Ranch jobs, ski jobs, and cruise jobs are a click away. Search by state, or use the menu of job categories. Cool Works links you to information about the job and the respective employer's Web page, if available, along with contact information so you can mow hay while the sun shines.

My Summers

mysummers.com

This site is abuzz with summer jobs, mostly in summer camps. The free registration is required, and you must be eighteen or older and a high school graduate to participate. Once you are registered, which includes filling in a bit of an application, your input will be forwarded to all of the camps that subscribe to this service (pretty much the same ones you can see advertising in Campfinders .com, their sister site with summer programs). You can also search the job postings and apply to any that grab you.

Summer Jobs

summerjobs.com

Spanning the globe: Search these summer jobs by keyword or geographic location, or link to other job sites and career or training resources. Among these listings from all over the world are many opportunities to exchange your skills for several weeks in locations such as the Caribbean.

Volunteer Opportunities

Do Something

dosomething.org

Do Something is a not-for-profit Internet company that believes young people have the power to make a difference. The website functions as "a place to connect, a place to be inspired, be supported, be celebrated." In a trice, you can search for volunteer opportunities within a certain distance of your zip code, or review the list of projects, causes, and available grants, and get involved!

VolunteerMatch

www.volunteermatch.org

If you are beating the bushes for something to do with your time and talent that can benefit your community and yourself, then plug in your zip code and get a list of organizations nearby that need you. You have the option of specifying how far you can travel, when you can start, and whether you want a one-time or ongoing opportunity. Each listing includes a profile of the organization plus a rundown of all activities associated with the group. You can even "Express interest in this activity" online by simply filling out the form provided, which will then be zipped to the sponsoring organization.

11

State and Local
Resources for the
United States

For a job hunter, the byword is that a focused search can take you further faster. Set your radar on a specific industry, target employers, and zoom in on the most promising networking opportunities. The more precise your focus, the better.

This chapter maps out geography-specific websites at the state and local level. Cities, states, regions, and dependencies of the United States maintain websites of interest to local job hunters, and you're depriving yourself if you bypass them. In fact, many go beyond the provision of employment information to flesh out assistance with child care, transportation, and other potential barriers, to empower today's workforce as never before.

We give you the URLs for all of the state-sponsored job-service sites and some of the larger county or municipal job sites. We also provide a sampling of initiatives developed by individual jurisdictions, grassroots organizations, or other local enterprises on the vanguard. U.S. colleges and universities are not represented in this chapter, except for a few of the best career-service centers maintained by these institutions. You can easily get contact information on colleges and universities through an online directory or search engine, or through a relevant site in Chapter 14. The schools often collect and publish information pertinent to their surrounding communities on their websites, not to mention listing their own employment opportunities.

Likewise, community-information networks frequently carry local job listings and provide all kinds of background for the region, such as the housing scene and data on businesses. Although each community net is organized differently, generally the most fertile ground for career information is among the listings of government resources and services, community centers, libraries, and business resources. As a bonus, some business or commercial resources provide the names for individual companies or personnel to contact about employment opportunities.

Remember too that local newspapers add fuel to your search. They will help you learn about a community and its employers, target potential contacts within those organizations and businesses, and even connect with local job listings. Most U.S. newspapers are now represented on the Web, making it a snap for you to locate the ones that circulate within your location of choice. Rather than pile on each newspaper available for each state, we cite the specific section of NewsLink that holds the titles for the state. A single source cannot educate you about everything, however, so we also suggest you use the other online newspaper collections laid out in Chapter 3.

We have grouped the states into four regions and encourage you to read about the resources for neighboring states, as they may well address your area too. This proximity factor looms large for jobs and job seekers near a state line, but it could also bear on any spot on the map where employers literally go the extra mile to attract the talent they need. The order of main entries is as follows:

- Each region begins with job resources that cover multiple states within the area.

- All the states within that region then follow in alphabetical order.

- Each state's job bank is listed first; then the newspaper link; and finally, any additional resources we have of note.

For jobs with state government, consult the respective governmental websites in Chapter 9.

Business directories are another time-tested resource for finding an employer eager to remunerate you for your skills. SuperPages (superpages.com) and other online telephone directories offer a search by category and by location. You can also explore an online directory such as Business.com (business.com) or Yahoo! (yahoo.com). If you're on the hunt for a specific business, try putting its name in quotes in the Google (google.com) search box.

And don't forget the library! It's generally a desirable first stop on the job-search trail. You can get your hands on some good local job links plus get a boost in fine-tuning your search, creating a resume, and honing your interview skills. Libraries also offer business directories and databases, directories of libraries and chambers of commerce, and, of course, knowledgeable librarians on the grounds to lend a hand. Use a search engine or business directory to look for a library in your target area.

While we have provided a lot of information here, it's possible that we still don't have exactly what you need. In that case, marshal the resources and strategies in Chapter 1 to probe for more local sources for employment. Keep in mind too that many of the job sites featured in other chapters of this book are also searchable by location.

Finally, The Riley Guide will have additional listings for the states, as well as updates for these listings, so don't be a stranger: rileyguide.com/local.html.

INTERNET TIP: RSS FEEDS

According to WhatIsRSS.com, RSS (Rich Site Summary or Real Simple Syndication) is "a format for delivering regularly changing web content. Many news-related sites, weblogs and other online publishers syndicate their content as an RSS Feed to whoever wants it." For people who visit specific sites regularly, RSS feeds allow you to keep up-to-date by automatically retrieving the latest content from the sites that interest you. You save time by not needing to visit each site individually while also ensuring your privacy because you do not need to join each site's e-mail newsletter. You can visit WhatIsRSS.com for more information on this format and the software needed to receive it.

General Resources

America's Career InfoNet	acinet.org
America's Service Locator	servicelocator.org
CareerOneStop	careeronestop.org

The federal government maintains these career and service websites. America's Career InfoNet provides a library of information to assist you in finding or building your career. America's Service Locator can assist you in finding some of the support services you need, and the CareerOneStop attempts to pull it all together for employees and employers alike. Can't find what you need? For direct assistance, dial 877/US2-JOBS or (TTY) 877/889-5627.

Note: Now that America's Job Bank has been disbanded, other job links that fill that function will be with their state employment services (and those of Guam, Puerto Rico, and other U.S. territories).

SuperPages.com	superpages.com
Yellowpages.com	yellowpages.com

The online telephone directories at these sites are searchable by business categories as well as name. SuperPages.com is provided by Verizon, and Yellowpages.com is provided by AT&T. We suggest using both, since each specializes in the calling areas covered by that vendor.

JobCentral National Labor Exchange

jobcentral.com

Representing a public service partnership between the DirectEmployers Association and the National Association of State Workforce Agencies (NASWA), JobCentral offers easy access to quality career resources and jobs nationwide. This site welcomes veterans, seniors, and students entering the world of work.

USA.gov

usa.gov

Click on Jobs and Education to access a page full of helpful information. Topics range from GI Bill enrollment, to finding child care, to information technology training and other work-related resources. USA.gov provides one-stop access to federal government information and more. The links to financial aid, government grants, labor law, and colleges are among many that can pay off for job hunters.

NewsLink

newslink.org

Read all about it: easy access to newspapers and other media simultaneously. Browse by state or media type. At the time of review, the links to newspapers were good, but the resource pages had many dead links. NewsLink is part of the HelloMetro Group.

State and Local Government on the Net

statelocalgov.net

Dana Noonan's outstanding collection of links throws open the gate to state and local government resources. These government websites can be fantastic funnels of information! Beyond informing users about themselves, they often list businesses, educational institutions, and other grist for the job hunter's mill. State and Local Government on the Net is now a member of the HelloMetro Group.

The Midwest and the Great Lakes

This region comprises Illinois, Indiana, Iowa, Kansas, Michigan, Minnesota, Missouri, Nebraska, Ohio, Oklahoma, and Wisconsin.

Illinois

Illinois's Job Bank

illinoisskillsmatch.com

www.ides.state.il.us

ilworkinfo.com

Illinois Skills Match (first URL) automatically connects your skills and requirements to thousands of jobs in the state; the job-matching website is maintained by the Department of Employment Services (second URL). The third URL takes you directly to the helpful career resources: "Countdown" for middle school students, "Career Clicks" for high school students and adults, and "Career Information System," a self-service, interactive body of knowledge about careers, training, and more.

Illinois Newspapers

newslink.org/ilnews.html

This gateway from Newslink.org will link you to many of the newspapers for this state.

ChicagoJobs.com

chicagojobs.com

Brought to you by the Sun-Times, Pioneer Press, Daily Herald, and other Chicago-area newspapers, ChicagoJobs.com offers a handy simultaneous search of job listings in all the participating newspapers.

ChicagoJobs.org

chicagojobs.org

chicagojobtalk.info

The definitive Chicago-area job and career guide, as it's known, continues to serve as a gateway to resources for local job seekers and career changers. Job postings, salary surveys, networking opportunities, and the new ChicagoJobTalk blog are all easily accessible here. Maintained by librarians at Skokie Public Library, ChicagoJobs now features Ask an Expert and a Career Coaching Q&A advice column, made possible through a partnership with Jewish Vocational Service.

City of Chicago

egov.cityofchicago.org

cityofchicago.org/personnel

Ease into community, business, and government information from the first URL. To access Chicago Career Works, the listing of municipal employment opportunities, look under "I want to . . ." and select Find Out About City Employment. The second URL will take you there directly. You may also call the twenty-four-hour job hotline at 312/744-1369 to find out what jobs are available and get help with online applications. Or apply in person at the Chicago Career Works Application Center at City Hall, 121 North LaSalle Street, Room 100, Chicago, IL 60602, open Monday through Friday from 8:00 A.M. to 5:00 P.M.

Illinois Department of Commerce and Economic Opportunity

illinoisbiz.biz

The DCEO site provides loads of good information about starting a new business and managing it successfully, plus fact sheets about doing business in Illinois, training and financial assistance, and up-to-date community profiles.

Illinois workNet

illinoisworknet.com

Newest among the state of Illinois job and career offerings, workNet represents a partnership among several educational agencies and institutions and the Department of Commerce and Economic Opportunity. At the time of review, workNet had just added the Online Resume Builder. You can create up to twenty resumes to store in your account. To get full access to the site, you must register.

Indiana

Indiana's Job Bank—Indiana Department of Workforce Development

in.gov/dwd

The DWD website offers access to career-planning assistance, from self-assessment to gaining new skills, unemployment assistance, and information for veterans in the workforce. From the main page, select Job Seekers to access DWD's Customer Self Service System (CS3), an interactive service that provides access to job-matching and labor market information.

Indiana Newspapers

newslink.org/innews.html

This gateway from Newslink.org will link you to many of the newspapers for this state.

Access Indiana: Linking Hoosiers to Government

ai.org

www.state.in.us

Indiana's official website speeds you to miles of good information. Either URL will take you to the main page, from which you can bone up on state agencies, educational resources, social services, and businesses. Click on Information for Residents, and then select WorkOne Centers to access the job leads and career information. Resources from Workforce Development are also accessible from the front page.

HoosierNet

www.bloomington.in.us

HoosierNet's mission is "to develop and maintain a quality information infrastructure" for its community. It does just that, paving the way to in-depth community information for the Bloomington area in a simple, easy-to-use format. You'll find links to educational and business resources, libraries, and local social-service organizations. Click on the Employment link to reach the career resources.

IndyGov

indygov.org

IndyGov provides simple access to lots of good resources—housing and relocation information, government agencies, educational institutions, business directories and assistance, plus job opportunities with the city of Indianapolis and Marion County.

Learn More Resource Center

learnmoreindiana.org

indianaintern.net

The Learn More website, the first URL, provides timely, useful information on education, financial aid, and careers. Complete the interactive Career Interest Checklist, or check out the profiles of colleges and universities nationwide. The new INTERNnet website features hundreds of internship opportunities; use the second URL for direct access to this source.

Iowa

Iowa's Job Bank—IowaJobs

www1.iowajobs.org/jobs

www.iowaworkforce.org

IowaJobs, the first URL, offers easy-to-navigate access to jobs. Browse or search for full-time or part-time work in the public or private sector. It was produced by Iowa Workforce Development, whose motto is "Putting Iowa to Work!" The second URL leads to the full range of job-placement, skill-development, and lifelong learning resources and services created for workers, job seekers, and employers. Also helpful are the business directory and the career resources designed for students.

Iowa Newspapers

newslink.org/ianews.html

This gateway from Newslink.org will link you to many of the newspapers for this state.

Kansas

Kansas Job Bank—Kansas JobLink

kansasworks.com

www.dol.ks.gov

Scroll down the page to start your Quick Search for jobs by location and keyword. Sort the results by title, date, salary, or location. Lots of other good resources are available here, including child-care referrals. Use the second URL to access the Kansas Department of Labor training and additional career resources, labor statistics, and business start-up information.

Kansas Newspapers

newslink.org/ksnews.html

This gateway from Newslink.org will link you to many of the newspapers for this state.

Blue Skyways

www.skyways.org

Blue Skyways is a service of the Kansas State Library. It brings together links to schools, towns and cities, counties, local government, and databases to use in your job and career research. Very helpful resources!

Kansas Educational Employment Board

kansasteachingjobs.com

Looking for a job teaching in Kansas? Use this site's online form to apply for teaching positions in several Kansas school districts simultaneously.

Kansas.gov

kansas.gov

The official website for the state of Kansas offers simple access to government and community information, assistance in doing business in Kansas, and links to educational institutions. Click on Business to open a helpful page of links to government jobs, resources organized by profession, and more.

KChasJobs.com

kchasjobs.com

KChasJobs.com is a collection of helpful resources maintained by the Kansas City Chamber of Commerce. Click on the Chamber link for the directory of chamber members, searchable by keyword or company name. Browse current job listings by occupation or employer. New to this site are resources for teachers and career resources for children from preschool through the sixth grade.

Wichita Area Chamber of Commerce

wichitakansas.org

A searchable membership directory and several helpful resources are accessible right from the opening page. Click on Find a Job to access the Wichita NationJob Network, which is updated daily. Browse by company or position, or use the search for more targeted results. The site has launched a Spouse Career Network to provide job-search assistance to the husbands or wives of professionals new to the area.

Michigan

Michigan's Job Bank—MTB: Michigan Talent Bank

www.michworks.org

The Michigan Department of Labor and Economic Growth, through its Michigan Works! initiative, maintains this customer-driven Talent Bank, supplying job seekers and employers with the help they need via a statewide system of service centers. Users have access to employment support services, internships, and thousands of job leads. Register your skills and post your resume, or link to the Career Portal, also listed here. Click on Job Seeker to start your search for employment.

Michigan Newspapers

newslink.org/minews.html

This gateway from Newslink.org will link you to many of the newspapers for this state.

Michigan Career Portal

michigan.gov

"Get Skills. Explore Careers. Find Work. Find Workers." Click on Jobs to reach Michigan's Career Portal. This website pulls it all together—support services, apprenticeships, tools for career exploration and planning geared to youth, retirees, college-age job seekers, and others wending their way through the world of work.

Michigan Electronic Library Internet Collection

mel.org

A joint project of the state's libraries, MEL is an excellent one-stop answer for your Michigan information needs, including businesses (potential employers) and job links. Click on Jobs and Careers Pathfinder to access the extensive collection of links and article and information databases.

Minnesota

Minnesota's Job Bank—"Where Job Seekers and Employers Click"

www.mnworks.org

Minnesota's Job Bank is a self-service job-matching system through which job seekers and employers can find one another. You'll find apprenticeships, internships, and volunteer positions, to go along with the job opportunities. To take advantage of the full range of services, you must register (free).

Minnesota Workforce Center System

mnwfc.org

iseek.org

deed.state.mn.us/cjs

Minnesota continues to deliver cutting-edge service to its job seekers and career changers! The first URL leads to the full range of career-related resources provided by the state: the Job Bank, the Creative Job Search, the Internet System for Education and Employment Knowledge (ISEEK), and more. The second URL goes directly to ISEEK's assessment tools and other resources. This site now includes "New to America" resources for recent immigrants. Also new is FutureWork, articles highlighting trends in business, education, and the workplace. The Health Care Channel provides an exclusive focus on the health care industry. The third URL accesses the Creative Job Search Online Guide, for insight on developing a job-search strategy and career plan. You can order a paper copy to read and work on at your leisure. These are wonderful resources!

Minnesota Newspapers

newslink.org/mnnews.html

This gateway from Newslink.org will link you to many of the newspapers for this state.

Minneapolis–St. Paul Star Tribune

startribune.com

The *Star Tribune* site offers news plus a new space for a community dialogue (buzz.mn). Click on Jobs to reach the employment opportunities. Search by keyword, or browse by category. Any or all of the jobs are now available as an RSS feed, making it easy for you to stay in touch using a newsreader such as Google News (news.google.com) or Bloglines (bloglines.com). You can also subscribe to Job Mate (JobM8) to have jobs of interest text-messaged to you wherever you are.

Missouri

Missouri's Job Bank—Great Hires

greathires.org

"Missouri's Workforce Resource" now requires registration before you can access the jobs and career resources. Start your search for employment opportunities by selecting Job Seekers and registering. Call the Career Information Hotline Monday through Friday from 8:00 A.M. to 5:00 P.M. at 800/392-2949 for information about education, training, or job hunting.

Missouri Newspapers

newslink.org/monews.html

This gateway from Newslink.org will link you to many of the newspapers for this state.

Missouri State Government Web

mo.gov

The state website links to the usual government agencies and services. A recent introduction is the Business Portal, featuring good resources for small businesses. Click on Working to go to a nice assortment of job and training links, including the State Park Rangers page, jobs for teachers, and the Great Hires Job Bank.

St. Louis, Missouri, Community Information Network

stlouis.missouri.org

The St. Louis CIN features information about housing, business development, the neighborhoods of St. Louis, and local and state governments. Click on Resources & Links to access the Community Resources database, listing several organizations that offer employment assistance and other helpful information, along with the Community Connection link for resources statewide. Click on Government, and then Jobs with the City, to access the current job leads.

STLtoday.com: St. Louis at Work

stltoday.com/jobs

St. Louis at Work, the self-described "#1 St. Louis web site," is part of the *St. Louis Post-Dispatch*. You have access to the news and business resources and will also find profiles of leading employers. Search by category, job title, and other qualifiers. Register for free to take advantage of the job alert and resume tools.

Nebraska

Nebraska's Job Bank—Nebraska JobLink

nejoblink.dol.state.ne.us

www.dol.state.ne.us

Brought to you by Nebraska Workforce Development, JobLink unveils all the standard resources. A nice addition is the zip code radius search, so that you can get at jobs within a chosen geographical area. Search by category or job title. Register to access company information and upload your resume. The second URL goes to the Workforce site, which hands you the scoop on the labor market, education, and training resources.

Nebraska Newspapers

newslink.org/nenews.html

This gateway from Newslink.org will link you to many of the newspapers for this state.

Career Link

careerlink.com

The Applied Information Management Institute supports "Better Communities Through Technology" by maintaining this database and others like it throughout the region. Nebraska and Iowa career opportunities reside here along with career tools for all ages.

Greater Omaha Chamber of Commerce

omahachamber.org

The chamber now offers access to job leads, primarily in Greater Omaha. This is a well-developed website with everything you need to know about living and working in the area. The business directory is searchable by company name or industry. You can also unearth helpful links to educational and business resources, rounded out by a special page for newcomers.

lincolnjobs.com

lincolnjobs.com

Visit this site for extensive information about Lincoln, Nebraska. Simple to navigate, Lincolnjobs.com offers career advice, links to several local employers, and a place to create and store your resume. A newer add-on is a listing of job hotlines.

University of Nebraska (UNL) Career Services

unl.edu/careers

UNL Career Services serves up detailed information on myriad topics, including internships and specific career paths, and backs it up with tips on resumes, cover letters, and interview presentation. The Husker Hire Link is available to students and alumni only; it matches job candidates with potential employers. All other job links are accessible to anyone.

Ohio

Ohio's Job Bank—WorkForce 411

scoti.ohio.gov/scoti_lexs

Using Ohio's Statewide Job Matching System database, you can breeze through loads of jobs plus career links and authoritative advice. Formally referred to as

Sharing Career Opportunities and Training Information, SCOTI also provides access to the SHARE database of human services, job and career help for youth and adults, and training and apprenticeship opportunities.

Ohio Newspapers

newslink.org/ohnews.html

This gateway from Newslink.org will link you to many of the newspapers for this state.

CareerBoard

careerboard.com

"Local Jobs. Local Talent." CareerBoard covers most of Ohio's metropolitan areas. Start the Quick Search with keywords or a selected category; browse by category, or search by keywords, type of employment (full- or part-time), or date of job posting using the Advanced Search. Register (free) to create and post your resume or to have job postings sent to you via e-mail.

Ohio Department of Job and Family Services

jfs.ohio.gov

The agency whose credo is "Helping Ohioans" delivers the goods. The ODJFS offers one-stop shopping for all your health and human services needs. Information on child-care referrals, transportation, and more is front and center. The site serves up career counseling, education and training, labor market information, and assistance in conducting your job search.

SuperJobs

superjobs.com

SuperJobs represents the bricks-and-mortar job centers in Cincinnati that assist with resume writing, job fairs, and programming for local job seekers and career changers. It also posts information of interest online at this site. The Youth Zone section is customized for the generation of young men and women considering or entering the world of work. Parts of the site may still be under construction.

Oklahoma

Oklahoma's Job Bank—Oklahoma JobLink

servicelink.oesc.state.ok.us

www.oesc.state.ok.us

Scroll down the page of the first URL to start your Quick Search for jobs by location and keyword. Sort the results by title, date, salary, or location. Lots of other A-OK resources are situated here, including child-care referrals. Use the second URL to access other programs and services from the Oklahoma Employment Security Commission.

Oklahoma Newspapers

newslink.org/oknews.html

This gateway from Newslink.org will link you to many of the newspapers for this state.

OK.gov: Oklahoma's Official Web Site

ok.gov

This nicely organized portal provides you hassle-free access to acres of educational and job opportunities in Oklahoma. The Business and Employment links take you to business start-up information, a business directory, employment resources, and a neat listing of professional associations. The state's libraries and schools are just as easily accessible. Real-time chat assistance is now available during regular office hours via the Online Live Help link.

Wisconsin

Wisconsin's Job Bank—Wisconsin JobNet

wisconsinjobcenter.org

www.dwd.state.wi.us/jobnet/mapwi.htm

At the first URL, click on Job Seekers to access Wisconsin's Job Bank. The handiwork of the Department of Workforce Development, the Job Center provides access to all of the services and programs for Wisconsin job seekers and career changers online. These include child care referrals, labor market data, and guidance for the job hunt. For the database of job leads, click on JobNet, or use the second URL to go there directly. You can gather the information you need fast and without a hitch.

Wisconsin Newspapers

newslink.org/winews.html

This gateway from Newslink.org will link you to many of the newspapers for this state.

City of Madison

www.ci.madison.wi.us

www.ci.madison.wi.us/jobs.html

If you'd like to live in the "City of Lakes," click on City Agencies at the first URL, and then scroll down to the Human Resources link, or use the second URL to dive right in. New job listings are posted weekly. You'll find additional links to other area job sites. City of Madison Employment Applications must be completed for all jobs and are not accepted via e-mail.

State of Wisconsin

wisconsin.gov

Here users have links to information about the state and to all aspects of state government, including the employment services. This server also offers start-up assistance (via the Business Wizard) and links to educational resources. Click on Relocation to access the job leads.

WISCareers

wisconsincareers.wisc.edu

A new addition here is a suite of tools developed by the University of Wisconsin that can help you enter the world of work, re-career, or fine-tune your career. The easy-to-use ePortfolio helps you build and store your resume and details about your skills, abilities, and achievements. WISCareers is available free through your local career center, most schools, and some public libraries; otherwise, the cost is $20 per year for an individual.

New England and the Mid-Atlantic States

This region comprises Connecticut, Delaware, the District of Columbia (Washington D.C.), Maine, Maryland, Massachusetts, New Hampshire, New Jersey, New York, Pennsylvania, Rhode Island, Vermont, Virginia, and West Virginia.

Regional Resources

JobCircle.com

jobcircle.com

With a mission to "help jobseekers and employers connect," the award-winning JobCircle rewards residents of the eastern seaboard with all kinds of job and career information. Read the articles, get help from the Career Coach, or browse the directory of employers. Enter a keyword into the handy radius search to locate a job.

Jobfind.com

jobfind.com

Brought to you by the *Boston Herald*, Jobfind offers a calendar of events, company profiles, and free resume posting. To find a job, type in a keyword, delineate your location, or select a job category in the Yahoo! Hotjobs Search for Jobs. Click on Search to view the results.

Connecticut

Connecticut's Job Bank

ct.gov/dol

jobcentral.com/ct

ctjobandcareer.org

The new Connecticut Job Bank is now available. You will easily find it from the Department of Labor home page (the first URL), or you can use the second URL to go there directly. The third URL goes to the state Labor Department's Job and Career ConneCTion with information about occupations, education resources, and resources for job seekers. The Career Express mobile career center is a recent introduction; check online to see when it will be in your neighborhood!

Connecticut Newspapers

newslink.org/ctnews.html

This gateway from Newslink.org will link you to many of the newspapers for this state.

CT.gov: State of Connecticut Online Access to Government

ct.gov

Click on Working to access help for working families, including child care and assistance for special populations. Education and training opportunities, the Career Resource Network, and related career help and job leads are at your fingertips.

CTJobs.com

ctjobs.com

Brought to your virtual doorstep by a dozen of the state's newspapers, CTJobs aggregates helpful career articles plus access to jobs throughout the state. Register (free) to use the resume tools or have job alerts sent to you. Use the handy Quick Search to look for a job; select the county and employment category in which you're interested, and add a keyword if it suits your fancy.

Delaware

Delaware's Job Bank—Delaware JobLink

delawareworks.com

joblink.delaware.gov

Delaware's new JobLink replaces the former state job bank operated through America's Job Bank. Connect to that service from DelawareWorks.com, the online home of the Delaware Department of Labor, or use the second URL to access it directly.

Delaware Newspapers

newslink.org/denews.html

This gateway from Newslink.org will link you to many of the newspapers for this state.

Bank of America Career Services Center (CSC), University of Delaware

www.udel.edu/csc

The University of Delaware's CSC originated this wonderful resource for students and alumni of the school. Most of the resources are accessible to the general public. Explore career opportunities and get sound advice for interviewing or constructing your resume. The CSC also has a first-rate collection of Major Resource Kits designed to connect academic majors to career alternatives and information on charting a career path. Web presentations feature lectures on a variety of topics. These require the RealOne Player (real.com), and the files are huge, so be sure that your network connection can handle them and that you have the proper audio equipment hooked up to the computer. What a great resource!

District of Columbia (Washington, D.C.)

District of Columbia's Job Bank—DC Virtual OneStop

dcnetworks.org

dc.gov

The District of Columbia provides this job database (first URL) for its residents and those beyond the borders in the suburban areas. Anyone can search for jobs and view partial results, including a summary of the position. You must register (free) to view all and take advantage of resume building, career exploration, and other services. Use the second URL to access DC's home page and everything you need to know to live in, work in, or visit the nation's capital.

District of Columbia Newspapers

newslink.org/dcnews.html

This gateway from Newslink.org will link you to many of the newspapers for this state.

USAJOBS: Working for America

www.usajobs.com

USAJobs is the official site for federal employment information and jobs listed with the U.S. Office of Personnel Management. From here you can get the heads-up on current job openings in the government, as well as pay and benefits. Download specific forms required for some applications and review instructions for applying for jobs with the U.S. government. USAJobs also features a resume builder you can use to create and store your resume in the system. While most government agencies post their jobs here, not all are required to do so; USAJobs will link you to those agencies for information on their openings.

For information on jobs in the federal government see Chapter 9.

Maine

Maine's Job Bank—Maine Employment Info Guide

http://198.182.162.220

mainecareercenter.com

Click on Services for Individuals at the first URL to access the job listings. The Quick Menu Job Search is your express train to the geographical and radius searches. The second URL leads to the Maine Career Center, a full range of resources and services. Examples are advice for transitioning if you are laid off or are re-careering, information about the Registered Apprenticeship Program, and links to the job bank and other job leads. A new offering here is Lifelong Learning Accounts (LiLAs), individual investment accounts that are matched by the employer to fund lifelong learning.

Maine Newspapers

newslink.org/menews.html

This gateway from Newslink.org will link you to many of the newspapers for this state.

State of Maine Official Web Site

maine.gov

The state of Maine has long conveyed a great deal of information through its server. Click on "How do I find a job in Maine?" Or click on Online Services to access the job and career information. The Services page links you to helpful business and education resources.

Maryland

Maryland's Job Bank—Maryland's Workforce Exchange

mwe.dllr.state.md.us

dllr.state.md.us

Maryland's new job bank has much potential but may still need some tinkering. We had a bit of trouble figuring out which fields to complete so that we could execute a job search. After clicking on Find a Job, we found it easiest to go to Step 1, select "Use the skills and keywords below" and type a keyword into the box (e.g., *baker*, *accounting*). You can then select a geographical location if desired. Click on the Search button to view the results.

The second URL offers an easier route to career resources. Scroll down the page to the Find a Maryland One-Stop Career Center link for a clickable map of Maryland counties. Select the county you want. This site includes some of the good content previously accessible through CareerNet, such as the Professional Outplacement Assistance Center, which provides information and services for individuals in professional, technical, and managerial occupations.

Maryland Newspapers

newslink.org/mdnews.html

This gateway from Newslink.org will link you to many of the newspapers for this state.

SAILOR: Maryland's Online Public Information Network

sailor.lib.md.us

From the opening page, SAILOR offers easy access to databases of local and subject-specific information and articles. These include the SHARE database of community organizations and services. SAILOR also offers access to select Internet sites in Maryland Links: A to Z. Select E for "employment" to access the career resources. Unfortunately, at the time of review, several of the links were dead, although the effort is still worthwhile. You'll also find education, government, and community information, and more. Just keep trying if you don't think of the right keyword to use for the information you are seeking.

Massachusetts

Massachusetts Job Bank—Massachusetts JobQuest

web.detma.org/jobseeker

web.detma.org

JobQuest offers a "bulletin board" of links to training programs in Massachusetts and beyond. Click on MJQ Job Bank at the first URL to start your search by keyword and/or category or region, use your zip code, or unearth only the newest jobs in your area. JobQuest is a cinch to use, and the additional job leads available through the EmployOn search are a great addition. The second URL offers best access to all of the job and career resources provided by the Department of Labor and Workforce Development.

Massachusetts Newspapers

newslink.org/manews.html

This gateway from Newslink.org will link you to many of the newspapers for this state.

Boston.com

boston.com/jobs

On this multipurpose site you can read the latest about area businesses—or find an apartment! Feast your eyes on the employer profiles, post your resume, or scan a job fair schedule. Boston.com claims to have the largest database of jobs in New England. Scroll down the page to use the Career Development resources, digest the latest job news, or participate in the Job Blog. Browse jobs by location, employer, or job title, or use the search box. Boston.com is a service of the *Boston Globe*, and the job site partners with Monster.com.

Boston Online Employment Links

boston-online.com

Boston Online maintains this collection of links that include the tongue-in-cheek "Wicked Good Guides" to Boston English and public restrooms. Click on the Boston Links to hook yourself to business and educational resources, housing, communities, libraries, and more! Use the Job Quick Search to locate jobs.

Commonwealth of Massachusetts Home Page

mass.gov

Mass.gov transports you to a variety of services online—you can download forms or pay or apply for many services via the website. Select the For Business header for links to community profiles and information of interest to experienced entrepreneurs and new business owners alike. The Virtual Gateway leads to health and human services galore. Click on Residents, and then select Labor and Employment for easiest access to all the other great resources for job hunters in Massachusetts.

New Hampshire

New Hampshire's Job Bank—Job Match System

www.nhes.state.nh.us/itsweb

nh.gov/nhes/jobseeker

www.nhes.state.nh.us/elmi/nhcrn/index.htm

Click on Job Seekers at the first URL to start your job search. The Take a Tour option allows you to search by keyword or Job Division without registering, but you must register to post your resume and take advantage of the Job Match System. The second URL provides access to other job and career resources in New Hampshire. Scroll on down the page to locate links of interest. The third URL leads directly to the NH Career Resource Network (NHCRN) and its many labor and career-exploration links.

New Hampshire Newspapers

newslink.org/nhnews.html

This gateway from Newslink.org will link you to many of the newspapers for this state.

NH.gov

nh.gov

The official website for the state of New Hampshire offers community profiles, links to state and local government, plus resources for living, working, and doing business there. You'll find additional links to the state's schools and colleges, as well as other resources of interest. Click on Residents to access the job resources.

New Jersey

New Jersey's Job Bank—Workforce New Jersey Employment Information Network

lwd.dol.state.nj.us/labor/wnjpin/findjob/findjobindex.html

wnjpin.net

The simple search is straightforward and easy to do. At the time of review, the extensive job links in the NJ Employment page were mostly current, although the links in the Job Search Tools section were almost entirely dead or out of date. Use the second URL to access the career links. A few of these were also outdated. You'll find help for students and others exploring the world of work.

New Jersey Newspapers

newslink.org/njnews.html

This gateway from Newslink.org will link you to many of the newspapers for this state.

New Jersey: The Official State of New Jersey Web Site

www.state.nj.us

New Jersey's official website provides information about the state, its agencies, and its communities. Government links include the towns and counties in the state. The Business section provides information on starting and maintaining a business in New Jersey. Child care referrals are accessible under Health & Social Services. Click on Employment to access the job resources.

NJ.com: Everything Jersey Best Local Jobs

nj.com/jobs

"Everything Jersey" offers yellow pages and some community information, along with access to several of the state's newspapers. This URL goes directly to the employment page, where you can easily search the classifieds of several area newspapers either separately or simultaneously. Register (free) to create a profile and post your resume.

New York

New York's Job Bank—New York State Department of Labor Finding a Job

labor.state.ny.us

New York's Job Bank offers easy access to resources for job seekers and career changers, and for the next generation entering the world of work. You'll find jobs, labor statistics, and links to many other career resources.

New York Newspapers

newslink.org/nynews.html

This gateway from Newslink.org will link you to many of the newspapers for this state.

DaVinci Jobs

davincitimes.org

Operated by the da Vinci Project of Upstate New York, this site represents a collaboration of local community organizations, area businesses, and educational institutions in central and upstate New York. You'll find links to arts, recreation, the economy, and other resources of interest to anyone contemplating a move to the Syracuse area.

New York CareerZone

nycareerzone.org

This site is better and easier to navigate than ever! Although New York State's interactive career-exploration system was developed primarily for its students, it also includes resources for adults. Select a topic to dig into: Career Interests, Skills Survey, Education and Training, Occupations, and so on. CareerZone provides information about the skills and education required for any of the careers selected, along with the tasks involved, and the job outlook and expected wages. You can then link from the job title to current job offerings in the New York Job Bank. The new Portfolio option helps you manage your career.

New York Times on the Web

nytimes.com

Although access to the *Times* site is free, the publisher of "all the news that's fit to print" asks that you register before you use the online paper. You do not have to register to access the job listings, although you must register to post your resume or use the e-mail job-alert system. Click on Jobs to start your job search. Type a keyword into the search box, and hit Enter to view the results. New to the site are RSS feeds for receiving job alerts.

NYC.gov: The Official New York City Website

nyc.gov

Scroll down and click on Business to view helpful resources for entrepreneurs—new and long-standing alike. For job and career information, select Residents, and click on Health & Human Services to reach the Employment & Training links. For employment opportunities with the city, click on Government, and then use the pull-down menu to access Human Resources or IT jobs.

Western New York Jobs

wnyjobs.com

"Your Source for Employment in Buffalo and Rochester" is published online in conjunction with the free print version, *WNY JOBS Weekly,* which is distributed widely in the community. Register for free e-mail alerts or to post your resume.

Pennsylvania

Pennsylvania's Job Bank—Commonwealth Workforce Development System

www.cwds.state.pa.us

Pennsylvania's "One-Stop On-Line Resource" is your access to mountains of information and services for job seekers, employers, and individuals looking for training or social services. Get help in preparing your resume, locate support services, and scope out training or career-related events. In addition to its internal job bank, this resource provides access to employer websites and other employment opportunities.

Pennsylvania Newspapers

newslink.org/panews.html

This gateway from Newslink.org will link you to many of the newspapers for this state.

Carnegie Library of Pittsburgh Job & Career Education Center

clpgh.org/locations/jcec

Drop by the highly regarded Job and Career Education Center if you're in the neighborhood—it could be just the boost you need to jump-start your career! If you're a resident of the area, be sure to bookmark this site. You'll find a great deal of assistance, including interview and resume tips, links to financial aid information, access to helpful career databases, and, yes, links to job leads!

Phila.gov

www.phila.gov

The "City @ Your Service" philosophy comes through loud and clear on this website. Click on Business to access directories and helpful resources for starting and growing a business. Click on "Find a . . . " to access health centers, child care and after-school programs, and jobs with the city. For the most comprehensive access to job leads in and beyond Philly, tap the Residents or Business links.

Rhode Island

Rhode Island's Job Bank

www.dlt.state.ri.us

www.networkri.org

Access Rhode Island's new job bank from the first URL, the Department of Labor and Training website. You can also use this page to access jobs in state government and other career resources, including the RI RED database—"Oceans of Information at Your Fingertips." You must register (free) for full access to all of its resources. Use the second URL to access netWORKri, the state's recruitment home. For financial aid and training information, choose the Out of Work? header.

Rhode Island Newspapers

newslink.org/rinews.html

This gateway from Newslink.org will link you to many of the newspapers for this state.

JobsinRI: Where Employers and Job Seekers Click!

jobsinri.com

Browse the company profiles, or read the helpful articles on the Career Central Advice page. JobsinRI offers links to other associations and organizations that may prove beneficial in your job search. Browse all the new jobs, or select a category or city. The Advanced Search allows a simple search by keyword only. The links in the handy On the Border section lead to job opportunities in neighboring states.

Swearer Center for Public Service, Brown University

swearercenter.brown.edu

The Swearer Center views service as an important component of a liberal education. This site links to the Providence Community Agency Directory, which carries volunteer opportunities. The Swearer Center also sponsors a Community Action Resource Night, at which more than one hundred area agencies recruit members of the Brown community for volunteer projects, and offers a Listserv featuring R.I. Community Jobs. The many helpful resources for people seeking "Careers in the Common Good" are now coordinated through Brown's Office of Career Development.

Vermont

Vermont's Job Bank—Vermont JobLink

vermontjoblink.com

labor.vermont.gov

www.vtlmi.info/career8.cfm

JobLink is a must-see for Vermont job hunters. At this first URL, you have a lot to soak up, including jobs. Use the second URL to take yourself to the easy-to-navigate Vermont Department of Labor page, with links to the state's training and education information, the 211 database of social service providers, and other employment resources and agencies. Click on Labor Market Information to access the assessment and career-development tools from the Vermont Career Resource Network, or use the third URL to go there nonstop.

Vermont Newspapers

newslink.org/vtnews.html

This gateway from Newslink.org will link you to many of the newspapers for this state.

State of Vermont Home Page

vermont.gov

Your entrée to the "Green Mountain State" features agency links and business, education, and relocation information. The Employment in Vermont link connects you to some helpful resources, including job opportunities in state government. At the time of review, the community profiles were six years out of date, and a few other links had up and died.

Virginia

Virginia's Job Bank—Virginia Employment Commission Job Bank

www.vec.virginia.gov

www.careerconnect.state.va.us

Virginia's electronic workforce-development system offers training and education opportunities, apprenticeships, financial aid information, career-preparation assistance, and job listings from the Virginia Employment Commission job bank—all at the first URL. Try the new VEC Job Search. You can also learn the ins and outs of child and elder care support, transportation, housing, and other community services. The easiest access is through the links on the right-hand side of the page. The second URL takes you to CareerConnect, the state's "One-Stop Workforce Development System," which links to business resources, regional profiles, and other career help.

Virginia Newspapers

newslink.org/vanews.html

This gateway from Newslink.org will link you to many of the newspapers for this state.

Gateway Virginia

gatewayva.com

This gateway from the *Richmond Times-Dispatch* offers links to cities, universities, government information, and more. Easily accessible from the opening page are links to other Virginia newspapers. Click on the Classified link or Search Jobs to access the Career Seeker page and start your job hunt.

Virginia Career Resource Network

vacrn.net

rureadyvirginia.com

vaview.org

knowhowvirginia.org

The Virginia Career Resource Network (VACRN) is the central access point to a phenomenal array of career tools for different stages of life. Each resource can also be accessed individually by URL. Use the second URL to go directly to r u ready? Life After High School, for information on choosing a career or paying for an education, now part of the Gateway Virginia website. The third URL goes to Virginia VIEW, which provides career and education information for all citizens from kindergarten through adult. VIEW is fun to use and informative, with links to exploration tools, a list of Virginia job hotlines, and much more. Know How, which is the fourth URL, brings you information about emerging and high-demand fields, career resources, and Career and Technical Education (CTE) and leadership opportunities. Let's not forget the VACRN links to the Guide to Career Prospects, providing detailed information about major careers in Virginia. Have your own report generated that shows the differences between Virginia and other states. The commonwealth bestows uncommon resources for current and prospective residents.

Washington, D.C.

See "District of Columbia."

West Virginia

West Virginia's Job Bank—Workforce West Virginia

www.workforcewv.org

http://129.71.177.40

Start your search for work by clicking on Find a Job, and then choose "Use the skills and keywords below"; type a keyword into the box (e.g., *baker, accounting*), and then select a geographical location. Click on the Search button to produce the results. The resume and preference links were confusing, as they led to a Civil Rights Statement, followed by a privacy statement. You need to sign off on both forms before going through the procedure of registering. The best access to career resources is by using the second URL, where a great deal of helpful information resides.

West Virginia Newspapers

newslink.org/wvnews.html

This gateway from Newslink.org will link you to many of the newspapers for this state.

WV.gov

wv.gov

The official website of West Virginia offers smooth access to all of the state's agencies and services. The links to colleges and job-training resources can be particularly helpful for job seekers and career changers. Click on Working in WV for the employment links, including state government jobs.

The South and the Caribbean Islands

This region comprises Alabama, Arkansas, Florida, Georgia, Kentucky, Louisiana, Mississippi, North Carolina, Puerto Rico, South Carolina, Tennessee, Texas, and the U.S. Virgin Islands.

Alabama

Alabama's Job Bank—Alabama JobLink

joblink.alabama.gov

Come to Alabama JobLink for an amalgam of job leads, job fairs, and other resources for Alabama job hunters. Scroll down the page to Quick Search—for jobs by location and keyword. Sort the results by title, date, salary, or location. Lots of other terrific resources are available here, including child care referrals.

Alabama Newspapers

newslink.org/alnews.html

This gateway from Newslink.org will link you to many of the newspapers for this state.

Alabama.gov

alabama.gov

This official state website provides simple-as-can-be access to business and educational resources and government information. Click on Working to access the job resources and employment opportunities in state government.

Everything Alabama

al.com

al.com/jobs

Everything Alabama is a comprehensive electronic source for news, business information, and classified ads. It is produced in cooperation with three Alabama newspapers—the *Birmingham News, Mobile Register,* and *Huntsville Times.* Use the second URL to access the job page and search for leads. Register (free) to post your resume or receive job listings via e-mail.

Arkansas

Arkansas Job Bank—Arkansas JobLink

www.arjoblink.arkansas.gov

discoverarkansas.net

Arkansas JobLink is the state's new job bank. Scroll down the page at the first URL to reach Quick Search, and kick off your job hunt by location and keyword. Sort the output by title, date, salary, or location. Among the suite of resources here are child care referrals. The second URL leads to the labor market information and career-exploration tools at Discover Arkansas. You'll also find helpful brochures courtesy of America's Career Resource Network, a pocket resume and job checklist, and access to training programs.

Arkansas Newspapers

newslink.org/arnews.html

This gateway from Newslink.org will link you to many of the newspapers for this state.

Arkansas Business

arkansasbusiness.com

arkansasjobs.net

The website of the business weekly published by the Arkansas Business Publishing Group is a portal to all manner of information. At this first URL, Arkansas Business offers up-to-date news about the state's business community and industries, resources for small businesses, and several business directories. Developed by arkansasbusiness.com in collaboration with dozens of statewide partners, ArkansasJobs.net offers access to internships and links to job opportunities. The second URL takes you there pronto. You'll find a handy collection of career tips and articles, the "Ladder" career blog, and job fair schedules.

Arkansas Next: A Guide to Life after High School

arkansasnext.com

Arkansas Next offers life and career advice for teens entering the world of work or contemplating additional schooling. The links include Go to School and Get a Life, along with more traditional links to Arkansas schools and businesses, associations, government agencies, scholarship and financial aid information, and more.

Florida

Florida's Job Bank—Employ Florida Marketplace

employflorida.com

floridajobs.org

The Employ Florida job-matching site, at the first URL, replaced America's Job Bank as the main source of job postings for residents of the state. Here you can pick up bushels of information and job leads. Use the second URL for one-stop access via the Florida Agency for Workforce Innovation to a range of helpful resources, including jobs in Florida government and schools, and job fairs and job leads in the Employ Florida Marketplace.

Florida Newspapers

newslink.org/flnews.html

This gateway from Newslink.org will link you to many of the newspapers for this state.

Employment Opportunities, Board of Governors, State University System of Florida

www.flbog.org/employmentops

The Board of Governors site connects you to open positions for the public universities, independent colleges and universities, and community colleges in Florida. Listings are for faculty, administration, and support personnel. Select a school to access the job information.

Georgia

Georgia's Job Bank—Job Information System

www.dol.state.ga.us/js/job_info_system.htm

www.dol.state.ga.us/js

To start your search at the first URL, you must select a category. You can search statewide or by city. The DOL (Department of Labor) website, the second URL, offers easy access to information on finding a job in Georgia: career-planning tools, the Re-Place Yourself job-search guide, training and education opportunities, and other tools for career building and job hunting are all accessible here.

Georgia Newspapers

newslink.org/ganews.html

This gateway from Newslink.org will link you to many of the newspapers for this state.

City of Atlanta Employment Opportunities

atlantaga.gov

Work for the city of Atlanta! Click on Employment for current job opportunities and instructions on applying for a position.

Fulton County Employment

ww2.co.fulton.ga.us

Selected as "Best of the Web" in 2006 by the Center for Digital Government, Fulton County's website is loaded with helpful information in several languages and is easy to navigate. Click on Employment to view job opportunities with county government, along with information about applying.

The Job Site

thejobsite.org

The Job Site offers easy access to jobs and information. Click on Applicant Resource Center, and select CareerSearch Now! to activate your job search. There are no career resources here, but it is a sweet site for finding, selecting, and applying for Georgia government jobs.

TeachGeorgia

teachgeorgia.org

TeachGeorgia serves as the official teacher-recruitment website for public schools in Georgia. You get information about the Troops to Teachers program, a job fair calendar, and other helpful resources. Click on Job Search to find a job statewide by location, subject, or position. You must register (free) to apply for jobs online.

Kentucky

Kentucky's Job Bank—Office of Employment and Training Self-Registration

selfreg.ky.gov

workforce.ky.gov

gohigherky.org

The commonwealth of Kentucky has endeavored on several fronts to support lifelong learning, access to information, and economic development. The resulting resources are a boon for job hunters, from kids entering the world of work to downsized baby boomers in need of a new career. To start your search for work, use the advanced search at the first URL. It's simple, but it gives you several options. Search statewide or by city or county, or specify new jobs only and a salary range. The Kentucky Cabinet for Workforce Development, charged with "Growing a Strong Workforce for the Bluegrass State," offers links to education, training, and resources designed specifically for youth. Use the second URL to view them all. The third URL leads to the website designed to encourage students of all ages to "Go Higher." Statewide resources include the Kentucky Virtual Library, online help for adults practicing for their GED, and a Virtual University that provides "Learning @ Your Convenience," all major resources that support lifelong learning and skill development.

Kentucky Newspapers

newslink.org/kynews.html

This gateway from Newslink.org will link you to many of the newspapers for this state.

Louisiana

Louisiana's Job Bank—Louisiana Works

www.laworks.net

www.ldol.state.la.us

Downloadable forms, career resources, and job services are all at your disposal! Users can access occupation and labor information, statistics, and more at the first URL. Scroll through the full range of career, community, and job seeker resources available via the simple menu structure. Use the second URL to load up on even more resources. New to this site is Louisiana Youth Works, doling out skills and interest assessments, job-preparation links, and school and financial aid information.

Louisiana Newspapers

newslink.org/lanews.html

This gateway from Newslink.org will link you to many of the newspapers for this state.

Nola.com: Everything New Orleans

nola.com

The *Times-Picayune* maintains this portal to oodles of practical information for both residents of New Orleans and visitors. At the "Moving to N.O." forum, users ask questions and share information about the community. Click on Jobs to get your search moving. All searches include local job leads as well as a link to national results. Sign up for the monthly job bulletin, or register to receive the e-mail alerts and to use the resume tools.

Mississippi

Mississippi's Job Bank

mdes.ms.gov

mscareernet.org

The Mississippi Job Bank, a partnership with Job Central, is fully functional and accessible. Visit the Department of Employment Security website at the first URL to look for a link to this new service and review the other good resources available here, including the schedule of upcoming events on the Governor's Job Fair Network. The second URL connects you to Mississippi's Career Resource Network with easy access to some helpful links and career videos detailing many occupations.

Mississippi Newspapers

newslink.org/msnews.html

This gateway from Newslink.org will link you to many of the newspapers for this state.

Mississippi.gov

mississippi.gov

The state of Mississippi home page serves as a gateway to resources throughout the state. You'll find information about the business community and links to Mississippi's schools and colleges. Click on Working in Mississippi to find jobs in state agencies and to access the links at the Department of Employment Security.

North Carolina

North Carolina's Job Bank

ncesc.com

This URL offers easy access to labor statistics, the Job Bank, and other trusty employment-related resources. Click on Individual Services to access the resources for job seekers. You'll find "Real Life Tips," with helpful advice to anyone out of work, and Smart Start, the program that assists with health and child care costs for families of young children, and the Teach4NC portal for state education jobs. Try the new Employer Websites link. Easy to use, it provides results from other North Carolina job sites.

North Carolina Newspapers

newslink.org/ncnews.html

This gateway from Newslink.org will link you to many of the newspapers for this state.

BizLink: Your On-line Business Resource

www.bizlink.org

Whether you're researching a company or starting a new business, you'll end up with good information from this business website sponsored by the Public Library of Charlotte and Mecklenburg County. Select the Career Corner link from the opening page to access career-exploration tools, along with local and regional job postings.

City of Raleigh Job Postings

raleighnc.gov

You say you're interested in working for Raleigh? View current offerings on the city's website. Click on Employment for easy access to the job page.

NCCareers

nccareers.org

ncsoicc.org

Although NCCareers went offline in March of 2007, job hunters are encouraged to use the State Occupational Information Coordinating Committee (SOICC) weblinks, now resident on the site. Explore occupations, find career information, and get good advice for your job search. Use the second URL for direct access to the SOICC website.

Puerto Rico

El Nueva Dia Interactivo

elnuevodia.com

The newspaper for San Juan offers this portal featuring news, lifestyle information, and more for residents of Puerto Rico. Click on Clasificados, and then select Empleos to access the job listings.

Puerto Rico Clasificados Online

clasificadosonline.com

Look here for business yellow pages and real estate offerings in Puerto Rico. Click on Empleos to access the job opportunities. Most areas of this site are in English and Spanish, but the job listings may be in Spanish.

Yellow Pages of Puerto Rico (Las Paginas Amarillas)

laspaginasamarillas.com

onlineyellowpages.com

Both URLs work for this site. Search by keyword and city, or browse the listings by geographic location. This is a good way to find out what businesses are here and how to contact them about opportunities. The site is available in English, Portuguese, and Spanish. From here you can search for results for all fifty states and the Virgin Islands.

South Carolina

South Carolina's Job Bank

www.sces.org

scois.net

South Carolina's Job Bank is now fully accessible. Click on Looking for work? to start your job search. The South Carolina Employment Securities website, the first URL, serves as a portal to job and support services provided by the state. Locate the closest employment office, link to jobs in state and federal government, or access South Carolina's new Job Bank. The second URL goes to the South Carolina Occupational Information System, offering up-to-date career and labor market information. Use these sites for career exploration and planning.

South Carolina Newspapers

newslink.org/scnews.html

This gateway from Newslink.org will link you to many of the newspapers for this state.

SCIway . . . the South Carolina Information Highway

sciway.net

"South Carolina's Information Highway" is chock-full of helpful information about the state and its communities. Use the simple menu structure to dig into exactly what you need. The home page leads on to libraries, newspapers, and government and education sites. The Directories link takes you to an assortment of yellow pages for the state, organized by topic. To get to the employment links, click on Jobs. The Jobs page alone offers hundreds of links to employment opportunities statewide and by community. SCIway continues to provide nicely organized, up-to-date information in an easy-to-navigate format.

Tennessee

Tennessee's Job Bank—The Source

thesource.tnui.net

tcids.tbr.edu

"The Source . . . for Tennessee Employment Information," a service of the Tennessee Department of Labor & Workforce Development, puts almost everything you need for the job hunt and career exploration here at your fingertips. Career resources, labor information, and the jobs, including jobs with state government, are all here. The Quick Menu Job Search serves as a shortcut to the Job Bank. Search by location and occupation group, employer, or job order. Use the second URL to explore the world of work and individual careers through the Tennessee Career Information Delivery System (TCIDS).

Tennessee Newspapers

newslink.org/tnnews.html

This gateway from Newslink.org will link you to many of the newspapers for this state.

Nashville Area Chamber of Commerce

nashvillechamber.com

nashvillejobslink.com

The chamber of commerce maintains a searchable database of local businesses. The first URL supplies concrete information about starting and growing a business in Nashville and helpful information about the community. The chamber also sponsors Nashville JobsLink, with job listings and employer information for the area. Browse the employer links, post your resume, or find a job. You can easily access JobsLink from the chamber's front page, or use the second URL to get there faster.

Nashville.gov: Metropolitan Government of Nashville and Davidson County

nashville.gov

Nashville's city and county governments maintain this website featuring links to local agencies and services. You'll also find information about business start-up. Click on Directory and scroll down the page to access Nashville's Public Library and its extensive collection of job and career sites in the Research and Subject Guides recommended websites. If you're interested in working for city or county government, click on the Employment link, or call the job line at 615-862-6660. Note: Civil Service applications are only accepted through their online INSIGHT system. Residents of the metro area can use the County's Career Centers for free.

Tennessee.gov

tennessee.gov

tennessee.gov/labor-wfd

The portal for the state of Tennessee is better than ever! It offers easy access to some good information. Using the first URL, click on Residents to access the Newcomers Guide or choose transportation information for bus schedules, or visit the comprehensive Business or Education links. The links to local government resources offer extensive information for those areas. When you click on Employment, you'll find links to the jobs offered by the state agencies plus access to the state's teaching jobs. The second URL leads to other resources at the Department of Labor and Workforce Development, including Boomer Careers and TN Teens2Work.

Texas

Texas's Job Bank—Work in Texas

workintexas.com

www.twc.state.tx.us

Brought to you by the Texas Workforce Commission, Work in Texas provides easy access to the job bank, jobs in state government, and career resources that include all the newspapers in the state neatly pulled together. Register to add your resume to the job-matching database. The second URL leads to more resources for employers and a full range of services, including child care, family and work support resources, health care, and transportation for employees and their families.

Texas Newspapers

newslink.org/txnews.html

This gateway from Newslink.org will link you to many of the newspapers for this state.

Austin City Connection

www.ci.austin.tx.us

Select from the many services accessible via this page, or choose a map from the collection that includes a bike map and area guides. Choose Employment from the menu to search for job opportunities with Austin's city government. If you have an Austin Public Library card, you can use the helpful article and information databases from home in your job search. Access the library's website by choosing Library from the Front Page.

Everything Austin

www.ci.austin.tx.us/library/ea_index.htm

Everything Austin, another service of the Austin Public Library, treats you to helpful business links, information about neighborhoods, access to local government resources, and job links. Click on Jobs to access the classified ads for government and private-sector jobs in the community.

TexasOnline: State of Texas Home Page

www.texas.gov

Sit for a spell at "Texas at Your Fingertips" to take in all the links to state agencies, along with barrels of information about the state. Get a load of the material on starting a business, training and educational resources, and information about the communities of the state. The Working link is prominently displayed in the menu on the left of the opening page. Resources include Youth Information and Services and the Texas Job Hunter's Guide.

U.S. Virgin Islands

The Virgin Islands Daily News

www.virginislandsdailynews.com

This website from the Pulitzer Prize–winning newspaper covers news and information regarding the U.S. Virgin Islands and Tortola. Job seekers targeting this region will light on a small area for classified advertisements here, and the Local Calendar includes meeting announcements for local business, social, and professional associations. The local Business Directory is accessible from the opening page.

St. Croix Source	http://stx.onepaper.com
St. John Source	http://stj.onepaper.com
St. Thomas Source	http://sts.onepaper.com

The websites for these sister news publications for the islands in this region are credible sources for local news and information. Each carries business and community news and information for its location. Job seekers will find some classifieds on each site, along with a calendar of events and an Island Directory that is useful for identifying potential employers.

Southwest, Mountain Region, Pacific Northwest, and the Pacific Islands

This region comprises Alaska, Arizona, California, Colorado, Guam, Hawaii, Idaho, Montana, Nevada, New Mexico, North Dakota, Oregon, South Dakota, Utah, Washington, and Wyoming.

Regional Resources

CascadeLink

cascadelink.org

CascadeLink is new and improved! It serves as a portal to helpful local and regional information for the Portland (Oregon) and Vancouver (Washington) area. Information on housing, transportation, businesses, libraries, and government is accessible here with no sweat. To view the Community Organizations OnLine (COOL) database of organizations, click on the Organizations link, and then select Search COOL. To access the employment information, click on the Jobs link.

Alaska

ALEXsys: Alaska's Job Bank

alexsys.labor.state.ak.us

jobs.state.ak.us

The ALEXsys job-search system is maintained by Alaska's Department of Labor and Workforce Development at the first URL. Select a region to view all job openings in that area, or limit your search by tacking on a category, job title, or keyword. The second URL goes immediately to the Alaska Job Center Network. Click on Job Seeker Resources to access a job fair calendar, Alaska newspapers, and resume tips. You'll also find apprenticeships, training and continuing education, jobs in local government, seafood/fishing jobs, employment at the University of Alaska, and a link to ALEXsys. If you are thinking of relocating to Alaska, be sure to read "Finding Work in Alaska" first; this guide was developed by the state's Department of Labor and Workforce Development.

Alaska Newspapers

newslink.org/aknews.html

This gateway from Newslink.org will link you to many of the newspapers for this state.

Alaska State Troopers

www.dps.state.ak.us/ast/recruit

The state troopers are always seeking candidates for duty in law enforcement, rescue operations, and fish and wildlife protection programs.

The Capitol City Home Page

juneau.org

The official page for the city and borough of Juneau offers business information, links to government and community websites, and jobs in city and borough government.

Fairbanks Alaska Internet Resources Network for Education and Training (FairNet)

fairnet.org

Fairbanks's electronic community network features links to organizations, educational resources, and government information. Click on Employment to access the career resources.

SLED: Alaska's Statewide Library Electronic Doorway

sled.alaska.edu

Since 1994, SLED has provided straightforward and nicely organized access to electronic information. The Alaska Communities link reveals all kinds of information about the state and its local communities, and the business links could be an asset in your job search. Click on Job & Employment Resources to go directly to a comprehensive page of career information.

Arizona

Arizona's Job Bank—Arizona Workforce Connection

arizonavirtualonestop.com

Select a region to view all the current job listings for that area, or limit your search by adding a category, job title, or keyword. You'll find easy access to career and training resources, labor market trends, and job-search tools. Register to save your searches and use the new resume wizard.

Arizona Newspapers

newslink.org/aznews.html

This gateway from Newslink.org will link you to many of the newspapers for this state.

Arizona @ Your Service

az.gov

The official website for the state of Arizona provides access to the 211 human services system, education and training links, community links and profiles, resources for small businesses, and jobs with state government. Click on Employment to reach the job links.

California

California's Job Bank—CalJOBS

www.caljobs.ca.gov

www.edd.ca.gov

www.worksmart.ca.gov

CalJOBS is brought to you by the state's Employment Development Department (EDD), linking Californians with jobs for more than sixty years. Enter your skills into the database to match with job openings posted by employers in the CalJOBS skills-matching database at the first URL. Use the second URL to access the EDD website, featuring labor market information, links to training resources and the One-Stop Career Center service system, assistance for youth entering the world of work and for other special groups, and job clubs. Use the third URL to access WorkSmart, featuring "Getting Ready for Work" advice, career-exploration tools, help with the job search, interviewing tips, and much more.

California Newspapers

newslink.org/canews.html

This gateway from Newslink.org will link you to many of the newspapers for this state.

CAJobs.com

cajobs.com

Click on the map to access the community job leads of your choice. Register to post your resume online and have job postings sent to you via e-mail. Browse by employer, or view the JobingVideos. Use the following URLs to go directly to specific major sites:

Los Angeles	losangeles.jobing.com
Orange County	orangecounty.jobing.com
San Diego	sandiego.jobing.com

California State Government

ca.gov

Open up this golden gate to education and training resources from preschool to adult ed and re-careering, business start-up and company information, government agencies, and more. Click on Employment to access jobs in state and local government and links to CalJOBS, the Community College Job Database, and other private-sector jobs.

California State University Careers

csucareers.calstate.edu

CSU Careers maintains a list of all available faculty and administrative positions for the twenty-three campuses of California State University, searchable by campus and discipline.

City of Los Angeles

lacity.org

Ignore the scrolling banner and take advantage of the simple menus on the left and at the top of the page. Business resources include the LA Business Team, whose question for you is "How May We Help You?" Check out the real-time bus and traffic information. Find government pages for nearby cities and counties, education links, and programs for youth. Click on Jobs Available under the Quick Links menu to access the employment opportunities.

JobStar Central

jobstar.org

JobStar brings you the most comprehensive listing of salary surveys available, along with resume-writing tips and a guide to the hidden job market. Search for jobs in specific California regions, choose Ask Electra for career advice, or find additional assistance with national and international job searching. Scroll down the page a bit to get past the advertisements and take full advantage of this highly regarded resource.

San Francisco Bay Area Volunteer Information Center

volunteerinfo.org

Don't give short shrift to this site if your heart is in the nonprofit employment sector: where there are volunteer positions, there might be job possibilities as well! Browse by title or geographical area.

SFGov: Official San Francisco City & County Web Site

sfgov.org

SFGov offers access to the SFBizInfo Great City Business Guide, tips for business start-up, and links to agency websites. Click on Government, and then select City Employment to access links to current openings in municipal and county government, or call the Job Hotline at 415-557-4888.

Colorado

Colorado's Job Bank—Connecting Colorado

connectingcolorado.com

lmigateway.coworkforce.com

You can use the simple Quick Job Search at the first URL without registering. Use the second URL to access the LMI (Labor Market Information) Gateway's career-assessment and career-exploration tools, learn about labor market trends, and locate education and training programs. You must register to take advantage of the full range of career and job-matching services through these websites.

Colorado Newspapers

newslink.org/conews.html

This gateway from Newslink.org will link you to many of the newspapers for this state.

Boulder County

www.co.boulder.co.us/jobs

Search here for employment opportunities with Boulder County government. You can also call the twenty-four-hour Jobline at 303-441-4555 to see what positions are available.

Colorado.gov: The Official Site of the State of Colorado

colorado.gov

Look to the Learning and Education page for information of interest to kids, parents, and professionals—including jobs in Colorado schools and libraries. Don't overlook the Business and Living sections for business start-up information, transportation and child care resources. This site also offers extensive links to local government and agencies. Click on Working to access the job leads and the career resources.

Denver: the Mile High City

denvergov.org

Get a leg up on starting your business at the Denver Business Assistance Center, maintained by the Department of Economic Development. Locate health services and transportation, and find schools, child care referrals, and programs of merit. If you are high on working for the city of Denver, click on Jobs. The links include volunteer and intern positions, job-search and networking assistance, and current opportunities in municipal government.

Guam

Guam's Job Bank—Guam Department of Labor (GDOL) Job Bank

guamdol.net/component/option.com_jobline

This is the job bank for Guam's state employment service. You can now upload your resume to the Job Bank for potential employers to see. You do not need to register to apply for jobs.

Guam Phone Book

guamphonebook.com

This searchable white and yellow pages directory for the territory of Guam includes a separate section for government agencies. The index makes it easy to browse listings of interest in the yellow pages.

University of Guam

www.uog.edu

Upgrade your skills via the extensive courses available for professional development and lifelong learning. Many of these fee-based classes are accessible online. Click on Employment Opportunities to view the current job listings.

Hawaii

Hawaii's Job Bank—HireNet Hawaii

hirenethawaii.com

careerkokua.org

Click on Find a Job at the first URL to access the maps of the state and start your search for employment statewide or within a specific geographic location. The second URL provides access to the Career Kokua self-assessment and career-exploration tools, which are available free for all through Hawaiian schools and career services. Click on Job Strategies to reach the links to jobs in Hawaiian agencies and institutions. You must register to create a resume or to use all of the resources available to you in both HireNet Hawaii and Career Kokua.

Hawaii Newspapers

newslink.org/hinews.html

This gateway from Newslink.org will link you to many of the newspapers for this state.

eHawaiiGov

ehawaii.gov

The state of Hawaii offers information aplenty through this portal. You'll find material of interest to citizens and visitors alike, including links to education and local community resources. Select Hawaii Business Express to reach additional links, including help for owners of small businesses. Click on Employment to reach the job and career resources.

Idaho

Idaho's Job Bank—IdahoWorks

idahoworks.org/jobseekers.shtml

cis.idaho.gov

IdahoWorks is a collaboration of the Idaho Department of Labor and state and local workforce development organizations. Use the first URL to access the job leads and career resources. Select Find Jobs to start your search for opportunities with state government or to search the IdahoWorks database. The links on the left lead to child care, training, and other support services. Use the second URL to access the Idaho Career Information System (CIS) and wield the career assessment and job search tools available there. You must register through your school or career center to use CIS.

Idaho Newspapers

newslink.org/idnews.html

This gateway from Newslink.org will link you to many of the newspapers for this state.

Montana

Montana's Job Bank—jobs.mt.gov

jobs.mt.gov/jobs

mtjoblinc.mt.gov

At the first URL, you can search for jobs by location or use the advanced search without registering. To apply for a position or to take advantage of the other resources, you must register. Use the second URL to access JobLINC, the page that brings it all together! Click on Job Seeker Services to access resume help, career resources, training, and the Job Bank. Other links lead to the Montana Career Information System (MCIS), jobs in state government, and labor market information. The MCIS is now available free to all Montanans through the schools and local career centers. The job bank is brought to you by the Workforce Services Division of the Department of Labor and Industry.

Montana Newspapers

newslink.org/mtnews.html

This gateway from Newslink.org will link you to many of the newspapers for this state.

Mt.gov: Montana's Official State Website

mt.gov

The official website for the state of Montana features agency and education information, tourist resources, and helpful guides to working, living, and doing business in Montana. Click on Working and Living to access the state's Workforce Services Division resources, the Native American Jobs Program, and opportunities in teaching. You can also come by child care referral, links to the Tribal Colleges, and more.

Nevada

Nevada's Job Bank—Nevada JobConnect

nvos.state.nv.us

nevadaworkforce.com

nvcis.intocareers.org

Use the first URL to access the JobConnect system and start your job search. You can do a simple search, but you have to register to submit a resume or apply for a position. The second URL leads to the Nevada Workforce Informer, your best source of labor and economic information about the state. The third URL accesses the Career Information System, which is available to Nevada residents only. To avoid confusion and save time, we suggest that you use the three URLs to go directly to each section.

Nevada Newspapers

newslink.org/nvnews.html

This gateway from Newslink.org will link you to many of the newspapers for this state.

ProNet

www.pronetreno.com

This northern Nevada networking association is for professionals seeking reentry into the workforce.

New Mexico

New Mexico's Job Bank—New Mexico Department of Workforce Solutions

www.dws.state.nm.us

jobs.state.nm.us

The New Mexico Department of Labor maintains this easy-to-navigate website at the first URL that matches the needs of employers with the skills of job candidates. Click on Jobseeker, then Find a Job to select statewide or regional areas of the maps to start your search for a position. The menu offers additional Job Seeker services, access to training programs, and links to career information and other useful resources. The second URL takes you directly to the extensive array of resources available for job seekers and career changers.

New Mexico Newspapers

newslink.org/nmnews.html

This gateway from Newslink.org will link you to many of the newspapers for this state.

North Dakota

North Dakota's Job Bank—Your Workforce Connection

jobsnd.com/seekers/find.html

onestop.jobsnd.com

ndcrn.com

From the first URL, you have passage to community services, training resources, and economic data about the state. Click on the link under Find a Job to access the Virtual One Stop, or use the second URL to go there directly. The handy menu invites you to choose from education and training links, resources for youth entering the world of work, resume assistance, support services, and more. You must register to create and post a resume and to sign up for the e-mail job alert. Click on a map of the state or a particular region to start your search for employment. Use the third URL to access the North Dakota Career Resource Network. Many of the career links are accessible to all. Contact your school's guidance counselor for access to Choices Explorer, the online career-guidance resources for middle and high school students.

North Dakota Newspapers

newslink.org/ndnews.html

This gateway from Newslink.org will link you to many of the newspapers for this state.

ND.gov: Official Portal for North Dakota State Government

nd.gov

Find helpful business information, and if you have a question, call the Business Hotline at 866-4DAKOTA! The Education links include the Tribal Colleges, K–12 school websites and profiles, and other educational services and institutions. The government links include state agencies, all of the county and city websites, branches of the military, and tribal government. Click on Agency by Alphabet, and then select H, to reach the Human Resources page offering jobs in state government. Lots of helpful services and resources are accessible here.

SHARE Network—Your Community Service Connection

www.sharenetworknd.com

Don't skip over this database of services in your job search! SHARE was developed by Job Service North Dakota to empower its users and provide easy access to programs and services in North Dakota. Resources include child care, financial assistance, and training programs. Search by service, location, or provider.

Oregon

Oregon Employment Department

www.employment.oregon.gov

oregoncis.uoregon.edu

mychildsfuture.org

Among its many Workforce services, Oregon's Employment Department oversees a system of safe, affordable, and high-quality child care services, including the Child Care Resource & Referral Network. The menu at the first URL offers Featured Links, from which you can select Browse Available Jobs to peruse listings by location, job title, and other descriptors; locate Apprenticeships; and easily access some of the other popular links from the opening page. Government Jobs, including municipal, education, and county websites, and the iMatchSkills job-matching service, are also easily accessible here. Select Job Seekers from the menu on the left to access a comprehensive listing of job fairs and other resources. The resources are available in five other languages. Use the second URL to access Oregon's Career Information System, offered through the state's schools and libraries. The third URL leads to MyChildsFuture.org, with tips, checklists, activities, and resources on career education for preschool through adult. Very helpful resources!

Oregon Newspapers

newslink.org/ornews.html

This gateway from Newslink.org will link you to many of the newspapers for this state.

Oregon.gov

oregon.gov

bluebook.state.or.us

Oregon's official website stands as an easy-access portal to reams of helpful information. The Education and Human Services links at the first URL include employment help for special populations, libraries, child care, and information about Oregon schools. Click on Business to get help starting or developing your business or to reach the Employment & Workforce link, which includes the Apprenticeship program, OLMIS (Oregon Labor Market Information System) career-exploration tools, and training resources. Use the second URL to go directly to the state's Blue Book, featuring links to community and regional Oregon information and more.

Portland Online

portlandonline.com

Portland Online offers links to area chambers of commerce, the Business Incubator developed by Multnomah Public Library, and government links that include community agencies, associations, and up-to-date business news. Click on Living to access jobs in local government.

South Dakota

South Dakota's Job Bank

www.sdjobs.org

The state's Department of Labor manages all aspects of employment and job training for the people of South Dakota. Click on Job Seekers to access a Quick Search that allows you to search state government jobs and to browse other job postings by location. Select a city or county, and then click Add to start the search. Register to post your resume or to do a more advanced job search. From the opening page, select Resources to access the Career InSite career-exploration tool and South Dakota Occupational Projections. The Programs section provides details about the Career Learning Centers and other DOL initiatives. The simple format makes finding the information you need a piece of cake.

South Dakota Newspapers

newslink.org/sdnews.html

This gateway from Newslink.org will link you to many of the newspapers for this state.

Sioux Falls Recruiting Cooperative

sfrc.com

The cooperative, established by a group of local businesses, has as its goal the recruitment of professionals and IT candidates for Sioux Falls industries. Select from among technical, engineering, professional, and sales and marketing positions. Visit the Links for Living or register to post your resume.

SiouxFalls.com

siouxfalls.com

Representing a partnership among the chamber of commerce, Convention and Visitors' Bureau, Development Foundation, and other Sioux Falls institutions, SiouxFalls.com provides information about the area's most important industries, links to educational resources, the city government page, and more. One of the most helpful features is the Chamber of Commerce Directory, which is searchable by category or business name. Click on SiouxFalls.com, and then select the Employment link on the Sioux Falls Living menu for employment agencies and the Argus classified job listings.

Utah

Utah's Job Bank—Utah's Job Connection

jobs.utah.gov

justforyouth.utah.gov

careers.utah.gov

As "Utah's Job Connection," the Department of Workforce Services (DWS) is the lead agency for job- and career-related services in the state. Find a job and access the job-search guides, career-outlook data, Utah Cares Community Services Directory, and child care resources at the first URL. DWS also links to Utah employers and the Electronic Job Board job-matching service, providing a customized searchable database of jobs. Just for Youth, at the second URL, offers resources to help young people successfully enter the world of work. Use the third URL to access the career-exploration tools at Utah's Career Connection. Your tax dollars created this trio of awesome resources, and we encourage you to put them to work for you.

Utah Newspapers

newslink.org/utnews.html

This gateway from Newslink.org will link you to many of the newspapers for this state.

Utah.gov

utah.gov

The state of Utah has harnessed some potent resources here. You'll find all the information you need for living, learning, doing business, and working in the state. From this page, you can link to the Job Bank, the state's universities, and other career resources and can access a helpful Newcomers Guide.

Washington

Washington's Job Bank—WorkSource Washington

worksource.wa.gov

workforceexplorer.com

The state of Washington has long been a leader in providing helpful online services and resources for its residents. The Employment Security Department's WorkSource at the first URL is no exception. It offers unique help for the state's job seekers and career changers. Do a Quick Job Search from the opening page. Use the extensive collection of Quick Guides for insight on creating and posting your resume, the basics of interviewing, the job-search system, and more. Find training and education resources, government jobs, and potential employers. The job leads include a handy collection of Washington-area newspaper classified ads neatly arranged by region, along with several other local career sites. Register for your own MyWorkSource account to use the resume, e-mail alert, and communication services. From the WorkSource page, you can easily access Workforce Explorer, the official source for labor market information and an ideal place for career exploration. Use the second URL to bypass the site and go directly there.

Washington Newspapers

newslink.org/wanews.html

This gateway from Newslink.org will link you to many of the newspapers for this state.

Access Washington

access.wa.gov

Use the menu system or the Ask George search engine to explore Washington's gateway to the Internet. The content includes a selection of online services, education directories and resources, an index to agencies by service category, and more. In addition, there are links to state, local, and federal agencies and services, as well as to business and consumer resources. Employment information is under the Working and Employment tab near the top of the page. You'll find information for teens entering the world of work, apprenticeship programs, the Workforce Explorer, and the Job Bank.

Seattle.gov

seattle.gov

Browse the official website for the city using the simple menu structure. Search by keyword or browse by service or agency. You'll find all the information you need to live in Seattle, start a business, get around the city, or access online services. Click on Find a Job to reach the current openings in city government.

Wyoming

Wyoming's Job Bank—Wyoming at Work

wyomingatwork.com

wyomingworkforce.org

Select Find a Job! at the first URL to start your job search by region of the state or statewide. Just click on the map that represents your area of interest. The easy-to-use menu system makes it possible to access the career resources and education and training links from this same page. You'll find labor statistics and workforce-development tools. Register to be notified by e-mail when a job matching your skills set becomes available, and to create and post your resume in the state talent bank. Use the second URL to access community profiles, support services, state agencies, associations, and other resources.

Wyoming Newspapers

newslink.org/wynews.html

This gateway from Newslink.org will link you to many of the newspapers for this state.

State of Wyoming

wyoming.gov

"Wyoming Welcomes You" with all these statewide online resources. Check out links to the University of Wyoming and the state's colleges, along with chambers of commerce throughout the state. Use the GoWYLD research tools, newspaper classifieds, and local government links made possible by the Wyoming State Library. And locate jobs in state government!

12

International Opportunities

More than ever, individuals are looking to go global with their careers. If this is true for you, you're on the right page. Internet resources for locating employment opportunities outside the United States are arranged in this chapter by region (Africa and the Middle East, Asia and the Pacific Rim, etc.) and then alphabetically by country. Many international recruiters based in one country often place employees in other countries, so it couldn't hurt to check neighboring countries for references. Sites featuring general advice, job leads, or career information lead off.

Again, think "focus." Using websites with a geographical or industry focus makes it easier for you to focus your search as well. Google, Yahoo!, and other regional portals have links to government agencies, embassies, foreign newspapers, career resources, and collateral information for specific countries. To access Google directories for other countries, just type google and the name of the country in the Google search box.

In addition, many of the larger job sites in Chapter 3 carry international postings, while some international sites that list jobs in a given specialty (mining, academe, etc.) appear in the chapter for that specialty, so peruse the entire book for nuggets!

General Resources

Escape Artist Jobs Overseas

jobs.escapeartist.com

This site features listings of jobs from many countries, brought to you by the website that offers advice on various aspects of living in, working in, and moving to another country.

International Career Employment Center

www.internationaljobs.org

For more than a decade, International Careers has published a weekly international employment newspaper for subscribers only. A few job listings are accessible via the website to nonsubscribers, including the "hot jobs" that employers are urgently seeking to fill, which can also be sent to you via e-mail. To view hundreds of jobs, you must be a subscriber.

International Rescue Committee

ircjobs.org

The IRC is the leading nonsectarian voluntary organization providing emergency relief and resettlement assistance for refugees worldwide. People registering for the Emergency Response Roster are considered for employment as it becomes available.

JobPilot AG

jobpilot.com

After selecting a region, you can browse this site by company or use the search form to locate job leads. Register to post your resume or have job listings sent to you via e-mail. A nice addition is the link to Expat Corner, a practical resource for job hunters who are thinking of relocating to another country. JobPilot is part of the Monster.com family.

Jobs Offered on Expatriates.com

www.expatriates.com

You'll arrive at many job listings at this site. Click on the country you want, or scroll down the page to the Jobs Offered link to browse all job leads. Beyond the job listings are pages of information about living and working in other countries, all provided by the "Online Community for Expatriates."

JobShark

jobshark.ca

Now featuring "JAWS," the skills database matching job candidates with likely employers, JobShark continues to offer hundreds of jobs, primarily in Canada.

Monster Global Gateway

globalgateway.monster.com

At the time of review, we had to scroll to the bottom of the monster.com page to spot the link to the international jobs. Use the Global Gateway link to go there directly. Career articles, tips and tools, a guide to salaries, and forums for communicating with all other job seekers are available from the main page.

OverseasJobs.com

www.overseasjobs.com

Part of the AboutJobs.com Network, using this website is a walk in the park. Browse by location, or click on the Search Jobs link to start your keyword search. At the time of review, there were just over a hundred jobs listed.

PlanetRecruit.com

planetrecruit.com

This site is simple to navigate and easy to search. From the opening page, scroll down to browse the mostly United Kingdom job listings. Use the Search Area feature to view the jobs listed for other countries.

Portals to the World

loc.gov/rr/international/portals.html

This database of "Links to Electronic Resources from Around the World" was created and is maintained by subject specialists at the Library of Congress. It is fast becoming a very good resource, offering quality information about many countries of the world, alphabetized for convenient access.

TopJobs

topjobs.co.uk

Browse jobs by sector or employer from the opening page. At the time of review, no dates accompanied any of the jobs we saw, so we cannot vouch for the currency of these listings.

Africa and the Middle East

Africa

Africa Jobsite.com

africajobsite.com

There are scads of job offerings here! This site also offers an opportunity for recruiters and potential employers to see your resume. AfricaJobsite.com is part of the Beyond.com network.

Career Classifieds

careerclassifieds.co.za

Simple to use, Career Classifieds offers a keyword search on the opening page and links to other job and career resources. You must register to apply for jobs online or to post your CV. Career Classifieds is now WAP (wireless application protocol) enabled.

Careernation: Africa—Your Job Destination

careernation.com

Search the job postings by category, geographical area, or keyword. Register to create and post your resume. At the time of review, it wasn't clear whether the jobs listed were current.

The Middle East

Association of Americans and Canadians in Israel (AACI) Jobnet

jobnet.co.il

The AACI brings you this online service. Click on All Companies to browse for jobs by employer. Search for jobs by field, keyword, or company. Mark your choices, and click on Indicated Jobs to get more details.

Gulf Job Sites

www.gulfjobsites.com

Gulf Job Sites is an independent directory of jobs and employment resources in the Persian Gulf region. Countries include Saudi Arabia, United Arab Emirates, Oman, Kuwait, Bahrain, Qatar, Iraq, and Iran. This site also maintains its own job board. Scroll down the opening page to read "How to Use This Site" for a practical overview of job-search resources.

Asia and the Pacific Rim

Regional Resources

JobsDB.com Interactive Recruitment Network

jobsdb.com

Browse the jobs by category, or click on a geographical icon to frame that region of Asia. Take advantage of the Talent Market by providing a brief resume for employers to view. All of the job listings allow you to contact the company directly. To use the Quick Apply option and get the full benefit of this job site, you must register.

JobStreet.com

jobstreet.com

Since 1995, JobStreet.com has offered online and interactive services for jobs in the Asia-Pacific region. The site features loads of very helpful career resources.

Australia

Australian JobSearch

jobsearch.gov.au

jobjuice.gov.au

Do a quick search at the first URL for jobs by location and occupation, or click on a section of the Australian map to browse the jobs in that geographic area. You can also access self-exploration and career information, in addition to pertinent articles. The second URL links to Job Juice, a site created for young job seekers in need of expertise to take on the world of work and jump start their careers.

Computerworld: the Voice of IT Management

computerworld.com.au

careerone.com.au

Computerworld, from IDG Communications, is designed to help IT professionals stay informed about the industry and locate training and educational opportunities. It also links you to thousands of job leads representing dozens of categories at CareerOne.com.au, the second URL.

JobServe Australia

jobserve.com.au

Simple to navigate, JobServe Australia is one of the largest sources of information technology jobs in the continent. Browse jobs by agency, or do a more detailed search by location and keywords. Select an industry to start your hunt. Register to receive the free newsletter or to have job postings that fit your specifications made available to you by e-mail or RSS.

My Future

myfuture.edu.au

Australia's Career Information Service offers information both for professionals assisting others and for the folks in need of the assistance. Click on the Facts section to access financial aid, career and business start-up information, articles, and work opportunities. You'll also find career events and an easy-to-use job-search page. Register to use the career-assessment resources. This is a terrific resource.

Seek

seek.com.au

it.seek.com.au

"Australia's #1 job site" offers tens of thousands of jobs, including separate Web pages for individuals looking for IT and senior-level or management jobs. Use the second URL to head straight to the IT jobs.

Sydney Morning Herald

smh.com.au

mycareer.com.au

To start your job search, select Jobs on the menu at the first URL, or use the second URL to go directly to the Job Search page. Choose a sector, or type in a keyword. You can now receive job leads of interest via an RSS feed. Register to have job postings sent to you via e-mail or to post your resume.

India

Naukri

naukri.com

Naukri has fast become one of the best resources for job hunters in India. Search for a job by keyword or location. Naukri has made it easy to add an RSS feed for specific job leads or register to receive e-mail notification of current opportunities. Naukri also offers assistance in composing cover letters and resumes for a fee.

Japan, Hong Kong, Korea, and Malaysia

CareerCross Japan

careercross.com

CareerCross is a bilingual recruitment resource serving the English-Japanese business community. Learn about living and working in Japan, and find jobs in Japan and overseas. First select the language: either English or Japanese. Visit the CareerClub for tips on interviewing, resume writing, and more. Search by job category, location, or other qualifiers. Register to receive e-mail updates or to post your resume. The site is highly informative.

Japan Association for Language Teaching

jalt.org

JALT offers resources for teachers of English as a foreign language, including an events calendar and links to some of its publications. At the time of review, JALT offered links to job sites only via Google.

O-Hayo Sensei, The Newsletter of (Teaching) Jobs in Japan

ohayosensei.com

O-Hayo Sensei is a free-subscription electronic newsletter that lists teaching positions at dozens of schools and companies in Japan. Have the newsletter e-mailed to you, or download it from the website.

Singapore and Thailand

Department of Employment (DOE), Thailand

www.doe.go.th

This is a good source of job leads for Thailand. The DOE supervises Thai nationals working overseas as well as foreign nationals working in Thailand.

Singapore Economic Development Board

www.edb.gov.sg

Look here for detailed information about specific industries in Singapore. Click on Why Singapore to learn more about the culture, along with facts and figures on the country and its standard of living. You'll find EDB job and internship opportunities, plus scholarships for "young, dynamic individuals."

Eastern Europe

Regional Resources

American Association of Teachers of Slavic and Eastern European Languages

aatseel.org

AATSEEL maintains this website for its members. Offering a handy calendar of events, it also links to interesting resources for teachers of Slavic languages, and to professional-development opportunities.

Czech Republic

CV-Online

cvonline.cz

The CV-Online job-search form is readily accessible from the opening page. Register to post your resume or to have job listings that match your profile delivered to you via e-mail.

Russia

American Chamber of Commerce in Russia

amcham.ru

The AmCham online directory of its membership is now available to nonmembers for downloading. You'll also find a calendar of events, news updates for Russia and for the organization, and advice on living and doing business in Russia.

The Moscow Times

themoscowtimes.com

careercenter.ru

The *Times*, whose site is at the first URL, is an English-language daily featuring news that bears on residents of Moscow. Use the second URL to access the job leads. Unfortunately, when we reviewed the site, resumes submitted could be viewed by any visitors.

Russian and East European Institute Job Resources

www.indiana.edu/~reeiweb

Indiana University offers this resource for people seeking jobs in Russia or Eastern Europe and for those with expertise in the languages, history, or cultures of these areas. Numerous up-to-date links here add to the value. Click on the Placement Resources links for internships and jobs and for other employment resources.

Europe

Regional Resources

EURES: the European Job Mobility Portal

europa.eu.int/eures

EURES offers a database of living and working conditions in all of the European Economic Area (EEA) member countries. Visitors also have access to all the European national employment services, an overview of labor conditions in each of the regions, and a helpful FAQs section. Select the language you speak from the opening page. Lots of employment opportunities are here. Register to post your CV or to receive e-mail notification of job leads.

Europa: Gateway to the European Union

europa.eu.int

ec.europa.eu/ploteus

The European Union maintains this list of links to its member nations and other European countries at the first URL. It offers a profile of each of the countries and links to the Portal on Learning Opportunities Throughout the European Space (PLOTEUS) and the job links at EURES. The second URL goes straight to PLOTEUS.

EuroPages: the European Business Directory

europages.com

EuroPages is searchable by product or service. You can also search by company name or browse by sector.

exec-appointments.com

exec-appointments.com

Click on Search for Jobs to start your executive job search. Search by location, role, industry, and salary, or browse by industry. Register to receive job alerts via e-mail and the free CV review.

StepStone

stepstone.com

StepStone is a major source of European jobs, primarily in Central and Eastern Europe. Under Talent Communities, select Find a Job. Scroll down the page, select the European country in which you wish to work from the pull-down menu, and click on Go. From there, select Employer, and then choose a category and/or add keywords. Click on Search to behold the results. Register to post your CV or to receive e-mail updates.

France, Belgium, Italy, and Spain

Association Bernard Gregory

abg.asso.fr

This association supports the training and employment of young French doctorates in engineering, the sciences, and the social sciences. It offers information on how to move from the academic world to the corporate world, and job listings.

Le Monde

lemonde.fr

www.talents.fr

The French newspaper of record, at the first URL, offers all the news that's fit to print. The second URL goes directly to the career page. Browse by category.

Prospective Management Overseas (PMO) Vacant Positions Overseas

www.pmo.be

The PMO specializes in the selection, recruitment, and management of experts such as technicians, engineers, and administrators for international projects. You can browse the listing of job leads and use the Submit CV form to apply for positions and forward your CV.

Trabajo.org

trabajo.org

Here you'll find listings for jobs in Spain—assuming you speak the language. Trabajo.org is available only in Spanish. Easiest search is from the opening page. Simply select Buscar to view all of the jobs. You can also browse by job category.

Germany and Austria

Breitbach Unternehmensberatung

breitbach.com

Breitbach is a German IT recruiter and consulting company. Click on Jobs to access a brief description of opportunities that are available. At the time of review, the job site was under construction but had expanded to include job leads from other European countries.

Ireland and Northern Ireland

IrishJobs.ie

irishjobs.ie

"Putting Power in Your Hands," IrishJobs.ie does facilitate the old job search. There are fistfuls of jobs here. You can browse by category or by location, or use the search boxes to combine it all into one set of results. Register to post your resume or receive job leads via e-mail. Click on Workwise to access the helpful career content, including articles on a variety of topics, advice from experts, and what you need to grasp before you settle in Ireland.

NIjobs.com

nijobs.com

This "sister site" to IrishJobs.ie has the same job-search form readily accessible on the opening page and similar content. All jobs are located in Northern Ireland.

Netherlands

Nederlandse Laboratorium

laboratorium.nl

The Laboratorium website offers information of note to employees of Dutch biomedical and chemical laboratories. You'll find news, training opportunities, associations, and job leads. Although resumes submitted to the site can be read by anyone, privacy is protected by the use of numbers to replace people's names.

Switzerland

Academic Job Exchange Board

www.telejob.ch

TeleJob is the electronic job-exchange board for the Association of Assistants and Doctoral Students of the institutes of Zurich (AVETH) and Lausanne (ACIDE). Use the quick search, or click on Job Offers to browse the positions available. Register to have job announcements sent to you electronically. The site is offered in four languages. At the time of review, resumes were easily viewable by anyone visiting the site, raising concerns about the privacy of the candidates.

JobEngine.ch

jobengine.ch

Search by category, or browse by employer. At the time of review, we found a little more than two hundred job leads. This site is mostly in German.

JobSafari Switzerland

jobsafari.ch

This Swiss job-search engine allows you to browse by category or region from the opening page, or to launch a keyword search. When you click on a job that strikes you, you're taken to the website of the organization advertising the job. This is part of the JobSafari International network. A new enhancement is the RSS feed, which brings the latest postings to you.

United Kingdom

Agency Central

agencycentral.co.uk

Easily access recruiters and job sites of all description for England, Scotland, Wales, and Ireland. Click on an industry to call for lists of businesses and job leads within that industry. Visit the Career Advice Centre for helpful articles.

British Jobs

britishjobs.net

Search for jobs in Scotland, Britain, or Wales. Browse by location or by sector, or use the search function that combines location, sector, and contract type (permanent or temporary), plus any keywords you want to add. This site has a good number of jobs for you to review.

CityJobs

cityjobs.com

CityJobs specializes in finance, accountancy, and insurance positions in the United Kingdom. The keyword search on the opening page allows you to get results quickly. Use as few terms as possible for best results. Register to post your CV or receive job leads via e-mail.

HERO: Higher Education & Research Opportunities in the United Kingdom

hero.ac.uk

jobs.ac.uk

The HERO website, at the first URL, serves as a portal for the academic community in the United Kingdom and offers news, career advice, and links to colleges and universities. HERO also links to research, science, academic, teaching, and management jobs in the public and private sector through Jobs .ac.uk, the "official recruitment site for Higher Education." Use the second URL to go lickety-split to the thousands of jobs featured via the site.

JobServe

jobserve.com

JobServe is among the largest sources of information technology jobs in the United Kingdom. It's easy to browse jobs by agency or to conduct a more detailed search by location, role, and keywords. Start out by selecting an industry. You can register to get the free newsletter or to have postings that fit your specifications sent to you by e-mail, RSS, or text messaging.

MediaWeek

brandrepublic.com/mediaweek

MediaWeek Online offers industry news and articles, industry directories, and job leads. Browse by location or sector, visit the blogs, or consult the Career Advice archives. Click on the Jobs link to start your job search. Register to receive news of interest via e-mail.

Reed Personnel Services

reed.co.uk

Browse the helpful career advice and industry information, or use the salary calculator at the "UK's biggest job site." Register to apply for the jobs listed. Once registered, you can also post your CV or have the latest job postings sent to you via e-mail.

THES: The Times Higher Education Supplement

thes.co.uk

thesjobs.co.uk

The *Times Higher Education Supplement* (*THES*) chronicles the latest developments in higher education. For subscribers only, *THES* makes available a searchable archive of articles and research funding sources at the first URL. New academic job opportunities appear every Wednesday. Browse them by broad category, search by keyword, or sign up for an e-mailed or text-messaged job alert. Use the second URL to zip right to the Jobs page.

TimesOnline, The Times (London)

timesonline.co.uk

jobs.timesonline.co.uk

Depend on the *Times* for world headlines and business news. Click on the Classifieds link at the first URL to reach the Appointments (jobs) section. Use the second URL to go directly to the advanced search. Browse the listings by industry, salary, or location, or search the jobs by industry or keyword. Register to post your CV or receive e-mail bulletins.

totaljobs.com

totaljobs.com

Billing itself as "serious about jobs," totaljobs.com delivers in spades! At the time of review, we counted thousands of jobs, mainly for the United Kingdom. All visitors have access to the career resources. Register to post your CV or develop a profile for the e-mail job alert. New at the site is the Graduate Zone, with advice, news, and more for the recent graduate.

workthing.com

workthing.com

hotonline.com

Workthing is one of the top job sites in the United Kingdom. Browse by industry, or search by location, minimum salary, and keyword. Jobs are also posted to niche sites maintained by hotonline.com.

Latin America and South America

Bolsa de Trabajo

www.bolsadetrabajo.com

Here you'll find employment opportunities and resumes for Spanish-speaking professionals. Register for full access to job openings or to post your resume.

Latin American Jobs

latinamericanjobs.com

ltj.com

Use either URL to access this site. Some business news is available to anyone visiting the site. You must register before you have full access to the job listings.

LatPro.com

latpro.com

LatPro is the "essential job board for Hispanic & bilingual professionals." Access immigration links featuring an H1B visa FAQs section, an event calendar, a salary calculator, and the other career aids. Use the advanced search to find jobs by location and category, or have job listings sent to you via e-mail or RSS feed. LatPro.com also offers several trade magazines free by subscription.

North America

Resources for the United States are in Chapter 11.

Canada

Sites with resources for the whole country occupy the beginning of the Canada entries. Individual provinces follow, in alphabetical order. Most sites in Canada have versions in French and English, with easy links to both versions from the front page. Note that the provincial agencies formerly affiliated with WorkInfoNet lead off the career resources for each province.

AllCanadianJobs.com

allcanadianjobs.com

"We Employ Canada" is the mantra of this website. During our review, the good news is that we saw more than fifty thousand jobs; the bad news is that there were no dates on them. The job search leads you to the respective job bank, employer, or recruiter that posted it. You then apply for the position using the tools supplied by that agency or business. Resume posting can be done on the companion site, Monster.com.

CanadianCareers.com

canadiancareers.com

CanadianCareers covers all facets of the job hunt, from career exploration to presenting yourself in an interview. Job links are accessible under the Job Boards section of the Finding Work page. At the time of review, the Daily Employment News feature was not available, and several other links were broken.

CanJobs.com

canjobs.com

The simple search is easily accessible from the opening page. You can search and apply for jobs without registering; however, to gain access to the career resources and job alerts, you must register.

Career Edge

careeredge.ca

Career Edge is a national, nonprofit organization whose mission is to improve youth employability. It provides recent graduates with internships and career-related work experience.

Charity Village

charityvillage.com

Charity Village is "Canada's supersite for the nonprofit sector" and includes hundreds of job listings, networking opportunities, and extensive online resources. The CharityVillage Campus offers access to continuing education and development opportunities for nonprofit professionals. Click on Jobs to browse the offerings by posting date or search by keyword.

Positionw@tch

www.positionwatch.com

Positionw@tch is an online IT recruiter. Search the entire database by keyword, browse by company, or use the advanced search to specify location, job category, and position type, including permanent or contract.

Public Service Commission

jobs-emplois.gc.ca

The PSC is responsible for the appointment of qualified individuals to Canadian federal government positions. You can toss your hat into this online ring of jobs, training opportunities, student work experience, and internships with the Canadian government.

Service Canada

servicecanada.gc.ca

jobbank.gc.ca

jobsetc.ca

Service Canada—People Serving People! The Canadian government provides access to a full range of human services. Among the items of special interest to job hunters at the first URL are the career-planning and self-assessment tools and the training and self-employment resources. The second URL goes directly to the Job Bank, which offers a special search for students entering the world of work. The third URL goes to the Training, Career and Worker Information page, which offers financial assistance, career exploration and training information, and the Career Navigator. Click on Services by Subject for one-stop shopping for helpful consumer, business, and education information, all searchable by audience or topic.

Industry Canada

ic.gc.ca

Industry Canada supports this wide-ranging business resource. Company directories, business information by industry, and labor statistics are complemented by details on starting a new business and the latest business news. Consumer information is accessible here too.

Working.com

working.canada.com

Working.com offers job leads from many of Canada's daily newspapers. The quick search is easily accessible from the opening page. Browse by industry sector, or use the advanced search to limit the dates, type of position (full-time, etc.), geographical area, and radius searched. You can also register to post your resume or have job listings sent to you via e-mail or RSS feed.

workopolisCampus.com

campus.workopolis.com

Students must register to access the job database and the full range of resources. Endorsed by the Canadian Association of Career Educators and Employers,

"Canada's Biggest Job Site for Students" offers its services free to students through the career centres of Canadian colleges and universities.

workopolis.com

workopolis.com

Workopolis offers thousands of job postings, including listings from some of the major Canadian daily newspapers. It also provides a bit of humor and some good career advice. New draws at the site are the industry news feeds for each job category and the ability to sign up for RSS feeds. Workopolis is working harder than ever!

Youth.gc.ca

youth.gc.ca

Originally created via input from Virtual Youth Canada in collaboration with the Canadian government, this site is the place to go for information about the world of work for Canadian young adults. With continuing input from the VYC's successor, the Canadian Youth Connection, the site offers job opportunities, career-assessment and career-planning tools, training and education resources, and other tips for preparing youth and young adults ages fifteen to thirty to start earning a living.

Alberta

Alberta Learning Information Service

alis.gov.ab.ca

This is the agency that serves as the primary source of career and training information for the province. It now includes a Career Information Hotline, an e-Resume Review Service, and RSS. You'll find everything you need for the job hunt and career exploration at your fingertips.

Career and Placement Services

www.ualberta.ca/caps

The University of Alberta offers this quality resource for its students. You'll find a wonderful collection of career-related tip sheets, and schedules for career fairs and workshops. Access to the job bank is password-protected for students only.

Edmonton Journal

www.canada.com/edmontonjournal

Part of the Canada.com suite of websites, this site from the *Edmonton Journal* offers standard newspaper content by subscription online. The jobs are easily searchable from the opening page on the working.com website. Register (free) to post your resume or cover letter, receive job alerts, or save your searches. Job alerts via an RSS feed are a recent rollout.

nextSteps.org

nextsteps.org

The city of Calgary, with generous support from Industry Canada, funds this career website for the youth of the community. Appealing colors, no-fuss layout, and quality information all contribute to the success of this site, now celebrating more than a decade of service on the Web. A white-hot resource for younger job seekers!

Personnel Administration Office

pao.gov.ab.ca

Name anything you want to know about working for the government of Alberta, and no doubt it's here—as are items of special interest to new residents. Click on the Alberta Government link to access the whys and hows of the provincial government, such as phone numbers, news briefings, legal information, and we could go on. The Employment Opportunities link leads to the current job offerings.

British Columbia

BC WorkInfoNet

workinfonet.bc.ca

This agency serves as the primary source of career and training information for the province.

BC Public Service Agency Job Opportunities

employment.gov.bc.ca

The Public Service Agency offers a wide range of employment opportunities. The Employment Opportunities link leads to the newest offerings and other job links. Click on the British Columbia logo for more information of value to new or current residents of the province.

British Columbia Chamber of Commerce

www.bcchamber.org

Dig through local business news or the business directories of many of the smaller chambers in the province.

Work Futures: British Columbia Occupational Outlooks

workfutures.bc.ca

At this turnkey career-exploration site, you can look up in-depth profiles of more than two hundred job groups covering most types of work available in British

Columbia's labor market. With the handy-dandy A–Z index, you're in and out in a wink. You can also browse by education requirements, type of work, or major occupational grouping, or search by job title.

Manitoba

Manitoba WorkInfoNET

mb.workinfonet.ca

This agency serves as the primary source of career and training information for the province.

Employment Manitoba

gov.mb.ca/employment

At this website, the provincial government puts Manitoba from soup to nuts into your hands. Career information, labor statistics, and employment information are listed in separate sections, so take the time to browse the selections as you go through the site. Don't overlook the business resources, including the Manitoba Business Information Service database, a good source of potential employers.

New Brunswick

New Brunswick Career Development Action Group

nbcdag-gadcnb.ca

This agency serves as the primary source of career and training information for the province. You'll find no job leads here, but this site offers news and an events calendar.

Newfoundland

Newfoundland and Labrador Work Information Network (WorkInfoNet)

www.gov.nf.ca/nlwin

This agency serves as the primary source of career and training information for the province.

Northwest Territory

Jobsnorth.ca

www.jobsnorth.ca

This site is recommended by the Human Resources Department of the government of the Northwest Territories for anyone seeking a nongovernmental position in the area.

Nova Scotia

Nova Scotia Department of Education

ednet.ns.ca

The Department of Education offers all visitors information on education and training opportunities in this province, along with career and employment guidance. Select Employment Opportunities from the menu to connect to job listings, labor market information, and the new Careersites (careersites.ednet .ns.ca).

Nunavut

Government of Nunavut

www.gov.nu.ca/

This official website includes a few government jobs for this province.

Jobsnorth.ca

www.jobsnorth.ca

This site is suggested by the Human Resources Department of the government of the Northwest Territories for anyone seeking a nongovernmental position in the north.

Ontario

Ontario WorkInfoNet

onwin.ca

This agency serves as the primary source of career and training information for the province. There are lots of good resources here.

The Career Centre @ Western

career.uwo.ca

The University of Western Ontario maintains the Career Centre for both students and alumni, and some areas of the website are reserved for those groups. The links, handouts, quizzes, and newsletters are accessible and helpful to any job seeker or career changer.

Employment News

employmentnews.com

You'll find some good information on this award-winning resource. Employment News is the online equivalent of the free publication by the same name that is distributed throughout Ontario. Job-search tips, school profiles, up-to-date news, and career articles supplement the job leads.

Sheridan College Career Centre

careercentre.sheridaninstitute.ca

The Sheridan Career Services page continues to offer helpful advice and career-planning assistance, although the links to these resources are a bit harder to find now. Select the topic of your choice to read through a pathfinder that details internal aid, online assistance for Sheridan students only, and online resources open to all.

Toronto Public Library: Career Bookmarks at the Virtual Reference Library

careerbookmarks.tpl.toronto.on.ca

The TPL's Career Bookmarks are a standout for anyone who is job hunting, exploring the world of work, reentering the workplace, or re-careering. Examples of these Bookmarks are strategies to use in the job search, help for specific audiences, and assistance in researching employers. Very well done!

University of Waterloo Career Services

careerservices.uwaterloo.ca

This university career service center offers all users quality tips for the job hunt, links to career-related websites, and thoughtful advice for successfully building your career. All users are also welcome to follow the "Steps to Success" outlined in the award-winning Career Development eManual.

Prince Edward Island

Prince Edward Island InfoPEI

gov.pe.ca/infopei

Click on Employment to reach the job and career resources. This agency serves as the primary source of career and training information for the province.

Quebec

Emploi Quebec

emploiquebec.net

This agency serves as the primary source of career and training information for the province.

The Montreal Page

toutmontreal.com (French)

moremontreal.com (English)

The main page is in French. Click on English Version, or select the second URL to access the English version in a New York minute. Montreal Page has nicely organized categories of information about living and working in the city, apartments for rent, ride sharing, and more. Click on the Businesses and Services link to access the Jobs.

Saskatchewan

Saskatchewan (SaskNetWork)

learning.gov.sk.ca

This agency serves as the primary source of career and training information for the province.

Yukon

Yukon WorkInfoNET

yuwin.ca

This agency (with the catchy acronym YUWIN) serves as the primary source of career and training information for the province.

The Scandinavian Countries

Job-Index

jobindex.dk

Job-Index offers a good collection of job opportunities in Denmark. Browse the jobs by category. Register to post your CV or to have job announcements sent to your e-mail account.

Ministry of Labour, Finland

mol.fi

Maintained by the Finnish government, this website is a fine place to start a job search. Included here are listings for job opportunities all over the country, with additional links to job openings in Scandinavia and the rest of Europe.

13

Resources for Diverse Audiences

The websites in this chapter offer information and job leads targeted to specific audiences based on gender, cultural background, or other affinity. They are certainly not the only places online where these groups can look for job listings, but users can be assured that the employers and recruiters advertising at these sites are concerned about equality and diversity in their organizations.

General Diversity Sites

Diversity/Careers in Engineering & Information Technology

diversitycareers.com

This website offers free online access to career articles and job announcements from the Diversity / Careers print journals for women, African Americans, Hispanics, Native Americans, Asian Americans, and people with disabilities in engineering and information technology. While at the website, qualified individuals can apply for free subscriptions to either the Minority College issue (published twice yearly) or the Professional issues (published six times a year).

Hire Diversity

hirediversity.com

This national diversity-recruitment service links qualified candidates from entry level to senior level with Fortune 500 companies and the government. Under Career Advice the Resource Links offer separate sets of resources for each population (African American, Hispanic, disabled, and more), but everyone will appreciate the heavy-hitting job bank.

IMDiversity.com

imdiversity.com

IMdiversity.com is an excellent resource for all minority and diversity candidates. It is set up in "villages" for African Americans, Asian Americans, Hispanic Americans, Native Americans, and women. The resources and information in each village are specific for each group, and visitors without their own village are welcomed to a marketplace of wares in the Global Village. Job listings here are updated frequently and are easy to access. This site was conceived by *The Black Collegian* magazine (see the listing under "African Americans" in the following section).

Minority Professional Network

minorityprofessionalnetwork.com

This site refers to itself as "Your Career, Economic, and Lifestyle Connection." It is a large site with many offerings in all of these categories, including a substantial diversity-recruiting service through which employers can find the range of professionals they want to hire. Come here also to learn about networking events that enable you to meet and greet employers and others all over the country.

WorkplaceDiversity

workplacediversity.com

This site offers not only numerous job listings but also employer profiles, news and information targeted to the various audiences it serves, and the background on organizations supporting and promoting minority and diversity interests, including military veterans and the "forty-plus" workforce.

African Americans

The Black Collegian Online

black-collegian.com

The print publication for college students and professionals of color set up this extensive online information resource. The website includes job resources, resume instruction, career guidance, and all kinds of other great articles and resources for everyone. *The Black Collegian* also sponsors IMDiversity.com (see the listing under "General Diversity Sites" at the beginning of this chapter).

National Urban League Employment Network

nul.org/employmentnetwork.html

The Urban League is the nation's oldest and largest community-based movement empowering African Americans to enter the economic and social mainstream. The free Employment Network features numerous job announcements from a wide variety of employers and organizations. Registration (free) is necessary to apply for jobs found here.

Asian Americans

AsianAve.com

asianave.com

This social and professional site for Asian Americans offers registered users the ability to post profiles, chat with others, and search for jobs. The site is operated by CommunityConnect.com, with the job section offered in cooperation with Monster.com.

Disabled Workers

American Federation for the Blind CareerConnect

afb.org/cc_employment.asp

CareerConnect is a "free resource for people who want to learn about the range and diversity of jobs performed by adults who are blind or visually impaired throughout the United States and Canada." Here you can learn what you have to offer an employer, explore careers, pick up tips for your job search, connect with a mentor to guide you through all of this, and, finally, take advantage of jobs posted here by a wide variety of employers.

National Business and Disability Council

business-disability.com

The National Business and Disability Council is the leading resource for employers seeking to integrate people with disabilities into the workplace as well as for companies seeking to reach this sector in the consumer marketplace. Job seekers with a disability who are college graduates or will graduate soon, or have the equivalent in technical training, qualify for the free job-search service, including a resume database and a nice job database.

Ex-Offenders and Others with Criminal Records

National H.I.R.E. Network

hirenetwork.org

Established by the Legal Action Center, the National Helping Individuals with criminal records Reenter through Employment Network is both a national clearinghouse for information and an advocate for policy change. The goal of the National H.I.R.E. Network is to increase the number and quality of job opportunities available to people with criminal records by changing public policies, employment practices, and public opinion. Visitors to this site will find a list of state-specific governmental agencies and community-based organizations to assist people with criminal records, practitioners, researchers, and policy makers, along with useful articles and advice.

Gay and Lesbian

GayJob.biz

gayjob.biz

GayJob.biz is an online community for gay and lesbian individuals looking for employment and for global businesses seeking diverse applicants. The job database is easy to search and is flush with desirable positions, but you must register to see the full listings. The site abounds with other good resources and information available to unregistered users, including many employer profiles spanning corporate, college, government and community, and small business. This is a priceless resource.

Hispanic Americans

iHispano.com

ihispano.com

Launched in 1999, iHispano.com is a vibrant resource where Hispanic and Latino professionals can meet top employers. The site offers users free job and resume databases, in combination with wise advice on interviewing, resume preparation, and a whole bunch more. You can freely search the job database and apply for positions listed here, but other features, such as saving a job search, require you to be a registered user (free).

LatPro

latpro.com

Created in 1997 and dedicated to Hispanic and bilingual (Spanish/English and Portuguese/English) professionals, LatPro.com offers a searchable resume database and job postings, accented with e-mail alerts. The site also features original articles and resume services, along with other career resources. This site is popular with Fortune 100 companies, among thousands of other employers.

Saludos

saludos.com

This site, dedicated exclusively to promoting Hispanic careers and education, is supported by *Saludos Hispanos* magazine. In addition to the career opportunities, it offers a free resume database, mentor profiles, and other job-search guidance.

Native North Americans

American Indian Science and Engineering Society (AISES)

aises.org

The AISES mission is to increase substantially the representation of American Indian and Alaskan Natives in engineering, science, and other related technology disciplines. Along with college scholarships and internships, the society offers an online career center that includes a free public database of job listings. (The resume database is restricted to AISES members.) Visitors will also want to look at the free public list of scholarships, internships, research opportunities, conferences and other useful information found under Career Services by clicking "Non-AISES Opportunities."

Native American SUNY: Western Consortium

www.fredonia.edu/na

This is one of two consortia created by the State University of New York to address the higher education needs of Native American students and communities. The

Western Consortium, based at the College at Fredonia, is a regional network of Native American communities and students as well as college campuses in central and western New York. Look under Student Development for the Directory of Internships and Fellowships for Native Americans, which lists opportunities specifically for Native American students or with relevance to Native issues, along with the Financial Aid directory, a list of resources for members of the Six Nations—Seneca, Cayuga, Tuscarora, Onondaga, Oneida, and Mohawk.

NativeWeb

nativeweb.org

NativeWeb is an international nonprofit organization dedicated to educating the public about indigenous cultures and issues, promoting communications between indigenous peoples and organizations supporting their goals and efforts, and furthering the use of technology by indigenous peoples. The Community Center area of the website includes job listings, while under the Resources header, users will find a category for Native Economy and Employment with links to Jobs and Opportunities.

The Tribal Employment Newsletter

nativejobs.com

This is a recruitment tool for employers who want to increase their efforts to hire diverse populations. For the job seeker, it is easy to access job announcements, all of which have the date of posting noted. There are other resources here of interest to Native Americans.

Older or Disadvantaged Workers

Experience Works

experienceworks.org

Experience Works is a national community group dedicated to providing training, employment, and community services for low-income senior citizens, who often face many barriers to finding suitable jobs. Check your state for programs operated by this group and others. The website also offers numerous tips and tools, but you must register (free) to access these.

Senior Service America

www.seniorserviceamerica.org

Senior Service America Inc. is a nonprofit organization that helps provide training and employment opportunities to older adults who work to fill real community needs. Persons over the age of fifty-five, as well as employers and community organizations interested in hiring participants, can contact the organization for more information.

Religious Affiliations

Christian Career Center

christiancareercenter.com

This service is run by professional career counselors who help job seekers to "integrate their faith with career/life planning and find work that fits their God-given design." A lot of job-hunting help is here, including career-consultation services, a resume bank, and related career resources and guides.

Christian Jobs Online

christianjobs.com

This site is intended as "a place where Christian job seekers and employers can meet." The service posts job openings, positions wanted, and resumes. Many of the organizations posting here are Christian-based nonprofits with a variety of personnel needs (social workers, architects with experience designing churches, etc.). You can search the job database without registering, but you will need to register to apply for any positions.

The Jewish Federation of Greater Washington Career Center

shalomdc.org/career_alljob.html

The Jewish Federation lists local jobs in the Jewish community in the Washington, D.C., area. These positions are posted by the many social services and other Jewish organizations in the vicinity, but most nonreligious positions are not limited to persons of the Jewish faith.

Transitioning or Former Military Personnel

These sites might work for folks preparing to separate as well as veterans.

Career Command Post

careercommandpost.com

This site helps bring active-duty military personnel and their spouses, as well as veterans of the armed forces, together with civilian employers. There is a wide variety of positions listed, with salaries ranging from $20,000 to $90,000 per year.

Corporate Gray Online

www.corporate-gray.com

This site targets job seekers transitioning from military to civilian careers, connecting you with military-friendly companies nationwide. The premise comes from the popular Corporate Gray books for finding jobs in the private sector after a military career—*From Army Green to Corporate Gray, From Navy Blue to Corporate Gray,* and *From Air Force Blue to Corporate Gray*—distributed by Competitive Edge. All users are required to fill out the free-registration form in order to search the job database.

HireVetsFirst

www.hirevetsfirst.gov

The President's National Hire Veterans Committee designed this website to help employers find qualified veterans, and to help veterans make the best use of a national network of employment resources. While the site does not offer anything new, it does provide a one-stop center with links to several extremely helpful resources and services available to veterans who need assistance in finding new employment as they transition out of the military.

Military.com

military.com

Military.com offers a variety of information and job opportunities for men and women in the military, those in transition, and their families. The site is a member of the Monster career and job network. Users must register in order to search the job database.

TAOnline.com, Transition Assistance Online

taonline.com

TAOnline.com provides free services to specific job seekers—separating military service members; armed forces retirees, veterans, and spouses and dependents; DoD employees; and related populations—to assist them in finding their next job or career with employers seeking to hire individuals with the unique training, education, skills, and leadership that only the military provides. The jobs here can be viewed by anyone, but contact information is hidden, and online applications can be submitted only by registered users. TAOnline.com is a division of LucasGroup.

VetJobs.com

vetjobs.com

This site is for all transitioning military personnel as well as longtime veterans. Users will find general career information, a resume database, and entry-level as well as middle-management positions posted here.

Women

Feminist Career Center

feminist.org/911/jobs/911jobs.asp

This service of the Feminist Majority Foundation Online is intended to increase awareness of a wide variety of feminist issues and to help feminist employers and job seekers unite. Search for jobs and internships by keywords and region, browse the full list, or view the twenty most recently added listings. You can also submit your resume to the public Positions Wanted database for free.

Tradeswomen Now and Tomorrow

tradeswomennow.org

Tradeswomen Now and Tomorrow is a national coalition committed to increasing the number of women in trade and technical fields and fostering equality in their working conditions. Women will appreciate the list of TNT member associations, many of which sponsor training programs in these fields, along with other resources and services.

Women for Hire

womenforhire.com

Founded in 1999, Women for Hire offers career fairs, an exceptional professional online network, inspiring speeches and seminars, a popular career-focused magazine, customized marketing programs, and an online job board—all of which connect leading employers and talented professional women in all fields. Some premium services impose a nominal fee, but much of what is offered is free.

14

Lifelong Career Planning

Whether or not you want to admit it, your work is critical to your happiness and your well-being. It affects your standard of living, your lifestyle, and how you spend most of your waking hours—and often your sleep. Decisions that affect your career affect your life, and those decisions are not limited to asking for a raise, accepting a promotion, or changing employers. They include actions such as taking a different job, transitioning to another field, physically moving to a new place because the opportunities there are better, and returning to college because you can get further with the degree than you can without it. Career planning is not just what happens when you are finishing high school or college. It is a lifelong process of exploration and decision making that colors and molds your life and the lives of those around you.

As you go through the years and encounter decision points, either by choice or by force, you need tools to help you evaluate options, make decisions, plan strategies, and execute those plans. The presentation of resources in this chapter is designed to help you with your job search, interview preparation, career exploration, and much more besides. These four dozen or so entries represent just a small fraction of the good things available online. You can always equip yourself with additional tools of the trade at The Riley Guide (rileyguide.com).

General Resources for Lifelong Career Planning

All of the sites in this section contain numerous resources to help you with planning and managing your career, from selecting a field to obtaining a job to moving up, sideways, or out of the market. Many even offer guidance for your life after work.

CareerJournal from the Wall Street Journal

careerjournal.com

If you use only one site for all of your career and life planning, make it this one. CareerJournal covers all the issues. Look over the Job-Hunting Advice, with its information on resumes, interviewing, changing careers, using the Internet, and much more. Check out the Salary and Hiring Info section for several articles and resources related to hiring activity, salaries, and other trends nationwide. Plan to spend some quality time here.

JobHuntersBible.com

jobhuntersbible.com

Richard Bolles, one of the foremost leaders in career exploration, has produced this attractive and informative guide to help job hunters and career changers make tracks to the best career sites and advice on the Internet. JobHuntersBible.com supplements Bolles's book *What Color Is Your Parachute?* and is also an unbeatable resource on its own.

USNews.com

www.usnews.com

The publisher of *U.S. News and World Report* has produced this outstanding resource for career and life planning. The Education section is one of the best guides to education on the Web, with dedicated sections on college, graduate school, and financial aid. Look under Money & Business for top-flight information on careers, including employment trends and job-search skills. Other areas of the website can help with budgeting, investing, and even retirement planning.

Career Exploration

If you are considering a career change, these sources can help with finding information and options, including how to transfer your current skills to new occupational areas and industries.

America's Career InfoNet

careerinfonet.org

This service tells you all about hundreds of occupations and what you need under your belt in order to do each job. The Occupation Information link shows you wage and trend reports, occupational requirements, and much more. Under the Career Tools header, you can assess your employability, dig deeper into careers, scout employers, and bone up on licensing information for various states. A financial aid adviser is ready to help you determine ways to pay for any training or education associated with a prospective move to the next best gig. America's Career InfoNet is a component of CareerOneStop (careeronestop.org), sponsored by the U.S. Department of Labor.

Career-Exploration Links

uhs.berkeley.edu/students/careerlibrary/links/occup.cfm

The Career and Educational Guidance Library, part of the Counseling and Psychological Services housed within University Health Services at the University of California, Berkeley, powers this well-organized set of links to career resources in a large number of occupational fields.

Career Guide to Industries

www.bls.gov/oco/cg

Turn to the hefty Career Guide to Industries for information on available careers by industry, including the nature of the industry, working conditions, employment statistics, occupations, training and advancement, earnings and benefits, employment outlook, and lists of organizations that have additional information. It is a nice way to find out who's needed by various industries and whether you fit the bill, all with the imprimatur of the Bureau of Labor Statistics at the U.S. Department of Labor.

Guide to Career Prospects in Virginia

www.careerprospects.org

This is a database of information about careers that are important to Virginia (and almost every other state). For each career, you get a written analysis that includes required educational levels and skills, earnings, and job outlook, along with a set of statistical tables enumerating wages and job outlook at the Virginia regional level as well as nationwide. While most of the salary data are specific to Virginia, descriptions of each career area are general enough to be relevant across the board and are very well crafted. Search by keyword, or browse the careers by job family.

Major Resource Kit

www.udel.edu/csc/mrk.html

The Bank of America Career Services Center at the University of Delaware devised these "kits" as a tool for undergraduates at the school. The Major Resource Kits link academic majors to career alternatives by providing information on career paths, sample job titles, and a short bibliography of printed materials available in many libraries. Each kit includes information such as entry-level job titles that previous graduates in that program have attained, brief job descriptions, and major employers for that field, along with additional materials.

O*NET Online

online.onetcenter.org

O*NET—the Occupational Information Network—takes the place of the *Dictionary of Occupational Titles*. This online version was created to provide broad access to the O*NET database of occupational information, which includes skills, abilities, work activities, and interests associated with more than 950 occupations. Search by keyword or code. You'll enjoy seeing what occupations are similar to yours and which ones call for the skills you already have.

The Occupational Outlook Handbook

www.bls.gov/oco

This is the current edition of the printed guide produced by the U.S. Bureau of Labor Statistics. You can use keyword searching in this valuable handbook to find out where your interests fit in the top 250 occupations in the country. You can also use the index to explore various occupations, or select an occupational cluster to see what is included within each group. Accompanying this information are well-written articles on how to find a job and evaluate a job offer, where to obtain career information, and what tomorrow's jobs look like. This is a top-shelf source for employment and career information.

Occupational Outlook Quarterly

www.bls.gov/opub/ooq/ooqhome.htm

Published quarterly by the Bureau of Labor Statistics, this magazine features articles with practical information on jobs and careers. They cover a wide variety of career- and work-related topics, such as new and emerging occupations, training opportunities, salary trends, and results of the latest studies from the BLS. The Grab Bag is a collection of brief items of interest to counselors and students, while "You're a What?" looks at unusual occupational fields and is fun reading for younger inquiring minds.

Career-Planning Processes

Career Decision-Making Tool from America's Career Resource Network

acrnetwork.org/decision.htm

This tool helps teachers, counselors, and parents assist their charges in identifying an appropriate career direction and selecting or developing an educational program that will provide the knowledge and skills needed to succeed in the chosen field. This online tool is also easy for any individual to use. The process of identifying a career direction and evaluating a preparation plan is presented in a six-step decision cycle that may be entered at any point and repeated until a satisfactory conclusion is reached.

Career Development eManual

cdm.uwaterloo.ca

Employ the six-step process suggested here for career- and life-planning success. Starting with self-assessment, it takes you through the full job-search process, right up to choosing which offer to accept. Kudos to the University of Waterloo Career Services in Ontario, Canada, for this site.

Minnesota Careers

iseek.org/mncareers

"What do I want to do with my life? What do the numbers say? Where do I go from here?" This guide from the Minnesota Department of Employment Security is here to help you answer these questions and plan your career path.

While it starts by talking to young adults just out of high school, older and more experienced people will also find this guide to be extremely helpful. It's not just for Minnesotans!

nextSteps.org

nextsteps.org

This slick guide to career planning, exploration, and decision making for persons aged fifteen to twenty-four includes interactive tools you can use as you work through the various steps and exercises tied to great resources. NextSteps. org originates in Canada and is a service of the Calgary Youth Employment Center.

Counseling Assistance

APA Help Center

helping.apa.org

Through this site, the American Psychological Association offers useful information and advice on how psychological services can help people cope with problems such as stress, depression, family strife, or chronic illness. The site provides sections devoted to psychology in the workplace, the health implications of the mind-body connection, family and personal relationships, and psychology in daily life. In addition, learn how and when to choose a psychologist—and obtain a referral to a practitioner in your area. A detailed site map and an easy-to-use keyword search facility aid navigation of these helpful pages.

International Association of Jewish Vocational Services

www.iajvs.org

This not-for-profit association conjoins twenty-nine health and human service agencies in the United States, Canada, and Israel. Through its member agencies, the IAJVS provides educational, vocational, career, and rehabilitation services to all individuals seeking to improve their lives. A list of member agencies can be found under Contact Us.

National Board of Certified Counselors

nbcc.org

The NBCC is a national certification agency for counselors. Certification from this group, or from a local licensing board, carries the assurance that a counselor has met certain professional standards. Select the Find a Counselor header for access to the NBCC's free CounselorFind, which will help you find board-certified counselors in your area. In addition, under the State Counselor Licensure header is the list of State Credentialing Boards. Many states require counselors to undergo a state certification process before they are allowed to practice. You can contact these agencies for names of locally certified counselors in your area who may not hold national certification.

National Career Development Association

ncda.org

This association is the career-counseling arm of the American Counseling Association (counseling.org), which has been instrumental in setting professional and ethical standards for counselors. Choose the Career Center option for the NCDA's "Consumer Guidelines for Selecting a Career Counselor," along with a list of frequently asked questions about career counselors and career counseling. The NCDA offers special certifications for Master Career Counselors and Master Career Development Professionals; for the names of those who have been awarded these titles, along with an outline of the standards that must be met, see Need a Career Counselor? under Career Center.

Distance Education

Distance Education and Training Council

detc.org

The Distance Education and Training Council is a nonprofit educational association located in Washington, D.C. Originally called the National Home Study Council, it serves as a clearinghouse of information about the distance-study/correspondence field and sponsors the Accrediting Commission of the Distance Education and Training Council, a nationally recognized accrediting agency. Through the website, you can find accredited high school and college degree programs, a directory of all institutions accredited by this group, and a list of study subjects available from the many programs.

Many of the following "Education and Training Resources" sites include citations for distance education and online programs.

Education and Training Resources

Don't forget to check USNews.com, mentioned in the first section of this chapter. It includes financial aid information as well as the annual college and graduate school rankings published by *U.S. News and World Report* (www.usnews.com/sections/education).

CareerAdvantage.org

careeradvantage.org

This site offers information on vocational schools and adult trade schools and colleges in the fields of business, culinary arts, information technology, graphic design, Web design, fashion design, interior design, and more. Select a field, and then review the list of online U.S., Canadian, and international schools offering programs. You can easily request more information from any program listed.

Carnegie Library of Pittsburgh: Education Resources

clpgh.org/locations/jcec/education

The librarians in the Job and Career Education Center at this Pittsburgh landmark have created a versatile online tool for locating information on educational institutions plus financial aid! Take a gander at their assemblage of print resources, databases, and Internet resources for anyone seeking assistance with the costs of higher education. A special area addresses foreign nationals.

College and University Rankings

library.uiuc.edu/edx/rankings.htm

This collection of links and references to print and online rankings of colleges and universities around the world is provided by the Education and Social Science Library at the University of Illinois at Urbana-Champaign. Be sure to read the note on the controversy regarding ranking services before you start comparing scores.

CollegeNET

collegenet.com

CollegeNET lets you browse information on colleges by various criteria, including geography, tuition, and enrollment. More than five hundred college applications are available here for you to fill out and submit online. Financial aid and scholarship information can also be found here.

College Navigator

nces.ed.gov/collegenavigator/

According to the site sponsors, "College Navigator is your direct link to nearly 7,000 colleges and universities in the United States. If you are thinking about a large university, a small liberal arts college, a specialized college, a community college, a career or technical college or a trade school, you can find them all here." College Navigator can be searched by location, program, or degree offerings—either alone or in combination. College Navigator is a product of the National Center for Education Statistics, a part of the U.S. Department of Education.

Peterson's

petersons.com

The well-known publisher of college directories has a tremendous amount of information online for students and parents. Select the appropriate education tab (college, grad school, online & continuing ed.) and then the category that fits you best to be directed to a page filled with free and fee-based services and products to help you in selecting a college, preparing for tests, and much more.

RWM Vocational School Database

rwm.org/rwm

This is a database of private postsecondary vocational schools in all fifty states offering certificates, diplomas, associate (junior college) degrees, and bachelor's (college) degrees in various business, trade, and technical disciplines. Except for the online programs, the site is organized by state and then the field for which you want to train, and all schools listed are state licensed or accredited. The Online Schools list is a short roster of institutions meeting the stated requirements of the site. The information provided for each school is either an address and telephone number or a link to its website, allowing you to easily contact the school to request a catalog and further information. Each state's page also includes a link to its Department of Education.

Employment Projections and Hiring Trends

Is your career field growing or declining? Is that trend just in your area, regional, or nationwide? Don't take a wild guess: get down to brass tacks by looking up the following sites.

Employment Projections from the Bureau of Labor Statistics

www.bls.gov/emp

This section of the BLS website lists many reports from the Office of Occupational Statistics and Employment Projections, which develops information about employment trends, the national labor market, and the implications of these data on employment opportunities for specific groups in the labor force. Assessments are also made of the effect on employment of specified changes in economic conditions and/or federal programs and policies. This page links to several useful resources, including the Occupational Employment, Training, and Earnings report; the Occupational Outlook Quarterly; the Career Guide to Industries; and the Occupational Outlook Handbook, all of which also carry information on projected employment trends and earning potential.

Labor Market Information State by State

rileyguide.com/trends.html#gov

Labor Market Information includes statistics on employment, wages, industries, and other factors affecting the world of work. These links from The Riley Guide take you to labor market information for the individual states so you can see how the industry or occupation you are exploring is doing wherever you want to be.

While the Bureau of Labor Statistics and the other federal agencies give us data based on national averages, the state you are targeting may turn out to be in a different, uh, state.

Occupational Employment Statistics, U.S. Bureau of Labor Statistics

www.bls.gov/oes

The OES program produces an annual survey of occupational employment and wages for more than 750 occupations. You'll find all kinds of very useful information, from wage and compensation data to occupational descriptions and employment projections.

State Occupational Projections

projectionscentral.com

This site contains projections of occupational employment growth for all states, as well as for the nation as a whole. Knowing state-level data enables you to make a more accurate estimate about what is going on in your neighborhood, rather than trying to guess based on the average for the country. One of the most important applications of the projections is to help individuals make informed career decisions. You can compare projected employment growth for a specific occupation among several states, or select several occupations and compare their growth projections within a specific state. At the time of review, the short-term projections were out of date, but the more important long-term projections are still updated on a two-year cycle, so new data are regularly added.

Financial Aid

College Is Possible

www.collegeispossible.org

This resource guide for parents, students, and education professionals is produced by the American Council on Education. This site walks you through preparing, choosing, and paying for college in a down-to-earth style, with links to additional information. Much of the cited resource material can be downloaded at no cost, and the advice and information are of high quality. The Jump Start Your Education booklet is available in Spanish, as are several related articles, which can be downloaded in PDF format.

FinAid, The SmartStudent Guide to Financial Aid

finaid.org

Established in 1994, FinAid is a gold mine of information and resources related to obtaining financial aid for education—including scholarships, loans, military aid, and other pools. The site also has calculators for figuring your debt load and payback, caveats regarding scams, and much more. Make this site your springboard for financial aid information.

SallieMae

salliemae.com

Founded in 1972, SLM Corporation, better known as Sallie Mae, provides funds for educational loans, primarily federally guaranteed student loans originated under the Federal Family Education Loan Program. Through its website, Sallie Mae allows you to access information to help you plan for college, apply for a loan, manage your loan payments, and even search for a job. There is information for parents as well as students. The family of services also includes information to help you plan for college.

Student Aid on the Web, U.S. Department of Education

studentaid.ed.gov

The Federal Student Aid programs are the largest source of student aid in the United States, providing nearly 70 percent of the total amount. This site gives you access to and information about the products and services needed throughout the process. There is information targeted to parents, counselors, returning (adult) students, and international students, as well as students in college and graduate school. Look under Applying for Financial Aid for links to information on state aid, tax credits, the department's Free Application for Federal Student Aid, and much more. Select the Federal Student Aid Programs header for a complete list of all education funding programs sponsored by the Department of Education. The entire website is available in English and Spanish.

Other Education and Training Options

Apprenticeship Information from the U.S. Department of Labor

www.doleta.gov/oa

Apprenticeship is a combination of on-the-job training and related classroom instruction in which workers learn the practical and theoretical aspects of a highly skilled occupation. Apprenticeship programs are sponsored by joint employer and labor groups, individual employers, and/or employer associations. This page will give you information on how to find and apply for apprenticeship programs in the United States.

Job Corps

jobcorps.doleta.gov

The Job Corps is the nation's largest residential education and training program for at-risk and disadvantaged youth between the ages of sixteen and twenty-four. It operates more than one hundred centers around the country and in Puerto Rico, offering participants the integrated academic, vocational, and social-skills training they need to gain independence and get quality, long-term jobs or further their education.

Professional and Trade Associations and Unions

These entries will take you to hundreds of associations and organizations representing many occupations and professions. These groups are good resources for finding out more about the areas they represent. See what they offer in the way of internships and apprenticeships, networking and support, mentoring, certification programs, professional development and training, and publications.

ASAE Gateway to Associations

asaecenter.org/directories/associationsearch.cfm

The American Society of Association Executives offers this terrific resource for anyone trying to locate a professional association for any field or interest. The Gateway can be searched by name, interest area, or geographic location, and the results will give you each association's address, phone number, and website (if available).

Business Organizations, from Yahoo!

dir.yahoo.com/business_and_economy/organizations

This is Yahoo!'s entry to its list of organizations, including professional and trade associations.

Labor Unions, from Yahoo!

dir.yahoo.com/business_and_economy/business_to_business/labor/unions

Yahoo! maintains this list of labor unions covering many occupations and industries.

The Scholarly Societies Project

scholarly-societies.org

You can search or browse this list of national and international associations, societies, and unions focused on "scholarly, academic, or research goals." This site has been online for several years and is maintained by the Library at the University of Waterloo, Ontario.

Salary and Compensation Information

In addition to visiting the following sites, surveying job listings in the many job banks will credit your account with some salary information. More sources lie in the resources already cited in this chapter, such as Careerjournal.com and the career guides. Also keep The Riley Guide (rileyguide.com/salary.html) in mind for salary-research purposes.

JobStar Salary Surveys

jobstar.org/tools/salary

JobStar has drawn together what many authorities assert is the finest collection of salary surveys online. Combining that constellation with recommended books and with articles from experts such as Jack Chapman, this site will steer you in the right direction for your salary search.

Salary.com

salary.com

This site is much more than just salary resources. It is dedicated to total compensation—not only what is in your paycheck but also the benefits and perquisites you receive as a part of your earnings. The Salary Wizard is fast and easy to use, allowing you to search for base, median, and top-level earnings in hundreds of jobs for many occupational areas, and much of the data applies to your local jurisdiction. Salary.com has a team of compensation specialists who add value to surveys conducted by others, such as the Bureau of Labor Statistics, and you can profit from their experience. If you are serious about your salary and compensation research, the Personal Salary Report is well worth the moderate fee. This site also includes articles and exercises to help you figure out benefits, stock options, bonuses (and how to get them), and even negotiations.

SalaryExpert.com

salaryexpert.com

A free service of Baker, Thomsen Associates, SalaryExpert.com offers access to extensive international compensation information prepared by these knowledgeable authorities. Use the Free Salary Calculator for basic salary reports covering the United States and Canada, or the International Salary Report for coverage of many other countries. Each allows you to select a job title and region and returns a nice report showing salary averages, salary levels, benefits, and cost of living. Other premium reports are available for a moderate fee. Scroll down the entire front page to see all the wares.

Self-Assessment

Sometimes a self-assessment test can help you to understand yourself better, but sometimes it can lead to more questions, best answered with the assistance of a counselor.

Campbell Interest and Skill Survey

pearsonassessments.com/tests/ciss.htm

"If you are interested in a career that requires some postsecondary education, the Campbell Interest and Skill Survey assessment can help you understand how you fit in the the world of work." Developed by David Campbell, Ph.D., the CISS uses targeted questions and analysis to help you understand how you fit into the world of work. This survey has been a popular tool with career counselors, and Pearson is now making it available to the public through the Internet for a fee. The report you receive upon completion of the survey compares your results with the results of people who are successfully employed in the same fields in which you're interested. Nearly sixty occupations are covered in your personalized report, which also includes a comprehensive career planner to help you interpret your results and plan for your new career.

CareerKey

careerkey.org

Developed by Dr. Lawrence K. Jones and based on Dr. John Holland's work (see the final entry in this chapter), this moderately priced career-tool game is designed to help you with career choices you make during your life. You can also access a lot of good career advice for free.

Keirsey Temperament Website

keirsey.com

This is the official website for the test developed by David Keirsey. Based on the Myers-Briggs Type Indicator, the Keirsey Temperament Sorter helps people discover their basic personality type as indicated by their preferences and personality. You can take the Keirsey Temperament Sorter II online and receive a brief report for free, learning basic information about your type and how it might affect your career choices and work style. Some of the tests are available in languages other than English.

Self-Directed Search

self-directed-search.com

The SDS was developed by Dr. John Holland, whose theory of careers is the basis for most of the career inventories used today. His theory states that most people can be loosely categorized with respect to six types—Realistic, Investigative, Artistic, Social, Enterprising, and Conventional—and occupations and work environments can also be classified by the same categories. People who select careers matching their own type tend to be happier and more successful. You can take the SDS online for a small fee, receiving a report indicating your three-letter Holland code along with occupations that match your skills and interests and recommendations on how to proceed with developing and planning your career.

15

Executive Job Searching Online

This final chapter contains selected resources for mid- to senior-level executives engaged in a job search. These sites were chosen because users have reported them to be especially helpful. Many other resources listed throughout this book also include job listings at this level. The good news is that, yes, executives can search for job opportunities online. The bad news is that most of the better sources are fee-based—but they are usually worth the expense, given the quality of listings and the confidentiality of your information.

General Services and Resources

CareerJournal from the Wall Street Journal

careerjournal.com

As noted throughout this book, this site is an excellent source of career news and job leads. The content changes daily and is made up of new articles written for this site as well as relevant articles from the print *Wall Street Journal*. While we feel that the articles are the best part of this site, we know that you likely care more about the job listings. Many of the postings derive from various search firms, others come direct from employers, and still others have been taken from the print version of the *Journal*. CareerJournal also offers several resources to assist you in your search, from directories of recruiters to salary surveys to interviewing and negotiation advice. Take the time to tap into all the offerings.

Exec-U-Net

execunet.com

Exec-U-Net is a career-management and job-search membership organization for $100,000-plus executives, offering listings of very good jobs along with a resume-review program and face-to-face networking meetings around the country. Several membership options are available, depending on how long you want to be active with the organization. This service has been in existence for several years and has always received positive comments from members.

ExecutivesOnly

executivesonly.com

This service offers $100,000-plus executives the opportunity to review job leads and get assistance from a career-management consultant in preparing your resume, presenting yourself, and planning your next career move. The people behind this service have extensive backgrounds in recruiting and outplacement. You can choose from several membership options, based on how long you wish to be a member and what services you'd like during your tenure. Discounted memberships may be available to people who are currently enrolled in an outplacement program or recently ended a program without successfully making a transition to a new opportunity. You can request more information about that.

TheLadders

theladders.com

TheLadders is a job site for the job seeker earning more than $100,000 per year. It offers specialized job-search engines for Sales, Marketing, Finance, Human Resources, Law, Technology, and Operations, as well as all other job and industry areas. Free membership entitles you to limited access to the job listings, but the real value of this site can be gained only through paid membership.

Netshare

netshare.com

Netshare is a fee-based service offering exclusive confidential job leads, a resume database, and career-management tools for senior executives earning $100,000-plus. If you haven't heard of Netshare, don't be concerned. Think of the company as "the quiet guys" who don't do as much general advertising as the competition but have a terrific reputation through word of mouth. The database is updated daily, and Netshare offers varying membership options designed to meet your current search needs.

RiteSite.com

ritesite.com

RiteSite's purpose is "to provide the strongest and most comprehensive possible help to job-hunting and career-building executives." John Lucht, author of *Rites of Passage*, offers members a Custom Career Service designed to "help you with everything you can do to advance your job search and long-term career development." This includes resume preparation and posting, the ability to confidentially forward your resume to others, and connectivity to his select group of retained executive-search firms, all for a low annual fee. This site is devoted to helping you know, contact, and build relationships with these firms. RiteSite has a job database that is open and free for anyone to view.

Additional Sources for Leads and Connections

These are services and resources you can use to locate job leads or present your information to various executive-search firms. Other resources and services appear throughout the book.

BlueSteps

bluesteps.com

BlueSteps is a service of the Association of Executive Search Consultants (AESC), a professional association representing retained executive-search consulting firms worldwide. BlueSteps offers two main services for executives seeking new career options: Executive Profile and SearchConnect. Executive Profile allows you to submit your resume for consideration by members of the AESC. SearchConnect is a searchable directory of all AESC members that you can use to make direct contact with firms that handle searches in your industry and functional field. With your membership, you also receive a free resume critique, newsletters, and opportunities to participate in seminars. There are various membership levels you can purchase.

CEO Job Opportunities Update

ceoupdate.com

This is the online presence for *CEO Job Opportunities Update*, a biweekly publication that lists senior-level nonprofit opportunities in trade associations, professional societies, cause-oriented organizations, and foundations. In addition to accepting announcements from HR professionals and executive-search firms, it actively seeks out listings in newspapers, magazines, websites, specialty publications, and newsletters; checks the status and accuracy of each posting; and verifies the compensation offered. According to the website, CEO Update "tracks over three hundred searches in a typical two-week publishing cycle." The print version of the newsletter is published every other Thursday and typically lists about 250 executive-level openings, along with many good articles. In addition, the website allows subscribers to access positions and news, updated daily. Current subscription information and costs are detailed on the website.

6FigureJobs.com

6figurejobs.com

6FigureJobs offers experienced professionals the opportunity to confidentially seek and be considered for some of the most prestigious jobs in the country. The free service is intended only for people who are qualified for executive-level placement, but it also offers those who are ready to move into the c-suite (chief executive suite) a great opportunity. You must submit your complete resume, which is then reviewed to verify that you qualify for membership based on your years of experience, educational background, prior job titles, career progression, job responsibilities, and current compensation. Once you are accepted, you have access to the job database, and your resume is included in the database. You then have the option of controlling how public your resume will be.

Directories of Recruiting Firms

You can use the following resources to locate recruiting firms in your local area and firms specializing in your target industry or occupation discipline. Many career consultants suggest that you contact the firms to let them know of your interest in being considered for searches that they might be handling and submit a resume for review. If you know the name of an individual search consultant, particularly one a colleague can recommend, then address your approach to this person. If you have never worked with this type of search firm or recruiter, we suggest checking out some of the articles in the Executive Recruiters section of CareerJournal (careerjournal.com) to help you understand and work effectively with these firms.

Avotek Headhunter Addresses

www.avotek.nl

Based in the Netherlands, Avotek is a marvelous resource for an international job search. It offers lists of recruiters from several countries, allowing you to contact them directly via e-mail and submit your resume for consideration in searches they are conducting. Each list tells you what country is covered, how many addresses are listed, when the list was last updated, and the cost. To access this site in English, just click on the British flag.

BlueSteps from the Association of Executive Search Consultants

bluesteps.com

See the entry earlier in this chapter.

Custom Databanks, Inc.

customdatabanks.com

If you are familiar with the CareerSeach product found in many college career centers and outplacement firms, then you have met Custom Databanks. This company provides the database of search firms used by CareerSearch, and it also makes this and other databases available to the public for a fee. To start your search, click on Download Data, select the database you wish to search (recruiters, companies, venture capital firms), and then select your search criteria. The results will tell you how many records have been found and the cost before you buy. They will also tell you how many firms have listed e-mail addresses, fax numbers, or merely postal addresses. You can buy whichever list you want based on your needs and contact plans, but we suggest you don't limit yourself to the firms with e-mail addresses. The data file you are buying can easily be imported into any word processor or spreadsheet program for mail-merge and campaign management. This is a competitive product to Kennedy's, described in the following entry, but in many cases we noticed that it provided more contact names for each firm listed.

The Directory of Executive Recruiters from Kennedy Publications

recruiterredbook.com

Kennedy's is probably the best-known name in this field, and the service is worth the cost of the search. For a one-time registration fee, you can have full access to the online version of the popular "Red Book," with its list of more than sixteen thousand search firms. If you wish to save money, you can obtain print copies of the directory in most major bookstores as well as in public and business libraries. Many colleges and universities also hold this title in their reference collections, and they usually allow the public to use materials in-house. Kennedy's also offers other career services to executives, including the ExecutiveRegistry.com job and resume service.

FindARecruiter.com

findarecruiter.com

Part of the Recruiters Online Network (recruitersonline.com), FindARecruiter is a free searchable database of third-party recruiters, headhunters, search firms, and staffing agencies. You can search the directory by job field or industry, location (not limited to the United States), or company name. See Chapter 3 for more information on Recruiters Online Network.

Recruiterlink.com

recruiterlink.com

Recruiterlink.com is a free directory designed to help hiring managers and executives create short lists of search consultants specializing in any of more than fifty areas, including financial services, consumer products, CEO search, information technology, marketing, and telecommunications. The directory entry for each consultant cites contact information, industries and functions with which this person works, and lowest salary level considered. You can then link over to learn more about the search firm with which this consultant is affiliated. Recruiterlink.com is operated by Hunt-Scanlon, a market-research firm and online data provider to the executive recruiting industry.

The Recruiting & Search Report

rsronline.com

These are print directories listing contingency and retained executive-search firms that specialize in various industry and functional areas. You can also order the directories on diskette for the cost of the directory plus an additional fee. The file is in Excel format for easy import into any spreadsheet or word-processing program. The list of available directories, including the number of entries in each and ordering information, is on the website.

SearchFirm.com

searchfirm.com

SearchFirm.com is a free searchable directory of retained and contingency recruiters and interim staffing firms from around the world. Though it is intended for employers, job seekers will find this very useful.

Executive Compensation Information

At some point in a successful search, you will be asked what compensation you expect. What salary are you asking? What additional perquisites and benefits might attract you to a particular position? The following resources, along with many that came before, can help you in preparing your answers and in holding your own in the negotiation process that will inevitably follow. Many of the resources noted earlier in this chapter will also have information and guides for you, as will the resources listed under "Salary and Compensation Information" in Chapter 14. You can find even more information in The Riley Guide (rileyguide.com).

Articles and Reports on CEO Pay from Forbes.com

forbes.com

Forbes publishes several articles plus special surveys on executive compensation throughout the year, including the annual report on best-paid CEOs. When you connect to the website, select Leadership to access both the Careers and Compensation sections.

CareerJournal from the Wall Street Journal

careerjournal.com

CareerJournal's section on Salary and Hiring Info contains articles and charts on pay, perquisites, options, and anything else you need to know before talking money.

DEF 14A Reports from the EDGAR Database of Corporate Information, United States Securities and Exchange Commission

sec.gov/edgar.shtml

Compensation for the top executives and members of the boards of directors of every publicly traded company in the United States must be reported to the SEC. While some fee-based EDGAR (Electronic Data Gathering, Analysis, and Retrieval) services will pull this information out for you, it is not difficult to get at it through this free database. First off, select two or three competitive companies similar in size and industry to your preferred employer. Then, go to EDGAR's Search for Company Filings, and select Companies & Other Filers to search EDGAR for each; select the most recent DEF 14A report, and use the Find command in your Web browser (usually control-F) to scan the long document for the word *compensation*. Not only will this reveal salary and stock information, but it also may give you some ideas for additional compensation considerations, such as cars, travel expenses for your spouse or partner, cell phones, and much more.

Index of Cited Sources

Subject Index